D1526766

How Leading Lawyers Think

Randall Kiser

How Leading Lawyers Think

Expert Insights Into Judgment and Advocacy

 Springer

Randall Kiser
DecisionSet®
550 Hamilton Avenue, Suite 100
Palo Alto, CA 94301
USA
rkiser@decisionset.com

ISBN 978-3-642-20483-8   e-ISBN 978-3-642-20484-5
DOI 10.1007/978-3-642-20484-5
Springer Heidelberg Dordrecht London New York

Library of Congress Control Number: 2011935044

Printed on acid-free paper

Springer is part of Springer Science+Business Media (www.springer.com)

Acknowledgments

Seventy-eight exceptional attorneys made this book possible. They generously contributed their time and insights to improve the quality of case evaluation and decision making for other attorneys and their clients. In interviews ranging from 30 minutes to 2½ hours, they patiently imparted the wisdom they had acquired during their combined 2,275 years of legal practice. Throughout the interviews I was aware that, for every hour spent on arranging our interview and responding to interview questions, the attorney would need to work on client matters an hour later that evening or week. Although they bear no responsibility for my imperfect efforts to distill and convey their knowledge, these attorneys are the force and inspiration underpinning this book. I express a deep sense of gratitude to them.

In writing this book, I have benefitted greatly from the opinions of many mediators, judges, consultants and attorneys. In particular, I thank Paul Gordon of Rethink LLP and Jonas Jacobson of Trial Behavior Consulting for their comments on portions of this book. I also have been fortunate to continue working with Blake McShane and Samantha Cassetta. I thank Blake for analyzing the datasets and producing the samples used to identify the attorney interview candidates and Samantha for reviewing and suggesting changes to previous versions of this book. The book also has been enhanced by discussions with Judge Allen Hurkin-Torres (Ret.), whose experience in settling more than 15,000 cases provided an invaluable perspective on case evaluation and settlement negotiations.

The bridge between a researcher and the reader is the publisher. For this book and my previous book, *Beyond Right and Wrong: The Power of Effective Decision Making for Attorneys and Clients*, Springer-Verlag and its outstanding editorial and production departments have served as that bridge. I am indebted to Anke Seyfried, my editor at Springer, for her precision, thoroughness, efficiency and foresight.

For the encouragement that enabled me to plan this project, conduct the study interviews and write this book, I thank my wife, Denise.

Contents

Chapter 1
Introduction

What is a legal claim worth? Should a case be settled or taken to trial? Will a jury believe a client's testimony? How do some attorneys accurately predict trial outcomes, while other attorneys are unrealistic and overconfident? When cases are settled, could the clients and their attorneys have negotiated better terms? These and other critical questions about civil litigation are answered in this book by 78 leading trial attorneys in California and New York.

The attorneys interviewed for this book have practiced law for 29 years on average, have achieved exceptional results in case evaluation, settlement negotiations and jury trials, and are recognized by their peers as leading attorneys. Based on their expertise and extensive experience in evaluating, settling and trying cases and training hundreds of associate attorneys, they explain how attorneys become skilled advocates and accurate evaluators. In discussing cases and clients, they also share a large part of their professional lives: their motivations, sense of justice, dedication, case strategies, negotiation tactics, opinions of juries, and expectations of other attorneys.

This Introduction provides an overview of the study attorneys, details the methods used to select the interview candidates, and summarizes the interview protocols and topics. It then describes how the attorneys' insights are organized and presented in this book.

1.1 Profile of the Study Attorneys

The study attorneys have extensive trial experience, are members of professional organizations imposing strict trial experience requirements and are highly regarded by their colleagues and adversaries. The California attorneys have practiced law an average of 29.4 years, and the New York attorneys have an average experience level of 27.3 years. The least experienced attorneys were admitted to the bar nine years ago, and the most experienced attorney has been licensed to practice for 58 years. Among the attorneys who specifically discussed the number of trials in which

R. Kiser, *How Leading Lawyers Think*,
DOI 10.1007/978-3-642-20484-5_1, © Springer-Verlag Berlin Heidelberg 2011

they acted as lead counsel, the lowest number of cases tried to verdict was eight; the number of trials handled by the other attorneys ranged from 30 to 175. Their practice areas include personal injury, premises liability, products liability, construction, professional negligence, eminent domain, public entity liability, employment, insurance, contracts and business torts.[1] At the time of the interviews, 42% of the study attorneys represented plaintiffs, 38% represented defendants, and 19% represented both plaintiffs and defendants.[2] Eighty-seven percent of the attorneys rated by Martindale-Hubbell received an "AV Preeminent 5.0 out of 5" rating, the highest possible peer review rating. Overall, 28% of the attorneys were members of the American Board of Trial Advocates (ABOTA), and 27% had been selected for inclusion in *Super Lawyers*; in California, 33% were ABOTA members, and 30% were listed in *Super Lawyers*. Many of the plaintiffs' attorneys are members of the Million Dollar Advocates Forum.

The study attorneys are not only exceptional trial attorneys but also are leaders within their firms and legal communities. Their careers are highlighted in trade publications, their voices are heard on radio programs and their cases are featured in newspaper articles. Many of the attorneys have taught undergraduate, law school and attorney continuing education courses, authored practice articles and books, led local and state bar associations and served on court advisory and civic organization boards. A large majority of attorneys who are members of ABOTA also serve as temporary or part-time judges or arbitrators and mediators in their local courts. About 20% of the attorneys maintain a solo practice; among the attorneys practicing in a group context, the majority are either founding or managing partners of their firms.

Apart from trial experience and professional distinction, one trait emerged early in the interviews: many of the attorneys had a previous career or extensive experience in other jobs or occupations before or after admission to the bar. At least 16% of the plaintiffs' attorneys and 10% of the defense attorneys, for instance, had supervisorial or executive responsibilities with insurance companies before bar admission. Other attorneys had spent years, sometimes decades, working exclusively for defense firms and then joined a plaintiff practice. A few had substantial prior experience prosecuting or defending criminal cases, a practice area that usually provides more courtroom experience than a general civil litigation practice. Another characteristic was immediately evident before the interviews began: nearly all of the attorneys were male; only 9% of the attorneys were female, and they tended to be partners in defense practices.[3]

---

[1] The study attorneys practiced in communities where the median household income ranged from $36,000 to $112,000 and the percentage of college graduates varied from 4% to 71%.

[2] The total is less than 100% due to rounding.

[3] This underrepresentation of female attorneys is roughly consistent with data regarding female lead attorneys in New York appellate court commercial cases and female equity partners in the United States. During the September 2010 – January 2011 period, "women were the lead attorney or argued the matter for one or both sides in 12 commercial cases (12.24%)," and of the 207 total attorneys who appeared in those commercial cases, "193 were male, 14 were female (7.3%)."

1.2 Selection of the Study Attorneys

The 78 attorneys interviewed for this study were selected from datasets of 8,114 attorneys who represented clients in 3,278 litigation cases. Those cases were reported in *VerdictSearch New York* in 2005 and *VerdictSearch California* between 2002 and 2007.[4] To be included in the datasets for New York and California cases, an attorney had to have represented a client in a case that was resolved by a judge, jury or arbitrator after the parties exchanged and rejected settlement offers and demands. The amount of the verdict, decision, award, offer and demand, moreover, could not be disputed. About 40% of all cases reported in *VerdictSearch California* and *VerdictSearch New York* during the designated periods met this criteria, requiring a review of more than 8,000 cases to find 3,278 eligible cases.[5]

To identify the attorneys whose representation was correlated with accurate case evaluations and financially effective trial results, the datasets were searched for cases that met two criteria: (1) the client's decision to reject an adversary's settlement proposal resulted in a superior financial outcome at trial or arbitration; and (2) the client's settlement demand or offer was within 20% of the ultimate award at trial or arbitration.[6] Thus, the criteria identified not only the cases where the client obtained a superior result through formal adjudication but also the cases where the client's pre-trial settlement position reflected a fairly accurate assessment of the ultimate outcome. The case, in short, had to represent both effective decision making and accurate calibration. Only 8% of the cases prosecuted by California

---

New York City Bar. (2011). *Appellate division, first department, civil and commercial litigation female attorney numbers.* Although female attorneys comprise about one-third of all attorneys in the United States, "women account for just 15 percent of equity partners – a level that has not changed in over five years." Behan, Wendy. (2011, March 23). Empowering female attorneys: How mentors and role models can close the gender gap. *San Francisco Daily Journal,* p. 5.

[4]*VerdictSearch,* a division of ALM Media, is the leading publisher of verdict and settlement case reports. It publishes a national verdict reporter and state reporters for California, New Jersey, New York, Pennsylvania and Texas.

[5]The search and coding methods for these datasets are described in Kiser, Randall. (2010). *Beyond right and wrong: The power of effective decision making for attorneys and clients* (pp. 32–35, 431–435). New York: Springer Science + Business Media.

[6]Any range selected to assess calibration is arbitrary. Because attorneys' fees play a major role in litigation, arguments can be made that accurate evaluation of plaintiffs' cases would dictate a settlement position below the anticipated verdict, reflecting plaintiffs' costs of proceeding to trial. Conversely, one may argue that a defendant's settlement position should be above the verdict amount, reflecting a defendant's aggregate cost of defending the case through trial and paying the judgment. The 20% range was selected as a compromise among competing arguments and is supported by cases in which the court determined whether a party's pre-trial settlement position was "reasonable." See *People ex rel. Dept. of Transportation v. Yuki* (1995) 31 Cal.App.4th 1754, 1764–1766 [offer of 77% of final award unreasonable]; *County of Los Angeles v. Kranz* (1977) 65 Cal.App.3d 656, 659 [offer of less than 80% unreasonable]; *Community Redevelopment Agency v. Krause* (1984) 162 Cal.App.3d 860, 865–866 [offer of 82% unreasonable]; *Los Angeles County Metropolitan Transportation Authority v. Continental Development Corp.* (1997) 16 Cal.4th 694, 720.

plaintiffs met the dual criteria, while 20% of the defendants' cases met the criteria. In New York, the results were slightly better. New York plaintiffs and defendants met the dual criteria in 9% and 26% of their cases, respectively.

To reduce the number of qualified cases to manageable interview samples, four random samples were generated. The first random sample of 100 cases was drawn from the 212 California plaintiff cases that met the criteria, and the second random sample of 100 cases was drawn from the 560 California defendant cases that met the criteria. The third random sample of 20 cases was drawn from the 49 New York plaintiff cases that met the criteria, and the fourth random sample of 20 cases was drawn from the 137 qualified defendant cases. The random samples thus represented an even division between plaintiffs and defendants, although a greater percentage of defendant cases met the criteria. The two New York random samples also reflected the smaller number of New York cases relative to California cases.

At a purely practical level, one may be interested to know how much money was actually gained by plaintiffs and saved by defendants in the random samples of qualified cases. The plaintiffs in the California random sample obtained an award at trial that was, on average, $626,300 *above* their opponent's settlement offer. For the defendants in the California random sample, the trial award was, on average, $605,000 *below* their opponent's settlement demand. The New York plaintiffs gained an average of $927,800 in excess of their adversary's offer, and the New York defendants saved, on average, $613,600 by proceeding to trial instead of paying their adversary's demand. The clients in both the California and New York samples placed big bets on their attorneys and won.

1.3   Attorney Responses to Interview Requests

After the four random samples were generated, the abstracts of each case in the samples were reviewed to identify the lead trial attorney. An interview inquiry letter was mailed to that attorney, describing the author's prior research in attorney-litigant decision making, explaining how the attorney was selected as an interview candidate, noting that the interview questions related to case evaluation and settlement negotiations and would not delve into protected attorney-client communications, and assuring the attorneys that their names would not be used in the resultant article or book (unless they preferred attribution). The letter also indicated that the author would telephone the attorney to arrange an interview at the attorney's office if the attorney was willing to participate in the study.

Fifteen percent of the attorneys in the random samples could not be located, had died, were now serving as judges, or were the lead trial attorney in more than one case in the sample. After adjusting for those attorneys, the total number of eligible interview candidates was 205. The interview inquiry letters were mailed to those 205 attorneys, and they received a follow-up telephone call. Eighty-one attorneys agreed to be interviewed and scheduled an interview time. Three of the attorneys later cancelled the interviews, reducing the response rate to 38%. For those readers unfamiliar with the declining response rate in social science surveys, it is important to note that a 38% response rate in a study requiring high-income professionals to spend an hour of their time without compensation is remarkably high.[7]

1.4   Interview Protocols and Topics

Most of the interviews were conducted in person at the attorney's office; only nine attorneys were interviewed by telephone. The average duration of the in-person interviews was 72 minutes, while the telephone interviews had a shorter average duration of 42 minutes. The interview protocol included nine general topics selected to probe the roles and practices of attorneys, insurers, clients, mediators and judges in case evaluation, negotiation and resolution. Due to time restrictions, however, many attorneys limited their comments to four issues: (1) attorneys' role in counseling clients about settlement and trial alternatives; (2) the most important factors in case evaluation; (3) mediators' role in case evaluation; and (4) common problems attorneys, clients and insurers encounter in case evaluation and settlement negotiations. When time permitted, other interview topics, ranked roughly in the order of precedence, included advice the attorney would offer new attorneys regarding case evaluation and negotiation; the interviewed attorney's evolution as a case evaluator and client counselor; jury selection and deliberations; the role of insurance companies in case management; whether case evaluation is an innate or teachable skill; and whether any course in law school had contributed to the attorney's case evaluation or negotiation skills. To meet privacy and confidentiality concerns, the interview notes did not show the attorney's name, and all identifying characteristics were omitted from the interview content later entered in a software program and manually sorted by subject matter.

The attorneys' responses to the interview questions were expansive and elaborate. Considering that they had spent a lifetime asking other people questions at depositions, client meetings, expert witness interviews and in direct and cross examinations at trial, the attorneys were surprisingly receptive and communicative. None of the attorneys declined to respond to an interview question, and only one attorney asked that a question be rephrased. (Another attorney said a question was "pretty wordy" but added, "I guess that's alright since you're a writer.") Many of

---

[7]As a reference point, the response rate in a recent study of state court judges, conducted by the agency that has policy-making authority over their court system and requiring 10–15 minutes to fill out a written survey in their office, was 20%. Robinson, Peter. (2009). Settlement conference judge – legal lion or problem solving lamb: An empirical documentation of judicial settlement conference practices and techniques. *American Journal of Trial Advocacy*, 33, 1. In another recent study, in which attorneys were asked to complete an on-line questionnaire in their office, the response rate ranged from 16% to 28%. Hinshaw, Art & Alberts, Jess K. (2009, June 10). Doing the right thing: An empirical study of attorney negotiation ethics. CELS 2009 4th Annual Conference on Empirical Legal Studies Paper. Available at SSRN: http://ssrn.com/abstract=1417666.

the statements quoted in this book were not directly responsive to any question but presumably reflected the attorneys' opinions on a topic they deemed to be necessarily related. Hence, the attorneys' most insightful and provocative remarks often were extemporaneous.

1.5   Purpose and Organization of This Book

The purpose of this book is to convey the insights and experiences of the interviewed attorneys. That purpose is best accomplished by allowing the attorneys to speak for themselves and, whenever possible, to quote them directly. The author's challenge in acting as a conduit for the attorneys is to transform about 90 hours of lively, interactive discussion into a few hundred pages of printed matter. In that process, many invaluable remarks are omitted, comments may be misunderstood or taken out of context, and the words in a chapter cannot reflect precisely the proportionate amount of time the attorneys devoted to a topic or the striking range of opinions they voiced on a subject. Nor is it possible from this highly opinionated group of attorneys to discern a consensus; when the term "the study attorneys" or "study attorneys" is used, it simply means that more than one attorney expressed that view. Attorneys being attorneys, one may assume that some study attorneys would object strongly to the views of other "study attorneys." Due to the personal nature of the individual attorneys' experiences, the limited sample size, and the discretion exercised in selecting salient, incisive and indicative interview excerpts, this book is necessarily narrative, not scientific. And the attorneys' statements, however well considered or adamantly expressed, are their personal opinions, not facts.

The chapters in this book are loosely organized and linked by themes, dilemmas, attitudes and controversies commonly encountered in civil litigation practice. The chapters are grouped into five parts, beginning with the attorneys' perspective on their work and ending with concrete evaluation, settlement and jury selection practices. Part I, "Roles and Responsibilities," describes the attorneys' professional values and motivations and their outlook on the respective responsibilities of attorneys, jurors and clients. In Part II, "Frameworks and Connections," the attorneys explain how they start to evaluate cases and develop strategies and themes and how they use various sources to test their assessments and stay connected with jurors' sense of reality and fairness. The cognitive skill set required for accurate case evaluation and effective client representation is examined in Part III, "Feelings and Traits." That part explores the persistent tension between zealous representation and objective case analysis and between empathy for the client and professional detachment. It also probes the relationship between superior attorney performance and emotional intelligence, perpetual learning and survivor personality traits. In Part IV, "Techniques and Strategies," the study attorneys identify and rank the tangible and intangible factors they regard as most important in evaluating, settling and trying a case. They also discuss how they interview and counsel clients;

interact with opposing counsel, insurers, judges and mediators; negotiate settlements; represent clients in mediation; and, when negotiations fail, select jurors for trial. In Part V, "Learning and Advice," the attorneys discuss how attorneys can become sound case evaluators and whether case evaluation skills can be taught. In that part, they also provide some cogent advice to accelerate other attorneys' development as astute evaluators and successful advocates.

Each part of this book is designed to convey to readers the skills, wisdom and collective experience of the 78 interviewed attorneys. That purpose will be accomplished if readers feel that, after listening to these attorneys, they have gained some insights into how other attorneys practice law and how they might improve their own practices.

Part I
Roles and Responsibilities

Chapter 2
Attorneys

The study attorneys' distinguishing characteristic is that they consider themselves responsible for litigation results. Although they believe the civil justice system is imperfect and individual jurors may be wayward, they assume personal responsibility for achieving clients' objectives. In describing how they work, they demonstrate that they are accountable, self-critical and resilient. Their time is devoted to trying to win cases, not blaming judges, juries, expert witnesses or other attorneys for outcomes that fall short of their expectations. It would be easy to conclude that they are goal-directed, but the more important conclusion is that they are self-directed.

The attorneys' sense of responsibility for results has major consequences not only for clients but also for the attorneys' professional development. Because their motivation is intrinsic, they define success by their own objectives, set stringent requirements for their own performance and continually monitor and evaluate their representation. The specific traits of responsibility, reliability, commitment, empathy, emotional regulation and self-motivation are described in this chapter.

2.1 Responsibility, Reliability and Commitment

The responsibility for case results, the study attorneys relate, rests squarely on their shoulders:

- I still worry about how the case will turn out. Most of my career, I've judged myself by how the case turns out. I recognize I'm the difference between an acceptable result for a client and an unacceptable result.
- I'm responsible for their [clients'] future, at least taking care of them monetarily. If something goes wrong in the case, I have always known it's my responsibility. I don't ever blame something else. . . . I put the case on, so if there's a bad result, I'm the one who did it.

R. Kiser, *How Leading Lawyers Think*,
DOI 10.1007/978-3-642-20484-5_2, © Springer-Verlag Berlin Heidelberg 2011

- I've only had three cases where the plaintiff recovered more than we offered. We keep track of these things, and it doesn't happen often. I remember them very well because my self-worth depends on what those 12 strangers do.
- You are the director. As a lawyer, you are putting the picture together. You are directing the show, and if the actors are not doing their parts, it's your responsibility.
- If a case does not turn out the way I expected, it's usually because of not paying attention to details at the beginning of the case. When you hear something from a juror that you had not considered, you didn't prepare. You should never hear something you hadn't expected from a juror.
- Attorneys – and I'm definitely one of them – say, "I won or lost." You don't say the case was lost or won. You take it personally.
- You have to have a competitive spirit. You have to enjoy litigation, and you have to be willing to working incredibly long hours. You have to put yourself on the line. If you don't have these qualities, all the intellect in the world will not be enough.

None of the attorneys was asked directly, "Do you feel responsible for results?" But in describing how they evaluate cases, counsel clients, negotiate settlements, and try cases, they convey an overriding sense of responsibility for outcomes.

The attorneys' sense of responsibility is unusual, as litigation practice presents a very broad field upon which to disperse responsibility for adverse outcomes. Clients may blame attorneys, attorneys criticize juries, judges chastise attorneys and insurers alternately disparage plaintiffs' attorneys and question their own defense counsel. Mediators, consistent with their role as neutrals, fault no one or everyone. Just as most medical errors occur in the obscure "handoff" between shifts and different health care providers, most case evaluation errors occur in an unmarked intersection where clients, jurors, judges, attorneys, insurers and mediators have converged but not cooperated. Consequently, responsibility for negative outcomes is either attributed to autonomous factors or consigned to a blame-free zone bounded by the participants.

The tendency to offload responsibility is illustrated in two studies. In one study, law professors Samuel Gross and Kent Syverud surveyed 735 litigation attorneys, asking, "Why did this case go to trial instead of settle?" They found that "each side says the other one did it." Successful plaintiffs' attorneys, for instance, said they were "forced to court by the defendants' stupidity," and successful defense attorneys said the trial was "caused by the plaintiff's greed or craziness." Almost none of the attorneys said "We gambled and lost" or "We decided to fight and we won."[1]

In the second study, conducted by Professor Jane Goodman-Delahunty and her colleagues, 481 attorneys were asked to specify their minimum goal for a litigation

---

[1]Gross, Samuel, & Syverud, Kent. (1996). Don't try: Civil jury verdicts in a system geared to settlement. *UCLA Law Review, 44*(1), 49.

case they were handling. After the case was resolved, the attorneys' minimum goals were compared with the actual outcome, and the attorneys were asked to rate "their feelings about the case outcomes." It turns out that the attorneys' subjective sense of satisfaction with the case outcome bore little relation to the actual case result. Only 18% of the attorneys were "very disappointed" or "somewhat disappointed" with the case outcome, although 43% of the attorneys did not meet the minimum litigation goal the attorney had set at the beginning of the study.[2]

This disconnect between performance and results in the Goodman-Delahunty study was presaged by the attorneys' perception of their role and impact. Before their case results had been determined, the attorneys were asked to list the reasons why they might not achieve their minimum litigation goal. "Case facts" and "judge and jury issues" were listed as the most likely reasons why their litigation goals might not be realized, followed by "witness factors," "client factors" and "court context." Goodman-Delahunty found that the "reasons least frequently cited were 'attorney factors,' comprising only 3.2% of the reasons stated and referring to the skill, preparedness or experience of the participant or opposing counsel."[3] Thus, among all possible variables determinative of case outcomes, the variable over which the attorneys have the most control is the variable they regard as having the least effect. Even if this perception is accurate, it eviscerates attorneys' motivation and stifles self-improvement. People simply do not develop skills absent a sense of accountability and consequence.[4]

The study attorneys stand apart from other attorneys in their explicit declaration of responsibility. In this respect, they exhibit the distinguishing characteristics of exceptional performers in domains as diverse as business, medicine, music and chess. Jim Collins, the author of the business bestsellers *Good to Great, How the Mighty Fall* and *Built to Last*, leads a team of researchers to determine how executives and companies consistently produce superior results. He sometimes asks executives to introduce themselves by describing their responsibilities instead of stating their titles. What separates the "wrong people" from the "right people," he concludes, is that the wrong people see themselves as having jobs while the right people see themselves as having responsibilities. "Every person in a key seat," Collins contends, "should be able to respond to the question 'What do you do?' *not* with a job title but with a statement of personal responsibility."[5]

Taking a similar approach, Harald Mieg, a professor at Humboldt Universität Berlin, finds that what separates "complete" professionals from limited subject matter experts is a comprehensive sense of responsibility and accountability.

---

[2]Goodman-Delahunty, Jane, *et al.* (2010). Insightful or wishful: Lawyers' ability to predict case outcomes. *Psychology, Public Policy, and Law, 16*(2), 147.

[3]*Id.* at 147–148.

[4]See Ackerman, Phillip L., & Beier, Margaret E. Methods for studying the structure of expertise: Psychometric approaches. In Ericsson, K. Anders, *et al.* (Eds.). (2006). *The Cambridge handbook of expertise and expert performance* (pp. 147–165). New York: Cambridge University Press.

[5]Collins, Jim. (2009). *How the mighty fall* (p. 57). New York: HarperCollins.

Complete professionals, he explains, are "units of expertise" as well as "units of accountability." They are not only accountable for the information they provide but also for "the complete professional task, including treatment."[6] Consequently, he writes, their performance is measured by effectiveness and efficiency, and their functions encompass all stages of professional performance – analysis, diagnosis, inference and treatment. Applying these concepts specifically to law practice, it becomes evident that a complete professional provides the expertise to identify, analyze and evaluate a client's problem *and* takes responsibility for solving the problem.[7]

2.2 Empathy and Detachment

The risk in assuming responsibility for case results – "putting yourself on the line," as one managing partner described it – is that attorneys may personalize the case and become so emotionally involved in the client's representation that they lose their objectivity. The study attorneys are keenly aware of this risk and have learned how to balance their personal sense of responsibility with their professional duty of objectivity. They continually monitor their own emotions to insure that their commitment to results is a positive motivational force and does not become a blinder. As shown by some of their comments, they have learned to be empathetic yet dispassionate, committed yet impartial:

- Don't confuse passion and emotion. I think it's a requirement of the job for an attorney to be passionate. But getting emotional is when the attorney takes on the client's emotions and they get upset and start yelling and screaming because they are feeling the same way as the clients.
- Part of the professionalism you develop and have to develop is rechecking and rechecking that you're not getting too emotionally involved in a case. As a part of my obligation to the profession, I have to ask, "Am I allowing my emotions to interfere with my judgment?"
- I will stop being a lawyer when I stop feeling empathy for my client. You have to feel for human nature. Compassion, empathy are important factors in my practice of law. But ultimately I have to be able to divorce myself from these aspects. This is called client control. For clients, this is the most important thing in the world for them. But this doesn't mean that I'm dragged along in the wake of my client's poor decisions. You don't want to beat up the client or [cause

---

[6]Mieg, Harald A. Social and sociological factors in the development of expertise. In Ericsson, K. Anders, *et al.* (Eds.). (2006). *The Cambridge handbook of expertise and expert performance* (p. 753). New York: Cambridge University Press.

[7]Effective attorneys, like physicians, generally are not legally responsible for outcomes, but they act as though they are responsible. Because this is an attitude, not a legal construct, it might be more precise (and cumbersome) to describe them as being psychologically responsible.

them to] be marginalized. On the other hand, you don't want the client running the store.

- You need to feel it, but you have to keep it in check.
- Yes, I think some of the more common misjudgments are – the mistakes attorneys will make – are getting caught up in the ebb and flow of a file, becoming emotionally involved with the client, the case. You have to become subjective to understand your client and the jury, but you also have to know where to stop.

These attorneys show an unusual ability to harness the power of emotion while recognizing the hazards of bias. Their remarks indicate they routinely step outside themselves to discern whether they have internalized the client's case and are starting to lose their professional objectivity.

The study attorneys' ability to remain emotionally committed to clients while preserving their objectivity demonstrates the critical difference between empathy and identification. Empathy is "the ability to accurately recognize the immediate emotional perspective of another person while maintaining one's own perspective."[8] Stated slightly differently, empathy is the ability to "perceive the internal frame of reference of another with accuracy, and with the emotional components and meanings which pertain thereto, as if one were the other person, but without ever losing the 'as if' condition."[9] Identification, in contradistinction, means that one "not only recognizes the emotional state of the other but also proceeds to feel it."[10] The danger of identification is that the attorney cannot serve the client as a counselor and loses the capacity to distinguish between the client's feelings and the attorney's sentiments. This distinction is clarified in the medical field: "a simple but important lesson to be learned from the study of empathy is that most patients are not searching for a person who feels as they do; they are searching for someone who is trying to understand what they feel."[11]

2.3   Emotional Self-Regulation

Expert performers routinely engage in the type of emotional self-monitoring and self-regulation practiced by the study attorneys. Expertise – whether exhibited by athletes, musicians, mathematicians or neurologists – "involves self-regulating three personal elements: one's covert cognitive and affective processes, behavioral

---

[8]Shea, Shawn Christopher. (1988). *Psychiatric interviewing: The art of understanding* (p. 14). Philadelphia: W.B. Saunders Company.

[9]Barrett-Lennard, G.T. (1981). The empathy cycle: Refinement of a nuclear concept. *Journal of Counseling Psychology* 28(2), 91–100. Quoted in Shea *supra* note 8 at 14.

[10]Shea *supra* note 8 at 14.

[11]Shea *supra* note 8 at 14.

performance, and environmental setting."[12] Checking, evaluating and changing one's emotional state, called "covert self-regulation," occurs when "an individual monitors and adjusts cognitive and affective states, such as when a basketball player begins to 'choke' under pressure and decides to form a relaxing mental image to counter-act the pressure. For all three self-regulatory elements, people's accuracy and constancy in self-monitoring of outcomes positively influence the effectiveness of their strategic adjustments and the nature of their self-beliefs, such as perceptions of self-efficacy – their self-belief in their capability to perform effectively."[13] Experts' awareness of their emotional states contributes to their keen sense of responsibility. Expert golfers, for example, downplay the importance of chance and "instead attribute their errors to personally controllable processes, such as poor concentration, tenseness, poor imagination and feel."[14] Experts, in sum, are self-reflecting and self-correcting.

2.4 Intrinsic Motivation

The distinction between "intrinsic motivation" and "extrinsic motivation" is helpful in understanding why the study attorneys establish performance standards above the level necessary to render competent legal services or achieve a comfortable standard of living. Intrinsic motivation has been defined as "the motivation to do an activity for its own sake, because it was intrinsically interesting, enjoyable or satisfying. In contrast, 'extrinsic motivation' was defined as 'the motivation to do an activity primarily to achieve some extrinsic goal such as a reward.'"[15] Intrinsic motivation is generated from within the individual – "the love of the thing itself" as Joshua Slocum, the first sailor to complete a solo circumnavigation, called it – while extrinsic motivation is an environmental reward, punishment or incentive.[16] Intrinsically motivated people have a high sense of independence and autonomy, rely on their own standards and goals and are persistent in solving protracted problems.[17] Not surprisingly, intrinsic motivation is a "core characteristic" of creative people and strongly affects how they define and solve problems.[18]

---

[12]Zimmerman, Barry. Development and adaptation of expertise: The role of self-regulatory processes and beliefs. In Ericsson, K. Anders, *et al.* (Eds.). (2006). *The Cambridge handbook of expertise and expert performance* (p. 706). New York: Cambridge University Press.

[13]*Id.* at 706–707.

[14]*Id.* at 712.

[15]Runco, Mark A. Motivation, competence, and creativity. In Elliot, Andrew J., & Dweck, Carol S. (Eds.). (2007). *Handbook of competence and motivation* (p. 613). New York: The Guilford Press.

[16]Teller, Walter Magnes. (1985). *The voyages of Joshua Slocum* (p. 84). Dobbs Ferry, New York: Sheridan House.

[17]Runco, *supra* note 15 at 615–617.

[18]Runco, *supra* note 15 at 612, 616–617.

The study attorneys, like other intrinsically motivated individuals, have developed their own standards of competence and strive to attain their own goals. Conventional attorney behavior, an extrinsic benchmark often considered the legal "standard of care," seems to have little effect on how they run their practices. Although he was not directly addressing the issue of motivation, one of the nation's most accomplished trial attorneys described a model of client service rooted in his own sense of values:

> I don't know who else you're interviewing or how I came up in your study, but one thing you need to know is I'm not representative of anyone. I don't run my practice the way anyone else does and that's why I have a small office, keep my overhead down, and take cases to trial that everyone else would settle.
>
> I do not take cases to settle them for ten cents on the dollar. On some of my cases the going rate [for settlement] is $675,000 – $1,000,000. I've never settled for less than $1,500,000. On other cases, one attorney gets $1,500,000. I settled the same type of case for $7 million.
>
> It's easy to talk a client into settling. I don't like this. That's not why I went to law school – just to process a [quadriplegic] case for $675,000 or $1,000,000.

"If you develop a reputation for settling cases for 60 cents on the dollar," this attorney relates, "everyone knows it and you lose your credibility. So I will not take a case unless I intend to take it to trial."

This sense of independence and dedication raises a plaintiff's risk of transforming a case with a positive settlement value into a defense verdict. But a cost-benefit analysis may not be determinative to attorneys who set their own standards and place dedication and fidelity to clients above economic conservativeness:

- When I lost, they were not really surprises. On one case, the judge told me I would lose and the attorney on the other side said, "Why are you trying this? You don't need it. The offer is still on the table. Why don't you take it?" But I had talked with the client and they wanted to have the jury decide it.
- I have lost cases but I always feel I gave it my all. A good lawyer should never go to bed thinking, "I gave up on my client." Clients who think, "My lawyer did everything and we still lost," do not sue, and they do not have fee disputes.
- During the trial the judge told me, "I think you're going to lose this case." I said, "Judge – news flash – so do I." If the client wants justice or someone to decide who is responsible for their son's death, I didn't care if I lost. The client was happy they had their day in court.
- If the case should be settled but the client does not want to settle, I will put it on the record with a court reporter. I put him or her on the stand and make sure they understand the decision they're making and the consequences. Ultimately, it's the client's decision. I tell them I have hundreds of cases in the office, and this is your one and only time to get the fair result you feel you are entitled to.

The attorneys' willingness to try a case, provided the client is fully informed of the risks, enables them to continually test jurors' sensibilities and avoid the extreme risk aversion exhibited by many other attorneys. "A lot of attorneys don't want a loss on their column," a prominent trial attorney observes, "so they don't take any chances and never find out what cases would actually be winners."

These dedicated attorneys, both plaintiffs' attorneys and defense counsel, often spoke of other attorneys who "are going through the motions." Distinguishing themselves from those legal functionaries, they describe their case analysis and preparation as an arduous but enjoyable challenge beginning the day they are retained.[19] One attorney's comments are illustrative:

> They never put the energy in. You have to know every nuance of the case and strategize. I'm thinking about what type of experts and who the experts should be right from the start, months before they are designated. They don't get what the case is really about. They're just going through the motions and they screw up by doing something like missing an expert designation. For them it's become more of a procedural thing to do, a calendar deadline, than something they've spent a lot of time thinking about, strategizing about how the expert's a part of winning your case.

The study attorneys are focused on the overall objectives, visualizing litigation not as a series of procedural deadlines but as an orchestration of strategies and actions that results in an advantageous settlement or a favorable verdict. "If you're going through the motions you won't be an effective litigator," observes a distinguished, 35-year trial veteran. "That's why I talked about enthusiasm earlier. This is my hobby."

Consistent with their intrinsic motivation, the study attorneys express a strong sense of professional pride and enjoyment in their practices. One attorney comments:

> I relish the whole advocacy preparation. Each trial is a gem-like legal experience. I keep sharp memories of every trial and the attorneys on the other side because we have shared the very pinnacle of the profession.

Another study attorney looks at his law practice from the vantage point of numerous previous endeavors:

> First of all, I'm a late bloomer. I did not become an attorney until I was in my 40s. I had done so many things trying to find myself. I sold newspapers. I was a real estate agent. I must have done 30 to 40 things before I became a lawyer, which I think is my calling. I have fun every day.

---

[19]According to a national survey of law students conducted by the American Bar Association Young Lawyers' Division, about one-third of law students identify extrinsic motivations (family pressure, financial opportunity, no attractive alternative, and escape family background) as their primary reason for attending law school. ABA Young Lawyers Division. (1990). *The state of the legal profession – 1990*. Chicago: American Bar Association. Thirty-three percent of the students in the Class of 2010 at the National University of Singapore also identified extrinsic factors (money, job security, social status and prestige, parents, and friends) as their primary reason for studying law. Tan, Seow Hon. (2009, December). Law school and the making of the student into a lawyer: Transformation of first year law students in the National University of Singapore. *Legal Ethics, 12*(2), 131.

A different attorney, when asked whether he had made many personal sacrifices in starting and managing a renowned defense firm and trying nearly 100 cases, responded, "If you like what you're doing it's not a sacrifice. I've enjoyed practicing law since I started."

2.5   Personal Values

Recognizing that these attorneys are strongly motivated and hold themselves to high standards of accountability, one inevitably wants to know the personal value system that underpins these traits. This was a difficult subject to broach in a one-hour interview and seemed to be pushing the boundary between professional and personal. But when directly asked, "What personal values have affected the way you practice law?", attorneys did not hesitate:

- How about, do unto others as if it was your dad, your mother, your sister. What would you want done? Lawyers are on a contingency and they have to move cases – the financial realities kick in. But I never looked at it that way. Gee, if it was my mom, what would I want? I have weak knees when it comes to telling clients to take [settlement] money. In one [wrongful death] case I told the client it was a loser but they wanted to take it to trial. I said, "it's your only son but it's not my only case. I'll try the case."
- I would turn to, I would say it's my upbringing, my mom. I like being able to stand up for people who cannot stand up for themselves. It makes me feel good. I like my clients. It makes me feel good to make a difference.
- My sense of right and wrong is built into my evaluation. There has to be some righteousness.
- I want people to respect me. I'm not expecting people to be like me – some of my partners are completely different from me – but I want to be an example they choose to follow. This is all self-imposed. It probably comes from expectations of myself I started growing up. I want to be perceived as someone who respects the dignity of other people. It drives my children's bar up, and I think it will make them better adults as well.

These attorneys see their practices as an integral part of their values and aspirations. Although it is unrealistic to assume that they can precisely identify the source of their professional motivations, something beyond court deadlines, financial rewards and extrinsic pressures to succeed defines their purpose and drives their practice. If they had been jazz musicians instead of lawyers, they might have related well to Art Blakey's advice to a young Wynton Marsalis: "If you want to play this music, you have to play it with soul, with intensity; and every time you touch your horn, you play your horn. This is not a game."[20]

---

[20]Quoted in Fine, Ralph. (2008). *The how-to-win trial manual* (p. 345). New York: JurisNet, LLC.

Chapter 3
Juries

An individual's sense of competence and motivation to be competent are closely tied to a sense of control and an assessment of whether one has "the capacity to interact effectively with the environment."[1] People are parsimonious in allocating their time and skills and thus direct themselves to endeavors that show some relation between effort and result, contribution and remuneration, and practice and improvement. When people perceive a system to be chaotic, unpredictable and arbitrary, they lose their motivation to excel in that system. How individuals perceive the system in which they work largely determines their behavior, motivation and, perhaps more importantly, desire to learn and improve performance.

The practical implication of human motivation research is that litigation attorneys who embrace the popular perception of jurors as erratic, ignorant and unreliable quickly give up on their own professional development as case evaluators and client advocates. In a system perceived to be rigged against solid evidence and sound argument, few attorneys will spend their time evaluating facts and honing communication skills. Disrespecting jurors thus becomes a mechanism for disregarding effort.

The study attorneys express a high level of confidence in the jury system. Although they recognize that individual jurors may be wayward and jurors do not always follow a strictly legal route in rendering a verdict, they believe jury decisions generally are correct. In seeing jury verdicts as the right results in most cases, the study attorneys align themselves with judges and professors who have spent years, sometimes lifetimes, observing and studying real juries.[2] These studies

---

[1]Plaut, Victoria C., & Markus, Hazel Rose. The "inside" story: A cultural-historical analysis of being smart and motivated, American style. In Elliot, Andrew J., & Dweck, Carol S. (2007). *Handbook of competence and motivation* (p. 472). New York: The Guilford Press.

[2]Kalven, Harry, & Zeisel, Hans. (1996). *The American jury*. Vidmar, Neil. (1998). The performance of the American civil jury: An empirical perspective. *Arizona Law Review, 40*, 849, 853. Kalven, Harry. (1964, October). The dignity of the civil jury. *Virginia Law Review, 50*(6), 1055, 1065–1066. Vidmar, Neil, & Hans, Valerie. (2007). *American juries: The verdict* (p. 149).

show that the judge would reach the same result as the jury in 74% to 78% of trials, contradicting views described by Cornell University law professor Kevin Clermont as "elitist perceptions of a biased and incompetent jury system." Although some lawyers hold onto "misperceptions" and "stereotypical" views of the jury, Clermont states, "There is, however, no actual evidence that juries are relatively biased or incompetent."[3]

3.1 Overall Assessment of Jurors' Decisions

The study attorneys recognize that the civil justice system is imperfect, but they generally trust the system and respect jurors' verdicts. Assessing the overall validity of jury verdicts, the attorneys remark:

- Facts control lawsuits. Juries ordinarily and predictably reach the right results based on the fundamental facts that make up the lawsuit. Some cases you will never win no matter how good or prepared you are.
- There's better than 500 years of experience on a jury panel. You cannot fool a panel, or at least you cannot fool nine of them.
- I've learned that usually what's right occurs if you're legitimately correct. I believe in the system. I don't think I felt that way initially.
- A lot of plaintiff attorneys see a massive injury and struggle to find a deviation from the standard of care. But juries understand that you can have a bad outcome without a breach of the standard of care. They know shit happens.
- First, there's no such thing as a runaway jury. They are very rational. You may not like the result, but they don't run away. They may get incensed, they may be offended by something, but that's different. That's what regular people do.
- Garden-variety working people do not want to be on the jury. Oddly enough, once they are on the jury and resigned to the fact they're there, they bring their best efforts to decide the case. If you read about a big verdict, they usually have someone who is badly injured and they deserved every nickel they got.

The attorneys thought that jurors were particularly adept in determining whether witnesses were truthful and whether attorneys sincerely believed in their clients and

Amherst, New York: Prometheus Books. Wissler, Roselle L., Hart, Allen J., & Saks, Michael J. (1999). Decision making about general damages: A comparison of jurors, judges and lawyers. *Michigan Law Review, 98,* 751. Heuer, Larry, & Penrod, Steven. (1994, February). Trial complexity: A field investigation of its meaning and its effects. *Law and Human Behavior, 18*(1), 29–52. Robbennolt, Jennifer K. (2005). Evaluating juries by comparison to judges: A benchmark for judging. *Florida State University Law Review, 32,* 469, 477.

[3]Clermont, Kevin M. (2008, May 10). Litigation realities redux. Cornell Legal Studies Research Paper No. 08–006, p. 32. Available at SSRN: http://ssrn.com/abstract=1112274. See Spencer, Bruce. (2007). Estimating the accuracy of jury verdicts. *Journal of Empirical Legal Studies, 4*(2), 305–329.

positions. "There is a number that sits with me very well," comments a defense attorney, "and I can be very persuasive when I really believe in that number. Juries feel it when you believe in your number, and they know when you're uncomfortable with it."

Some attorneys said they considered juries to be more impartial and objective than arbitrators. An arbitrator, one attorney commented, "may be concerned about potential loss of business" because some companies "won't use an arbitrator who has made a big award against them."[4] Another attorney believes that "a jury can make a tougher call than an arbitrator. Defense verdicts are not as common in arbitration because arbitrators tend to split the baby and jurors do not."

Although a few study attorneys said that juries are unpredictable, the attorneys usually seemed to be referring to jurors' deliberative processes rather than the ultimate result. In describing an employment discrimination case in which the jurors discussed their own experiences with employment discrimination, for instance, one attorney said, "If you have been to trial you learn there is no way in hell you can predict what will happen. You find out that some of your best evidence just goes right by them, and they reach a decision based on something entirely different from what I thought." Another remarked, "When I talk to juries even when I've won, I've thought, 'My God in Heaven, I never thought that is what they were thinking was important.'"

3.2 Shortcomings in Juror Deliberations

The attorneys acknowledge that the ascertainment of "truth" is often a subjective determination, jurors sometimes ignore critical evidence and their decision-making processes may deviate from legal standards:

- Some people internalize what is justice. I tell them [clients], "Justice is the application of our system of jurisprudence to specific events by fallible people." This means that cases that ought to be won are lost every day and vice versa.

---

[4]Although the attorney did not reference any studies, one 1999 study of medical malpractice arbitrations reported that "plaintiffs had a 26 percent chance of winning with a repeat arbitrator, compared to a 30 percent chance of winning with a non-repeat arbitrator." In the "three cases in which the plaintiffs were awarded over $1,000,000, the arbitrator was only employed in that case." Nieto, Marcus, & Hosel, Margaret. (2000, December). *Arbitration in California managed health care systems* (pp. 22–23). California Research Bureau, California State Library. The results of a more recent study of AAA employment arbitration decisions between 2003 and 2007, conducted by Cornell University law professor Alexander Colvin, "indicate the existence of a significant repeat employer-arbitrator pairing effect in which employees on average have lower win rates and receive smaller damage awards where the same arbitrator is involved in more than one case with the same employer, a finding supporting some of the fairness criticisms directed at mandatory employment arbitration." Colvin, Alexander. (2011). An empirical study of employment arbitration: Case outcomes and processes. *Journal of Empirical Legal Studies, 8*(1), 1.

- Two people will see the exact same event and come away with irreconcilable views. There's truth – like God – and there's legal truth. We don't have a perfect system for understanding what juries and judges will believe. That's why a common theme is your credibility – your credibility with the client, the client's credibility, your credibility with the other side.
- Jurors see unfairness. If jurors perceive injustice, they don't always follow the law – they try to fix it.
- They can be very intuitive about credibility. That's why I tell clients they must always be scrupulously honest.
- They [jurors] look at the people; they see the story of the case. The jury does not get all the details, but they do the right thing.

Although these remarks indicate that the study lawyers generally trusted juries, they were critical of individual jurors. In describing their trial frustrations and disappointments, the attorneys directed their criticisms at specific jurors rather than juries in general. This distinction is illustrated by one attorney's comment about a minority faction: "After we settled that case, I talked with the jury about some of the plaintiff's testimony that I found shocking. A couple of them were making excuses for him [the plaintiff], but they would not have carried the day."

The attorneys' perception that jurors overlook details but generally reach sound conclusions is consistent with research regarding the psychology of jury decision making. As law professor Neal Feigenson explains, jurors try to achieve "total justice":

> They strive to square all accounts between the parties (even though the issues the law asks them to resolve may not be framed in those terms), to consider all information they deem relevant (even if the law tries to keep them from relying on some of it), to reach a decision that is correct as a whole (even if they reach it by blurring legally distinct questions), and to feel right about their decision (even though the law discourages them from using their emotions to decide). The decisions that result are often, like common sense itself, "right for the wrong reasons": consistent with the law but not necessarily the result of strict adherence to legal rules and procedures.[5]

Legal blaming, Feigenson elaborates, is multidimensional. In determining liability and damages, jurors rely on four main factors: (1) their common sense; (2) the formal law; (3) the thinking of experts; and (4) the facts of the case.[6] Jurors see justice as the "righting of an imbalance," and they "are more concerned with making things come out right than with strictly following the relevant legal rules."[7]

---

[5]Feigenson, Neal. (2000). *Legal blame: How jurors think and talk about accidents* (p. 5). Washington, D.C.: American Psychological Association.

[6]*Id.* at 10.

[7]*Id.* at 16. See Diamond, Shari Seidman, Murphy, Beth, & Rose, Mary R. The "kettleful of law" in real jury deliberations: Successes and failures. Available at http://www.law.berkeley.edu/files/Diamondpaper20oct1Nov.pdf.

3.3 Jury Stereotypes and Caricatures

While discussing juries, the study attorneys frequently mentioned the famed "McDonald's Coffee Case" and the O.J. Simpson criminal trial. Both plaintiffs' and defense attorneys decried the public misperceptions regarding those cases, and plaintiffs' attorneys often expressed concern about how other well-publicized cases were affecting jurors' attitudes:

- Unsophisticated consumers – which could be plaintiffs or businessmen – get ideas about juries and cases from the media, the source of all the other misleading information, which glorifies bad cases and misrepresents the good ones. People talk about the McDonald's case, but they don't understand what happened in that case. That woman's private parts were burned and it was McDonald's decision to serve it at 180 degrees. There's a misrepresentation of how the system operates and a massive increase in the amount of misunderstanding.
- People point to the O.J. Simpson case as a perfect example of a runaway jury. That's not the way I see it. The prosecution did a lousy job in my opinion and Johnnie Cochran and Robert Shapiro and the other attorneys on their [defense] team knew what they were doing. Remember that thing with the glove? Well, it didn't fit.
- It has become profitable for people on the other side [defense attorneys and insurance companies] to publicize cases like McDonald's and the burglar who fell through the roof and sued the owner. The point is, they do this to create the expectation by the jury that plaintiffs are making frivolous clams. Juries determine every question you asked me, and if you can convince a jury that claims are excessively overstated, fabricated and fraudulent, then you will have a much easier time with juries.

One attorney pointed out that publicity regarding "frivolous" claims has the ironic effect of raising client expectations more than pre-conditioning jurors. Clients with meritorious cases, he explains, have developed unrealistically high expectations because they reason, "If a bad case is worth millions, a good case like mine must be worth much more."

3.4 Trusting the Process

Closely related to the attorneys' confidence in the jury system is their ability to maintain a sense of proportion throughout the trial and discriminate between serious setbacks and minor glitches. Although novice trial attorneys may vacillate between hoping that the jury will overlook a damaging fact and worrying that the jury will detect a missing element of proof, the study attorneys have an underlying sense of trust in the process. This trust is not based on their ability to outsmart the jury but rather is based on an attitude of respect and candor, thorough pre-trial case preparation and a frank recognition that case weaknesses are better confronted than concealed:

- Many cases have very weak defenses. Jurors see it right away. They're real people saying, "You're stupid and you're wasting my time."
- You cannot hide anything from the jury.
- If a case has negative aspects, you take the lead on the DUI [driving under the influence] conviction, on the felony conviction. They hear it in your voir dire, they hear it in your opening statement, they hear it on your client's direct examination. You take that negative and run with it. By the time the defense brings it up, the jurors are like, "Yeah, we already heard about that."
- Your credibility is absolutely critical. I want the jury to know I am scrupulously honest and straight with the facts. I will also call opposing counsel on it if they're being dishonest.
- If you're afraid of juries, you have no business representing clients. A lot of attorneys don't want to go to trial because they don't like juries. They don't want to take a risk. The clients don't know this.

One attorney described how she meets with jurors after trials and elicits their opinions about her representation: "Anything you do to lose your credibility you need to know about. When you lose your credibility, you're done – you can't give them any excuse to go against your client."

The study attorneys are comfortable with jurors and many are known for their extraordinary ability to establish a rapport with jurors. The attorneys' experience has taught them to communicate respectfully, have faith in the process and allow it to run its course:

- I tell them, "You are not here to rubber-stamp anything but to evaluate. People tell you stories all day, and you decide whether it's right, whether it's true. It's the same in this court."
- You cannot be nasty. You cannot be cynical.
- I tell the jurors, "We know what the facts are. We just disagree about what the result should be. We brought it to you to decide."
- When you catch a witness lying you just say, "Tell me more." You let the lie go on because lying witnesses think the more they talk, the more credible they'll become. You have to learn to be patient and trust the process.
- I was trying a case with one of our associates. She said, "the plaintiff's attorney is changing his theory all the time. First he argues the x-rays are the most important evidence. Then at closing he says the jury should disregard the x-rays." I told her, "Just relax." She was able to see how the case unfolds.

Some study attorneys said that jurors later became their clients. One attorney, who describes herself as "not the type of person who walks into a courtroom and my ego walks ahead of me," said, "I like juries and I do well with juries. I usually get one or two clients from every jury trial."

Juries, of course, are only a part of a larger civil justice system. For some study attorneys, their trust and confidence in jurors reflects a broader appreciation for the American system of justice. One study attorney, who travels extensively, said:

> I get my sense of justice by spending a lot of my time in places without justice. When I'm in court, I tell the jury, "We're in a very sacred place. This is what makes us different from Afghanistan. This is the rule of law." I've had a lot of experience in lawless societies and that's why I say, "This is sacred ground."

His respect for the jury system is set in an historical, comparative and deeply personal context. Although other study attorneys may share his allegiance but not his reverence, their positive statements about jurors' decisions, their enthusiasm about their work and the sheer amount of time they devote to trial preparation suggest that they, too, are strongly committed to this civil justice system.

Chapter 4
Clients

An attorney's relationship with the client is at the core of every important decision made about case evaluation and resolution. That relationship is complex and dynamic – at times concordant, at times contentious. To understand how the attorneys view clients and the attorney-client relationship, this chapter addresses four topics: (1) attorneys' ethical obligations to clients; (2) attorney-client counseling models; (3) allocation of authority, control and power between attorneys and clients; and (4) sources of client control problems.

4.1 Ethical Obligations

Attorneys' ethical standards require them to fulfill multiple, sometimes conflicting roles: advocate, advisor, negotiator and evaluator.[1] They perform these roles in an adversarial context depicted by one attorney as a surgical suite where one surgeon tries to save the life of a patient while another surgeon, similarly trained and equally competent, tries to wrest the scalpel from his hand. The stakes are often enormous, the outlook is uncertain and the participants are anxious. In this tense and antagonistic setting, attorneys find it challenging just to fulfill the two roles of advocate and advisor:

> I wear two hats – my advocate hat and my advisor hat. That is a very difficult balance to strike. It's especially tough because so many clients ask, "Do you believe in my case?" They are so emotionally invested and stressed from the litigation that they want to believe that you believe in me. In a lot of cases, their credibility is under attack and they need to know whether you're behind them, whether you believe in them.

---

[1]Center for Professional Responsibility. (2007). *Model rules of professional conduct* (p. 1). Chicago, Illinois: American Bar Association.

R. Kiser, *How Leading Lawyers Think*,
DOI 10.1007/978-3-642-20484-5_4, © Springer-Verlag Berlin Heidelberg 2011

As an ethical and practical matter, an attorney is continually confronted with the challenge of convincing the client she can be a powerful advocate while maintaining the objectivity of a prudent advisor.

Simultaneously advocating a client's position, by presenting it in the most persuasive light to an opponent and the court, and objectively advising a client, by pointing out all of the strengths and weaknesses of the case to the client, can seem paradoxical if not impracticable. Some of the study attorneys see these roles as conflicting, at least in their potential to confuse clients and raise unrealistic expectations about the case outcome. "Clients are hearing you tell the other side what you argue the case is worth," explains a plaintiffs' attorney. "You have to talk with the client and indicate this is argument, not a value or a number for settlement." Another attorney is preemptive: "I tell clients, 'Don't believe the figure in the demand letter. It's at least two times what you could possibly recover.'" Yet another attorney believes the attorney's roles as advocate and advisor are complementary, not conflicting: "There's a tension, but it's a tension that works well. It creates credibility for the client to see the attorney as an advocate and then to understand their role as advisor; it can help clients come to good decisions."

4.2   Client Counseling Models

The legal profession's attempt to integrate all of the attorneys' roles into their law office practices has yielded at least three different counseling models: directive, collaborative and client-centered. Derived, in part, from psychological counseling research, these models can be seen as a continuum of client autonomy.[2] In the directive model, the attorney attempts to impose his legal and moral judgment upon the client.[3] Its extreme form is articulated by Judge Clement Haynsworth: "The lawyer must never forget he is the master. He is not here to do the client's bidding. It is for the lawyer to decide what is morally and legally right."[4] A more balanced and participative view of attorney-client decision making is reflected in the collaborative approach. Attorneys and clients, acting like friends, share and respect each other's opinions, and the attorney probes gently to ensure that the client is considering all possible consequences. When properly executed, the collaborative model produces mature, considered and morally defensible decisions that, in the long term, reflect the client's better nature. The third model, the client-centered approach, shifts decision-making authority completely to the client. It promotes the client's autonomy, emphasizes the attorney's neutrality, facilitates a narrow

---

[2]For an overview of psychiatric interviewing techniques, see Shea, Shawn Christopher. (1998). *Psychiatric interviewing: The art of understanding*. Philadelphia: Saunders.

[3]The discussion of counseling models in this paragraph relies on Cochran, Robert F., Jr., *et al.* (2003). Symposium: Client counseling and moral responsibility. *Pepperdine Law Review, 30*, 591.

[4]*Id.* at 595.

cost-benefit analysis and minimizes moral issues and societal consequences. Not surprisingly, it has been characterized as the "attorney as hired gun" version.[5]

4.2.1 "Forceful Educator" Model

The study attorneys do not fit squarely into a directive, collaborative or client-centered model. If forced into a model, many would be characterized as directive with a large measure of collaboration. A more descriptive model for the study attorneys would be the "forceful educator," maximizing the attorney's knowledge, experience, conviction, and commitment while preserving the client's autonomy in deciding to settle or try a case. When asked how they perceive their roles, many attorneys referred to themselves as educators:

- A teacher more than anything else. I have to explain to the client what is compensable and not compensable, what is settlement and ADR [alternative dispute resolution], and I have to explain the law and the American system that you don't get your attorneys fees when you win. I also have to explain what is relevant and what is not relevant.
- My role has to be an information gatherer and an educator. I need to gather the information, explain the expert testimony, and tell them about the juror pool, and run comparable jury verdicts.
- I'm a coach also, a coach and an educator. I teach them how to ask the right questions and to understand the budget and to know that stuff like loss of time won't ever be recovered. Witness preparation can win or lose cases.
- Teacher, coach and sometimes [long pause] the principal. I want to teach them.
- Part of the education process is explaining what is realistic and what are the problems in the case. If a client comes in telling me what a case is worth, he's not going to be a client unless he's a CPA or there's a liquidated damages clause.

The role of attorney as educator is broad, encompassing civil procedure, substantive legal principles, deposition and trial preparation, representative case outcomes and likely juror perceptions. If the limited range of remedies afforded by the legal system may disappoint the client, the educator's role is yet more critical and difficult. "There's an element of psychology," notes a plaintiffs' personal injury attorney, "that plays a role in educating a client about how we have an imperfect system that cannot compensate every type of injury like the death of a child at trial."

---

[5]For a discussion of the diminishing independence of outside counsel, see Galanter, Marc, & Henderson, William. (2008). The elastic tournament: The second transformation of the big law firm. *Stanford Law Review*, *60*, 102, 147–148.

4.2.2 *"Benevolent Authoritarian" Model*

Although the study attorneys cited the educator role as the most common counseling model, their views spanned a wide range of counseling styles from strongly
authoritarian to consistently dispassionate. Representative of the more authoritarian
styles are these comments:

- I take a very strong position and I've gotten stronger about this the longer I'm in
  this business. You don't sit back and just say, "It's the client's decision so that's
  what I've got to do." I don't believe in taking the passive role. I hate to lose so I
  can't take a passive role with the client's expectations. I really don't like to lose.
  I can remember every loss. I have to win at least four cases before I can get over
  one loss.
- I tell them what they should do whether they like it or not. You have to be
  assertive because most clients do not have the background and experience.
- What I do is to try to set them straight on the ups and downs of the case, and
  they have confidence in me to guide them. I expect them to exercise sound
  judgment and follow my advice. If I can't get them educated, I'll just have a
  larger Excedrin bill. I give it to them straight – "just because you've been off
  of work, and you've lost $200,000 in wages, that doesn't mean you'll get that,
  especially if you're 40 to 50 percent at fault. Your own fault will come down like
  a meat cleaver in your case." That's what I tell them.
- In one case I could tell the client thought he had done a great job on the [witness]
  stand. The client asked me, "How did I do?" I said, "You were terrible." He said,
  "You're a bitch." That doesn't bother me. I give it to them straight.
- You beat it out of them real quick. They tell you, "I heard it from my friend or a
  family member." I tell them, "You don't know how this works. I will tell you the
  reality. Back in the 70's, you could get three times specials [medical expenses] –
  there's no way you're going to get that now."
- I try to be personal with all of my clients. I try to be supportive of them. I try to
  be the one sitting with them at their depos. I rarely let another attorney do that.
  They know I am very involved. Sometimes it doesn't work out and I've said,
  "You're fucking messing up. What happened to that kind, compassionate doctor
  I saw when we first met?"

Although the authoritarian style may seem unilateral and dictatorial, it often reflects
the client's high level of trust and confidence in the attorney. "I give them a lot
of emotional support," comments a medical malpractice defense attorney. "One
physician told me, 'You are my doctor. You are taking care of me.' When you have
that bond with your client, they are willing for you to take the lead."

4.2.3 *"Dispassionate Advisor" Model*

On the spectrum of client autonomy, the counseling model that affords the greatest
degree of client autonomy could be called the "dispassionate advisor" model.

Employed most often in the insurance defense context, its communication style is neutral, and the attorney's attitude ranges from detachment to deference:

- On the defense side, we represent clients who have insurance, but it may be large retentions or deductibles. They are all proactive, very sophisticated. I make recommendations. I would never tell a client what to do.
- Corporations have in-house counsel and when the attorney is the client, he knows better than I do what the case is worth. Corporations certainly generally have a much better idea of what a case is worth because they've been through a lot in the past.
- The first thing in advising a client to settle or try is I have no personal interest in whether the client settles or doesn't. Whatever happens – whether it's the right or the wrong one – it's not my case. The longer I do this the longer I realize it's the client's case, not my case.

The dispassionate advisor role may be more a reflection of the client's sophistication than the attorney's personality. Many attorneys noted that their approach to counseling is highly individualized, and they may simultaneously represent a client needing a high level of assurance and direction and another client functioning with minimal input from the attorney.

4.2.4 Client's Decision to Settle or Try

Whether assuming the forceful educator, benevolent authoritarian or dispassionate advisor role, the study attorneys acknowledged and respected the client's right to determine negotiation positions, reject an adversary's settlement proposal and take a case to trial. When the client's decision conflicts with the attorney's recommendation, the attorney continues to act as an independent advisor and committed advocate:

- I do tell them it's their decision – "whatever your decision is, I'll support you, and I'll tell you when you're screwing up."
- I will tell clients if they want me to demand $2 million I will. But usually they always ask me what do I think. I give clients the freedom they deserve. But when clients have disagreed with me, they have always been wrong.
- I've had two cases that went to trial against my advice. Both times either the client did not tell me something or did the opposite of what I told him to do. The problem usually turns up in the medical records. Ninety percent of the time there is something in the records the client has not told you.
- The obligation of the attorney is to provide an informed consent talk – discussing the strengths and weaknesses of cases. I always indicate that I'm willing to try this case, but they need to understand the perils of the jury system.

For both the client and the attorney, the option of trying the case often enhances their negotiation leverage. "If an attorney loses the willingness to try a case," comments a managing partner, "he has basically given up his ability to effectively negotiate. I have to have the ability to walk away and know what will happen at trial."

4.3   Authority, Control and Power

At an early stage in law school, nearly every attorney learns that the client makes substantive decisions like the decision to settle a lawsuit, and the attorney is permitted to make non-dispositive, procedural decisions like granting an extension of time to respond to discovery requests. This principle is embodied in Rule 1.2 of the Model Rules of Professional Conduct:

> [A] lawyer shall abide by a client's decisions concerning the objectives of representation and, as required by Rule 1.4, shall consult with the client as to the means by which they are to be pursued. A lawyer may take such action on behalf of the client as is impliedly authorized to carry out the representation. A lawyer shall abide by a client's decision whether to settle a matter.

This rule allocates but does not elucidate decision-making responsibility.

In actual practice, the attorney often defines the problems, identifies the critical issues and formulates the alternatives, leaving the client as the nominal decision maker and the attorney as the functional decision maker. As one attorney noted, "The attorney is the decision maker in 99.5% of the cases. The client will only consent to what they understand to be the risks. It's my job to be the educator." This decision-making paradox – "the same expert who is diagnosing the flaw is the one who will be paid to fix it"[6] – is called the "expert service problem." It occurs whenever an expert has superior knowledge required to both understand and solve a problem; and the customer, patient or client must have as much confidence in the expert's diagnostic skills as he has in the expert's problem-solving capabilities. Like a patient consenting to a surgical procedure recommended by a physician, the client relies heavily, if not exclusively, on the attorney's risk assessment.

When asked, "Who is the actual decision maker – the client or the attorney?" the study attorneys made two general observations: (1) the attorney has a major influence and may be the actual decision maker in most cases; and (2) decision-making power varies greatly between plaintiffs and defendants and insured and uninsured parties. The oft-cited rule that the client must consent to a settlement does not comprehend the nuances and realities of attorney-client communication and may underplay the attorney's practical responsibilities and power.

---

[6]Leonhardt, David. (2007, November 7). When trust in an expert is unwise. *New York Times.* Available at http://www.nytimes.com/2007/11/07/business/07leonhardt.html.

4.3.1 Actual Decision Makers

Looking first at the general issue of decision-making power, most attorneys credit the attorney with substantial influence, if not control:

- For all intents and purposes, ethically it's a joint decision but, truthfully, the attorney decides. The client looks to them for guidance. The client asks, "What is this case worth?" and the attorney explains.
- If I don't want to try the case, I will emphasize my fears. If I want to try the case, I'll emphasize the good aspects. It's an ethical dilemma. You can move the client to the decision you want.
- You have strong clients sometimes. They clearly drive the decision sometimes. Most clients rely on the lawyer. If you are strong and confident, they will listen to you. Lawyers have a lot to do with the decision.
- Your role varies with the client. In 75% of my cases they're relying entirely on me to evaluate the case, work up the case and tell them what it's worth. I have all the information.
- A lot of my clients are out-of-state, so they rely completely on me. I have strong and close relationships with them.
- I think it's the attorney for the most part. If I tell them what I would do, they're essentially going with my recommendation.

Although formal decision-making authority rests with the client under Rule 1.2, the study attorneys recognize that their opinions frequently underpin the client's exercise of that authority. "The lawyer has tremendous influence," states an attorney who represents both plaintiffs and defendants. "One thing that has struck me over the years is how much control the attorney has over the settlement, how much the client is looking up to the attorney."

4.3.2 Plaintiff and Defendant Decision-Making Authority

Just as counseling styles are affected by the roles and sophistication of the parties, decision-making authority seems to vary between plaintiffs and defendants, novice and serial litigants, and insured and uninsured defendants. Both plaintiffs' and defense attorneys – but predominantly defense attorneys – believe that plaintiffs' attorneys hold considerable sway over their clients:

- On the plaintiffs' side, two-thirds of the time it's the attorney who is the decision maker. The client will cede – "get me whatever you can." In the other one-third, the client has determined what should happen. On the defense side, I don't make any decisions – in only 5% of the cases do they say, "this is a range and get me whatever you can." It's more of a collaborative decision.
- Generally, a plaintiff's attorney can get the client to do what he wants. In general, the plaintiff's attorney makes the decision.

- I think when you are bringing a suit on behalf of a company or an individual, the attorney is the decision maker more often than not because he will make the recommendation. People listen to their lawyer's advice. On the defense side, someone is saying, "You need to pay me money." You often have an institution, an employer or an insurance company. You are dealing with sophisticated clients used to litigation, more forensically astute. This is how I see it in my practice.
- On the plaintiffs' side, if it's a good lawyer, he's the decision maker. That's what a good lawyer does. Absolutely, that's what they should do. A bad lawyer is not the decision maker.

One plaintiffs' attorney thought about the cases she had handled throughout her career and said, "I've never had a client who said 'take it to the mat' if I recommended the settlement." Other plaintiffs' attorneys may not elicit this degree of trust, according to a defense attorney: "On the plaintiff side, some plaintiffs do not trust their lawyers; they do not listen to what they say. This is why plaintiff attorneys are happy to go to mediation – to have someone push their client."

4.3.3   Insurer Effect

For defense attorneys, the existence of insurance sometimes shifts decision-making authority directly to the insurer:

- I would love to say our word is golden, but it's not. I make recommendations, but they [insurers] do not always take them.
- The auto claims people treat us as lackeys. They always have the option to take the cases to another firm. They decide whether to settle, mediate or go to judicial arbitration.
- We have to prepare reports, but they don't give a damn. They have committees that make decisions. They have seven people sitting around and trying to show who is the most macho and will pay the least. Some want your input; few do.
- The real person rarely has any say in whether the case settles. So if we're talking about the insured defendants, it's the insurer that has the ultimate say. That's how the policy's written.

From the perspective of plaintiffs' attorneys, the existence of insurance frequently takes defense counsel "out of the loop." In the opinion of one plaintiffs' attorney, "Everything is done by the adjuster or a committee. The tail does not wag the dog; the dog wags the tail. The lawyer is the tail."

4.4   Client Control Problems

The erosion of trust and confidence in an attorney-client relationship is often characterized by a mediator or judge as a "client control problem." It usually is raised as a question – "Is there a client control problem?" – that serves as a shorthand way of asking whether the attorney has one view of the case value and the client has quite another. Reflecting a serious breakdown in the attorney-client relationship, client control problems often propel cases into trials that yield outcomes inferior to the settlement alternatives or verdicts that are, at best, Pyrrhic victories. Because client control problems are the worst-case scenario in client counseling, foreshadowing poor quality decisions, damaged reputations, unpaid attorneys' fees and legal malpractice claims, it is essential to anticipate and avoid these problems.

The study attorneys reported very few client control problems but were quite familiar with their manifestations in adversaries' settlement negotiations. When asked their opinions about the sources and causes of client control problems, they emphasized overconfidence, inaccurate case evaluation, inadequate client counseling and distrust:

- When attorneys have client control problems it occurs because the attorney has built up an image of the case and gave that to the client. It's very hard to make that mental turn and potentially lose that much confidence in the face of the client. Other times it's the Dunning-Kruger effect.[7] The client or the attorney – sometimes both – does not know enough to know what he doesn't know.
- When cases go to trial because the attorney has a client control problem, on the plaintiffs' side it usually happens when the attorney did not give enough guidance at the start of the case. One thing that makes a case most likely to go to trial is a client who has misperceptions of the case. Defense lawyers have a tendency to be confident because they want to endear themselves to the client and figure it will settle anyway. Sometimes they have to change their evaluation at the last minute, and carriers really hate that. Sometimes you get professional clients who think they know more about case evaluation than you do.
- The source of client control problems is plaintiffs' greed and lack of understanding of reality – lack of appreciation of trial risks. I want to make sure our clients are advised of risks. With other attorneys sometimes there's an inability by the attorney to communicate the true reality and counsel the clients that their view may not be agreed to by the judge or jury. Some attorneys start right in advising clients of risks, but if the clients have a strong position they just leave it at that. In some cases, it seems that the client could not have been given a comprehensive, relatively accurate evaluation of the risks if they made the decision to try a case. Arrogance is another factor.

---

[7]"Dunning-Kruger" refers to the research conducted by professors Justin Kruger and David Dunning. They "found that college students who scored in the bottom 25 percent on a course exam handed in their papers feeling like they had outperformed the majority of their peers. Some of the students were so blind to their ineptitude that even after scoring poorly on a test, they spent hours attempting to convince their professors that their answers were actually correct and the test was wrong." Brown, Jeff, & Fenske, Mark. (2010). *The winner's brain* (p. 62). Cambridge, Massachusetts: Da Capo Press.

- They have to trust you and if you don't have that client relationship it will be difficult. You have to take the time not to be dismissive with clients. If you create that type of relationship, you don't have client control problems.
- Some attorneys have no client control and the mediator has to work with the client because there's no trust between the client and the attorney. Right from the beginning of the case, before you take it on, you have to make a judgment as to whether the client will take your advice. If the client doesn't trust you, you're not benefitting anyone.

Some client control problems seem to be an inevitable part of every attorney's career, an unavoidable consequence of the client's personality, immaturity or overreaching. "It's a personality type, a style, people who are just going to have difficulties no matter who is representing them," notes one attorney. Another attorney comments, "Sometimes you get clients who have no clue about what they're facing. They're just unreasonable. You run into four or five in your career who are totally off the mark." After stating that client problems are rare, one of the younger attorneys in the study paused and reflected, "I have one this week, so it's on my mind. It's a great settlement, but the client thinks it should have been more."

Part II
Frameworks and Connections

Chapter 5
Frameworks

In Part II of this book, the emphasis shifts from the roles and responsibilities of attorneys, jurors, and clients to the mental frameworks and evaluative sources of the study attorneys. Having discussed how the attorneys perceive themselves and the major legal actors in Part I, we now examine how the attorneys put a case together – how they visualize and meld case facts and personalities to achieve exceptional results.

Like experts in other domains, the study attorneys are largely unaware of the distinct phases of their planning and implementation processes and can describe only what they have done, not necessarily the specific sequences that preceded a particular action, the information they considered before taking that action and the justifications for their choices. When asked what enables them to understand jurors' sensitivities or see something in a case that other attorneys overlooked, the most common explanation was simply, "experience." In this respect, they display the expert trait of "automaticity," the unconscious selection of alternative explanations for ambiguous events and the rapid execution of successful strategies based on previous experiences that are cognitively accessible but consciously infrangible. Like chess masters, they quickly evaluate the positions and "identify weaknesses and associated lines of attack."[1] Their processes "involve rapid perception and encoding, and thus only the end products of these encoding processes are verbalized."[2] This rapid acceleration of the evaluative process is described succinctly by a managing partner: "As you become more experienced, you use the same processes but don't go through the steps as slowly."

When examined closely, the study attorneys' methods – their perception, conception, construction and presentation of a client's case – appear to have seven

---

[1] Ericsson, K. Anders. Protocol analysis and expert thought: Concurrent verbalizations of thinking during experts' performance on representative tasks. In Ericsson, K. Anders, *et al.* (Eds.). (2006). *The Cambridge handbook of expertise and expert performance* (p. 233). New York: Cambridge University Press.

[2] *Id.*

major features. First, they employ a technique known as "backward mapping" or, more simply, starting at the end of a case and working backward to realize that end. Second, they form a composite view of the case, taking a global outlook on the evidence and eschewing a narrow, deconstructionist approach. Third, they create overarching themes to link facts and hook into jurors' values and sense of morality. Fourth, they recognize that jurors process information visually, and they are visual thinkers themselves or have learned how to convey vivid pictures of critical case facts and events. Fifth, they see the case through multiple lenses, assuming the roles of jurors, judges, mediators, insurers, and opposing counsel to develop a persuasive argument and presentation. Sixth, they integrate both explicit knowledge and tacit knowledge into their legal representation, enabling the client to obtain the benefit of their technical legal knowledge and their personal judgments about people. Seventh, they have peripheral vision, a habit and skill of scoping, scanning, interpreting, and probing beyond the immediate field to anticipate problems and avoid mishaps. None of the attorneys cataloged their methods using these exact terms, but in listening to them, repeatedly reviewing the interview transcripts and relating their comments to the general research on expert performance, these seven methods correspond very closely with their explanations.

5.1 Backward Mapping

Superior strategists organize a case around the trial, the decisive event in the case. Even when a case is settled instead of tried, the anticipated trial is the reference point for negotiations, and the settlement is premised on assumptions about the likely trial outcome. Law professors Stefan Krieger and Richard Neumann assert that, although the attorney's identification of the decisive event is logical, the visualization of that event is subliminal:

> But often the event first enters the lawyer's consciousness as a picture imagined in precise and vivid detail. It is not usually selected in some more rational way. For example, a trial lawyer "sees" decisive courtroom events that have not yet happened – such as the direct examination in which the client relives the misery that led to the lawsuit or the cross-examination that discredits the adversary's leading witness – and then the trial lawyer patiently develops the testimony and tangible evidence needed to reproduce those scenes in front of a jury in the way they had first been fantasized.[3]

This visualization of the trial, Krieger and Neumann explain, enables the attorney to "cause the decisive event by planning backward – from the future to the present – identifying the things that must be done to make that event happen, and developing sub-strategies to cause each of them." This is the most important strategic concept, according to Krieger and Neumann, "because it concentrates

---

[3]Krieger, Stefan H., & Neumann, Richard K. (2007). *Essential lawyering skills* (p. 37). New York: Aspen Publishers.

your work on those things that are most likely to resolve the situation on desirable terms."[4]

Instead of woodenly plotting the next procedural step – filing a complaint or a responsive pleading – the study attorneys visualize a successful outcome and work back from that result.[5] They start with the last events before juror deliberations – closing argument and the court's instructions to the jury – and use those final actions as the anchor for their advice and strategies:

- Research the jury instructions. Don't start off with researching the law in general – start with the instructions the jury will get. At the beginning of cases, I send clients the jury instructions. This is what the jury will be told. That gives them a much better idea of what their position is and what the trial will be about.
- I also look at what the jury charges will be. Can I prove my affirmative defenses?
- Case analysis is really important. In the first meeting with the client, you should be thinking about your closing argument. Think about what you are going to say about this client.
- I've done a whole lot of trials. I figure out from the beginning what I need to win. You need a story. Look at the jury instructions early on in the case; figure out what you need to prove. Attorneys have a shoot from the hip attitude, and they don't always focus on the right things.

When a study attorney first started practicing law, one of the partners in his firm said, "You start your opening statement when the client walks in the door and you work backwards from there." After trying many cases, he notes, "That was good advice I got when I was young."

Thinking first about the jury instructions and trial arguments is part of a broader effort to focus on overall objectives and outcomes. Pre-trial procedures, case strategies and client advice are viewed through the prism of the ultimate trial:

- I spend the first month of a case thinking about how a jury will feel about the case – that's where the case value is.
- You have to think about, "Where am I going to be at the end of this?"
- When I see how other attorneys handle cases, I wonder, "Are they thinking about what they're doing to get to winning or just going through the motions?" Attorneys now are overwhelmed with cases. Hence, no thinking. It's always the same conventions – send interrogs, take depos. There's no deep thinking. In my practice, the whole process has to be thought through. Other attorneys don't do this because they are overwhelmed by things, too many cases.

---

[4]*Id.*

[5]This process should be distinguished from "top-down" decision making, where the objective is determined before the facts are analyzed and the facts are "spun" or contorted to support a pre-determined result. As one study attorney remarked, "You can't make chicken salad out of chicken you-know-what."

- Every case I look at, my question is, "How does this play out at trial?" Maybe that's why I prefer to settle cases after a trial starts – let's put some jurors in the box and then we'll have a value.
- When you deal with the things we deal with over the years, you get a little jaundiced. When you're handling these cases, you have to ask, "How do you win? How the hell do you win that case?" Each case requires a strategy for the weaknesses of that particular case. You have to show the plaintiff is not a good person, not credible.

Although clients continually ask attorneys for their opinions, these attorneys deflect that question because ultimately it is irrelevant. "My opinion doesn't matter," one attorney tells his clients, "because I'm not the one who will be deciding the case."

5.2 Global Outlook

Effective trial lawyers tend to be deductive thinkers, reaching conclusions from general or universal themes, while "litigators" often are inductive thinkers, drawing tentative conclusions about general propositions from a small set of experiences. In representing clients,

> [a] good litigator will know all the facts and issues. He or she will be brilliant at motion practice, discovery and preparing briefs ... and if you want to know the most minute point of evidence, the good litigator can tell you about it. In contrast a good trial lawyer ... can try any kind of case on any subject. They can do that because they know how to create a story. They build a team they can rely on for support and, more importantly, they can successfully connect with the jury.[6]

The brilliance of the trial attorney lies in the ability to create that story, to develop a plan "that cuts through a maze of difficulties to solve in one effort a large, complex problem. This is possible only if you can step back far enough to see the big picture – the whole forest instead of only the individual trees – and if you can keep that big picture in mind as you think about each smaller portion of the problem."[7] Seeing the "entire problem as an integrated whole," an outstanding trial attorney conceives a strategy that comprehends, explains and links all key events and actions.[8]

---

[6]DecisionQuest. (1993, October). Wanted: A good trial lawyer to take my case to court - litigators need not necessarily apply. DecisionQuest Litigation Library. Available at http://www.decisionquest.com/utility/showArticle/?objectID=537.

[7]Krieger & Neumann *supra* note 3 at 38. This "big picture" perspective is congruent with jurors' cognitive processes. As Michael Tigar explains, "Jurors and judges decide cases based on a gestalt, or total picture, from which the decision occurs to them as a just resolution." Tigar, Michael. (1999). *Persuasion: The litigator's art* (p. 7). Chicago: American Bar Association.

[8]Krieger & Neumann *supra* note 3 at 38.

The study attorneys display the deductive reasoning and global perspective that epitomize effective trial attorneys. They search for universal premises and develop a strategy that embraces all aspects – strengths and weaknesses – of the case:

- The most common mistake is allowing yourself to get swallowed up by the problem and getting afraid. Nobody likes to lose, but you cannot let fear take control. Laziness, financial insecurity, and fear are the biggest reasons attorneys don't go to trial. People do not walk into a room and think, "I'm going to get a big verdict." They focus on details and let those loom so large that they lose sight of the big picture.
- Every case will have problems. The question is how big or small the problem is. For me, this is problem solving. I have attorneys here who think every problem is a huge fucking problem. They don't try cases. They settle them.
- With every case, I know the main parts of it. I may not know every detail, but I have developed a strategy.
- It is a symphony. A trial, when it plays well, is well composed, well structured. It has to play well.
- You also have to have a sense of the whole proceeding, not a series of steps.
- Part of being a good lawyer is being a good strategist. If you cannot see beyond one move, you're not going to make it. The object is not to take the most pieces off the board but to get the king. Attorneys get caught up in discovery battles and motions and start thinking they're winning the case – they lose sight of the goal. As a counselor, my job is to figure out how I can get them to checkmate.

One study attorney sums it up this way: "Taking everything and putting it into some kind of whole – that's how you convince jurors."

When asked whether they had evolved as case evaluators and strategists, the study attorneys often commented on their graduation from "micro" to "macro" litigation strategies:

- I would say it has changed. What kind of witness and person, the credibility the claimant has, has a lot more weight than it did at the beginning. Earlier in my career I emphasized numbers and percentages. I see that jurors don't weight those factors as much as I did. Frankly, I'll pay more for a plaintiff who comes across well. I evaluate the specials [medical expenses] numbers less and now more the generality of the treatment. I look more at the treatment provided to understand the person. It's not just the numbers. I now look at the big picture.
- Over the years I think I've placed more of an emphasis on the fundamental fairness of a potential result. When you're a newer lawyer, you tend to be kind of clinical – adding up the evidence on each side and trying to make a precise determination. Whether it's a bench trial or a jury trial, the fairness is the most important issue.
- Attorneys need to ask whether they are arguing something you could not reasonably hope to win – something a trustworthy person would not do.
- I see cases differently now as someone who has gone to trial. I now see certain things as more important. When I was younger, I was sure this case hinged on

winning a discovery motion. Now I look at those motions and realize they were not as important as I thought. The questions I ask myself now are: Can I get the evidence in? Is this a case that requires expert testimony, and how will the expert be viewed? Is the client subject to punitive damages? How will the jury see the client? Is this a case where the plaintiff could get attorneys fees? Instead of little bumps in the road, I'm looking all the way out. I see the entire case in front of me, not just the specific procedures or motions along the way.

Ironically, litigation attorneys who reach an expert level seem to return to the broad perspectives they held when they first entered law school, having traversed the stages of initial dissonance when their personal ideas of fairness and justice clash with case law during the first year of law school, immersion in the minutiae and moral neutrality of general law practice as a novice attorney, and then a return to broader concepts of fairness and justice after years of trial experience. Considering "big picture" concepts of fairness and justice turns out to be an essential trial skill, not a first-year law student's pipe dream.

5.3 Themes

Closely related to the development of a global perspective is the construction of narratives and themes. Although novice attorneys describe their cases with detailed time lines and witness testimony summaries, expert attorneys know that jurors understand cases through compelling narratives and themes. Like other major life experiences, trials are seen as conflicts, opportunities and challenges animated by ambitions, values, prior experiences, insecurities, threats and hopes. At their core, trials are a struggle for personal dignity and vindication – whether the parties are a landlord and tenant enmeshed in a residential lease dispute or corporations whose officers accuse each other of intellectual property theft. For both plaintiffs and defendants, lawsuits charge the parties with actions and motivations that are irreconcilable with their self-concepts and social norms. Nearly every case, however mundane and dry, has a personal impact and a moral dimension that can be transformed into a theme.

Psychology professors Nancy Pennington and Reid Hastie have studied jurors' deliberations for decades. One of their major contributions is the "Story Model," a theory describing jurors' cognitive strategies. Jurors, they find, "impose a narrative story organization on trial information" from three sources: trial evidence; personal knowledge about similar events; and expectations about "story structures," e.g., how motivations affect human actions.[9] Like effective trial attorneys, jurors "rely on deduction from world knowledge" and attempt to form analogies between the

---

[9]Pennington, Nancy, & Hastie, Reid. (1991). A cognitive theory of juror decision making: The story model." *Cardozo Law Review*, *13*, 521, 527–528. See Hastie, Reid, & Dawes, Robyn M. (2001). *Rational choice in an uncertain world* (pp. 237–244). Thousand Oaks, California: Sage Publications, Inc.

case and that world knowledge.[10] Jurors choose the "best story" – the most persuasive explanation of the trial evidence – by comparing its coverage (the extent to which the story comprehends the trial evidence), coherence (the consistency, plausibility and completeness of the story) and uniqueness (whether only one story presents a coherent explanation for the evidence).

An attorney's ability to craft a story with coverage, coherence and uniqueness can be dispositive. In experiments conducted by Pennington and Hastie, 78% of the mock jurors convicted the defendant when the prosecution presented its evidence in story order ("a temporal and causal sequence that matched the occurrence of the original events") and the defense presented its evidence in witness order ("the sequence of evidence as conveyed by witnesses").[11] When the type of presentation was reversed – the prosecution presented its evidence in witness order and the defense presented its evidence in story order – only 31% of the mock jurors convicted the defendant. Pennington and Hastie also found that jurors who heard each side's case described in story order were more confident about their decisions than jurors who heard only one side or neither side in story order. Story order thus affects not only the jurors' decisions but also their confidence in making those decisions.

Although the study attorneys did not reference academic studies of juror behavior, they consistently emphasized the importance of organizing evidence into themes and narratives:

- Looking at what were the most favorable facts, I ask, "What theme can I come up with, knowing the facts and the law, that I can sell?" You have to capture their minds, and be able to say to yourself, "We can hang our hat on that."
- The most effective attorneys can present a theme, not just a technical tort or breach of contract. Successful cases always have equitable themes. It might be "be careful what you ask for" and "look before you cross." Every case needs to have a theme. Emotions and ethical levers – lawyers who get that tend to win a lot of cases.
- I tell even some of the best attorneys they need a theme. Attorneys to this day still think of an argument instead of a theme. Most attorneys are so darned focused on – to use that expression we used 10 years ago, anal-retentive – they want to dominate all the facts. But you have to do something with the facts. You have to have an equitable, resonating theme. The classic example is O.J. Simpson. There was DNA evidence all over the place but Johnnie Cochran [O. J. Simpson's attorney] said, "If the glove does not fit, you must acquit." This speaks volumes to how lawyers should prepare their cases.

"I start to develop a theme early in the case," states Robert Gilliland, whose practice emphasizes homeowner association, construction, and general business litigation. "Every case needs to have a theme, needs to have a nice theme. In the case you mentioned for this interview, it was a contractor ripping off elderly homeowners. I start thinking about themes early."

---

[10]Pennington & Hastie *supra* note 9 at 524.

[11]Pennington & Hastie *supra* note 9 at 542.

Themes are grounded in the attorneys' sense of fairness and "how ordinary people will see things – is this person attractive, deserving, but not greedy?" A defense attorney who has tried more than 100 cases to verdict always asks himself whether he believes in the position he is advocating:

> One thing I would say to myself is, "How will I feel about this case on Sunday evening [before the case is called for trial on Monday morning]? Is my position fair, just and reasonable? Do I feel good about my evaluation or do I have anxiety?" I know what anxiety is. When I had my first trials, I was assigned the worst cases – that's what happens when you start off – and I would look at them and say, "This isn't right." If I can say Sunday night in my heart of hearts, "I can argue this to a jury, it's fair, just and reasonable," and truly believe it, then I'm satisfied.

The attorneys also recognize that equitable themes have the power to overcome technical legal defenses. Describing another attorney who "seriously misevaluated" a case, one of the study attorneys commented, "He relied on legal defenses that were good – statute of limitations defenses – that should have won the day but for a jury did not amount to a hill of beans."

The study attorneys understand the necessity of story coverage, coherence and uniqueness, although they apparently are not aware of Pennington and Hastie's research. One attorney notes that adversaries often outdo themselves in constructing multiple alternative arguments that seem to ensure victory no matter how the evidence is viewed but in fact present a muddied case devoid of consistent themes:

> Another mistake is to argue too much and take too many inconsistent positions. This is encouraged by alternative pleading, where a party can allege too many different legal theories. Irving Younger [best known for his "10 Commandments of Cross-Examination"] got this right when he talked about the lawyer who argued that "my goat did not eat your grass, but if he did he didn't do any damage." At the end of the day, trials are morality plays. Jurors are looking for who has the whiter hat, who has the darker hat. This is why it can be a problem believing what the client says and disregarding contrary information.

Because consistency and coherency are paramount, the case themes must be constantly reevaluated and modified as necessary to match new evidence: "If stuff doesn't fit your theme, you don't want it in there either, or your theme may have to be changed. You may have to abandon your theme. The defendant you thought was most at fault may have settled or may have little insurance."

5.4 Visual Thinking

Jurors process information visually.[12] To communicate persuasively with jurors, the study attorneys have developed the capacity to form a vivid mental image and convey the full impression and force of that image to jurors. They think visually, not

---

[12]See Pinker, Steven. (1997). *How the mind works* (pp. 284–298). New York: W.W. Norton & Co. Just, Marcel A., *et al.* (2010). A neurosemantic theory of concrete noun representation based on the underlying brain codes. PLoS ONE 5(1): e8622.

literally, in relating to jurors. In this respect, they have overcome an occupational hazard – the tendency to rely on words instead of pictures. As attorney Charles Babcock and jury consultant Jason Bloom write,

> [J]urors retain very little, perhaps as little as 20 percent, of what they hear. The retention rate goes up significantly, to as high as 60 percent, when they see something, and research has proven that jurors retain over 80 percent of what they simultaneously hear and see. This should not surprise us. Yet, I see many younger lawyers in my firm and lawyers on the opposite side of cases fall prey to the potentially devastating misperception that if you say it in the courtroom, then the jury will hear it, understand it, and retain it.[13]

Attorneys' over-reliance on "saying" instead of "showing" may reflect their own learning styles. Research conducted by litigation consultant Kenneth Lopez indicates that "the majority of the general public are visual learners, and the majority of practicing attorneys are not."[14] An attorney representing a plaintiff in a products liability case, consequently, might tell a jury that corporate officers failed to investigate reports of a defective lawn mower; and "if you had been at Mark Stein's house on August 23, 1993, when Mark was mowing the front lawn, you would have seen the result of that corporation decision." An attorney trying to create a more vivid image, however, might speak to the jury this way: "Unfortunately for Mark Stein, their powers of prediction were no greater than their ability to make a lawn mower that was safe. And, as a result, Mark Stein has no legs and until he is old enough to get fitted with artificial limbs, he will have to roll around in a wheel chair while his friends and classmates frolic and play."[15]

An attorney's ability to develop a mental image and to transfer that image into a juror's mind does not ride on a few rhetorical twists at trial; that ability is grounded in the attorney's pre-trial preparation and willingness to get out of the office and into the setting. This includes the physical setting where the key case facts have occurred and the "social and cultural environment" in which the major witnesses have interacted. Juror consultant Susan Macpherson explains the critical importance of the setting and how it is overlooked in juror persuasion:

> The setting is the story element that attorneys are most likely to neglect, perhaps because it is rarely the subject of any dispute and generally requires little discussion. You gradually acquire an understanding of the setting as you get to know the client, the opposing party, and various witnesses. From a variety of conversations, you develop a sense of what it was like to work in that environment.
>
> Even so, if you spend a few days visiting the work site, you may come away with a significantly different picture of what happened or how it happened. For example, two people who were thought to be working in isolation turn out to be sharing an office. Or the

---

[13]Babcock, Charles L., & Bloom, Jason S. (2001). Getting your message across: Visual aids and demonstrative evidence in the courtroom. *Litigation*, 27(3), 41.

[14]Lopez, Kenneth. (2007). The animators at law attorney communication style study (p. 4). For a study challenging the use of learning-styles assessments, see Pashler, Harold, *et al*. Learning styles: Concepts and evidence. *Psychological Science in the Public Interest*, 9(3), 106–119.

[15]Fine, Ralph. (2008). *The how-to-win trial manual* (pp. 36–38). Huntington, New York: JurisNet, LLC.

boss who was thought to be an unapproachable tyrant turns out to have an open door and regularly sits down to eat a bag lunch with members of his staff. The jurors can gain the same types of insights if you provide them with a vivid description of the setting.[16]

This image of the setting is pivotal for the attorney as well as the jurors; it accelerates the attorney's understanding of the case and forms the picture presented to the jury. Describing his firm's success in resolving a partnership dispute with a manufacturer, trial attorney Jeffrey Valle of Valle Makoff tells a reporter that "the first thing the lawyers did was visit the factory." That visit, he explains, "informed everything we did in the case because we understood the facts better."[17]

Although the study attorneys did not explicitly describe themselves as visual thinkers, their work habits demonstrate the value they place on visualization and imagery. They immerse themselves in the critical scene, whether that is the client's executive suite, the intersection where an accident occurred, the undeveloped parcel being appraised or the liquor store in which a police officer shot a suspected burglar. An attorney specializing in eminent domain cases, for instance, does not just read the appraisers' reports and look at the photographs in the reports but rather gets in a car and views the property and comparable properties with the experts: "What I've gotten really good at is understanding the appraisers and engineers. I work with my experts. I drive around and look at what they're looking at." A personal injury attorney travels to the accident site immediately after accepting a case: "You can't do it in your office. You can't rely on the guy you send to take photographs. He's not trained as an attorney and may not see the things you see."

A veteran civil rights defense attorney demonstrates the "hands-on" discipline that compels an attorney to personally view and absorb every detail of the setting. In defending police officers against excessive force and civil rights claims, he physically integrates himself into the station, the site of the shooting and the selection of expert witnesses. His trial preparation is visceral:

- I always meet the clients at their station. [Interviewer: Why do you meet them there instead of your office?] One, it's ten of them and only one of me, so it's more convenient for them. Two, I see how they interact with each other and how others react to them. If they're at my office, I have no way of seeing what the people they work with think about them. This gives me a good start on understanding how jurors will feel about them.
- Go to the scene. I want to see where everyone stands so I can see what they saw. In one case, I stood where the shooter was and saw that a witness could not have even seen the shooter. I never would have seen that if I had stayed at my office and met the clients there. Always go to the scene and take the clients with you.
- Interview the expert [witness] yourself, not over the phone. The jury will see them face-to-face, so you have to evaluate them the same way the jury will.

[16]Macpherson, Susan. (2000, October). How to hook jurors in commercial cases. *TRIAL*.

[17]McRae, Susan. (2010, October 29). Be afraid, be very afraid. *San Francisco Daily Journal*, p. 4.

Recognizing that jurors inevitably develop mental images of scenes and events in every case, this attorney creates those scenes and events directly from his personal experience. A less effective attorney forgoes the on-site work and may not realize that his images are inferential and, being derived from secondary sources, inevitably lack vividness, detail and force.

This defense attorney's intensive, experiential preparation enables him to see and understand how the case must be presented to the jury. He can relate to the police officers in their own language and setting and ensure that the trial evidence captures the features he has personally observed:

- I need to have my officer express and articulate to the jury to make that jury feel what you felt and see what you saw when you pulled that trigger. So they will feel they would have done exactly what the officer did. He needs to go into great detail of what he saw, and based on his experience and training what was going through his mind the split second before you shot, the state of mind and that person's background. He needs to say everything that was going through his mind. And if he thought he was not going to see his wife and son again that night, that's what he needs to tell the jury.
- I will have anywhere from four to six meetings with each set of defendants. I express to them initially that they will need to tell the jury what their feelings were. I tell them everyday in your life you meet people you like or dislike, find some people believable or unbelievable, reasonable or unreasonable. The jurors are doing the same thing, making the same calls in their own lives.
- If you cannot get access to the scene, make sure someone does a reenactment of the scene to reconstruct the rooms as they appeared at that time. Make sure your expert walks through each room in the same way the shooter did. This gives you the advantage over the other side's expert because an expert would have to agree it's better to testify based on a reenactment than without one.

"In sum," instructs Michael Tigar in his book *Nine Principles of Litigation and Life*, "you must put your witness in the scene, and give the jurors a vicarious experience of having been there. You want them to have a mental image of what the witness observed."[18]

Although attorneys tend to regard visual thinking as a skill limited to jury persuasion, it actually enhances all forms of legal persuasion. The quality of briefs, negotiations and client communications is heightened when attorneys have a solid

---

[18]Tigar, Michael. (2009). *Nine principles of litigation and life* (pp. 162–163). Chicago: American Bar Association. Prominent trial attorney David Berg provides similar advice: "Every case includes at least one site you should visit, whether it is the scene of an accident or the boardroom where merger documents were signed. A site visit forces you to walk in your client's shoes – or those of an opponent. You will see things through trial eyes – painting pictures in your mind that will make the case more vivid to a jury." Berg, David. (2006). *The trial lawyer* (p. 18). Chicago: American Bar Association.

image of the facts, damages and interactions that underpin their clients' cases. Explaining the benefits of imagery, Pulitzer Prize-winning author Donald Murray states, "I see what I write and many times the focus of my writing is in my image."[19]

5.5 Perspective

In 1984, Bell Laboratories, whose scientists had won several Nobel Prizes in Physics, faced a threat to its existence. To settle an antitrust action brought by the United States Department of Justice, AT&T, its corporate parent, had entered into a consent decree that would result in the splintering of AT&T into seven local exchange carriers, commonly called the "Baby Bells." As part of the breakup of AT&T, Bell Laboratories would no longer act as a centralized research and development facility for a national telephone system; the Baby Bells set up a separate company, Bellcore, to perform research and development functions for the local exchange carriers.[20]

Because the fate of Bell Laboratories was uncertain, it sponsored an ambitious research project to identify the characteristics of its "star" performers and teach other employees how to replicate their successes. Only 10% - 15% of Bell Laboratories' scientists and engineers were considered to be "stars," yet they all scored at the top of IQ tests. The researchers first surveyed Bell Laboratories' executives to identify 45 "star" employee attributes. These attributes fell into four categories: cognitive abilities (logic, reasoning, IQ scores and creativity); personality factors (self-confidence, ambition, and risk taking); social factors (interpersonal skills and leadership); and environmental factors (work history and job satisfaction). They then subjected 200 of the best performers to two days of testing to ascertain the most important attributes of star performance. This intensive testing produced one conclusive result: "there was no appreciable relationship between status as a star performer and any of the cognitive, psychological, social or environmental factors." Neither the executives nor the star performers "could explain what attributes were responsible for high productivity or star performance."[21]

For the next two years the researchers watched the star performers' work habits and strategies. After carefully observing what star performers actually do – instead of relying on traits cited in executive or peer surveys – they found that top

---

[19]Zimmerman, Barry. Development and adaptation of expertise: The role of self-regulatory processes and beliefs. In Ericsson, K. Anders, *et al.* (Eds.). (2006). *The Cambridge handbook of expertise and expert performance* (p. 710). New York: Cambridge University Press.

[20]This description of the Bell Laboratories study is derived from Henderson, William D. (2008, April). Are we selling results or résumés?: The underexplored linkage between human resource strategies and firm-specific capital. Indiana Legal Studies Research Paper No. 105. Available at SSRN: http://ssrn.com/abstract=1121238.

[21]*Id.* at 17.

performers consistently exhibit nine key work strategies. "Perspective," the ability to see one's job in the larger context of the company's objectives and adopt the viewpoint of customers, managers and other employees, was ranked fourth among the nine strategies – behind taking initiative, networking, and self-management, and ahead of teamwork, leadership, organizational savvy, followership, and persuasion.[22] In describing the importance of perspective, the researchers noted that the Bell Laboratories scientists had similar academic credentials, but the average performers did not relate their job functions to overall objectives and did not anticipate, recognize or understand other viewpoints. A typical engineer, for instance, spent hours "mastering a software tool for organizing files, which ended up delaying the delivery of a customer's product." A star performer, in contrast, understood that "the customer comes first" and "stressed the need to 'shift gears' between the narrow focus required for certain tasks and a broad view of how their project fit into a larger one."[23]

The study attorneys consistently display the attribute of "perspective," assuming the jurors' viewpoints and seeing their work in the overall objective of jury persuasion. Because the jury determines the ultimate case outcome, the attorneys counsel clients and evaluate their own performance from the jurors' perspective. They know that the jurors' views are determinative and that an attorney's opinion may be irrelevant:

- It's your perspective. You have to have an open mind. You also have to remember it's not your opinion that matters; it's the life experience of 12 jurors. You have to anticipate that they'll see things differently than you would.
- The most commonly overlooked component of case evaluation is the hardest thing to communicate to clients and the hardest thing to learn – it's the human component. You cannot put it in words. It's basically seeing the case through jurors' eyes. It helps to talk with non-lawyers and family to get a better idea of how jurors will see things. Clients are looking for my opinion, but my opinion letters say, "The jury is likely to . . ."
- Our job is not to make the client hear what we think about the case but to tell them what 12 jurors will do with the case. That's different from what *you* think.
- Good lawyers talk to family, friends, and other attorneys to see, "How do other people look at this?" The natural tendency is to want to believe clients, and in competitive games, there's a drive to win. Really effective lawyers look at how my case will be seen by others, not themselves.
- Knowing that jurors are hostile to legal claims, I have to make them feel they could be in the same position. I have to enable them to empathize. I have to take the temperature. I'm the 13th juror. Assuming I'm not getting paid, just like a juror, I ask, "Is this the person I want to devote my time to?"

---

[22]*Id*. at 17.

[23]Kelley, Robert, & Caplan, Janet. (1993, July-August). How Bell Labs creates star performers. *Harvard Business Review.*

- What I rely on most is just being able to put yourself in the juror's shoes. I've handled a few appeals, and in appellate work I've read transcripts of opening statements and wondered, "What were you thinking?" They [jurors] would have no idea what the case is about, especially if it's dry material. If you lose sight of being able to put yourself in the shoes of the average jurors, you can't communicate with them and you can't get your case across.
- The biggest single failure in the plaintiffs' bar – at least the few hundred I dealt with – is the failure to do the back-seat question of what jurors will do. Jurors are skeptical. Almost every juror knows or has heard of somebody trying to get more than what they're entitled to. I would use that attitude as a background fertilizer when I did defense work. I used to work that to death.

Although it may seem logical to assume the juror's position, it is unnatural. Clients seek attorneys' advice, and the natural response is to provide one's personal opinion. "Most attorneys shoot from the hip at the beginning," notes one attorney. "They feel they have to have an answer immediately for their clients, and clients want at least a range of opinions." Especially in cases with a strong personal dimension, the attorney's opinions and perceptions may not comport with the jury's verdict. In employment cases, for example, "an attorney can look at the facts and think it is worthless. But employers take some big hits in cases an attorney personally thinks is worthless."

The study attorneys' emphasis on the jurors' perspective is more than philosophical; it governs how the attorneys look, speak, gesture, sit, stand and listen:

- I'm always amazed to see the attorneys who just walk into the courtroom and put their stuff on the table without greeting the bailiff or the clerk. Jurors look at everything about you – your shoes, your socks and how you treat other people.
- At one of my first trials, I was working under an older attorney who taught me a lot of what I know about trial practice. I was at counsel table, and we were selecting a jury. I started to pour myself a glass of water, and he leaned over to me and seemed really irritated. "What are you doing?" he asked me. I said, "I'm getting a glass of water. I'm thirsty." He said, "Look at those jurors. Do they have water? No. It's a status thing and you have to level the playing field."
- I've tried more than 80 cases to verdict. I started off working for an attorney who tried one case in the morning and one case in the afternoon. I learned by listening to the silver-tongued, white-haired fox. . . . He said the jury is always looking at you to see how you're reacting. So you always look relaxed on the outside and inside you're on the edge of your seat and hope that a plum falls off the tree. If opposing counsel shows you a document that you've never seen before that kills your case, you act like it's nothing [animatedly shrugs his shoulders].
- The people here are not stupid. They're military, retired military, contractors, civil service. They get paid in full while they're on the jury. They pay attention. They're [the defense attorneys] driving up in a $200,000 Mercedes, and the jurors have dusty, ordinary cars. Some of them may be doing OK, but they don't like it to be flashed.

To understand the jurors' perspective, the attorneys watch the jurors closely and imagine the questions running through the jurors' minds. "I'm sitting there thinking about what they're thinking, watching how they're impacted by it," explains a plaintiffs' attorney. In describing direct and cross-examination, a different attorney says, "It's a way of relating to them – asking the questions they want to ask." Another attorney comments, "We see a lot of robots in this business. They're into their books, but I'm listening to the jury. I go to trial with a pad and if it has three pages of notes at the end, I'd be surprised."

5.6   Explicit and Tacit Knowledge

Gary Klein, one of the nation's leading decision scientists, notes that experts rely on both explicit and tacit knowledge. Explicit knowledge, he explains, consists of facts and rules. It is "easy to write down, easy to communicate, easy to teach, and easy to learn." Tacit knowledge is quite different from explicit knowledge but is equally important. It is "being able to do things without being able to explain how. We can't learn tacit knowledge from a text book."[24] Declarative information, routines, and procedures are examples of explicit knowledge, and perceptual skills, workarounds, pattern matching, judging and mental models are examples of tacit knowledge. Klein describes how these two types of knowledge are integrated in the practice of law:

> I recently had the pleasure of watching an experienced lawyer scrutinize a contract, and I realized that I was seeing tacit knowledge in action. Good lawyers have mastered all the relevant laws in order to pass the law exams and get certified. That's the explicit knowledge. However, in scrutinizing the contract, my lawyer wasn't just trying to remember the statutes. He was also imagining what could happen to create headaches for me. He looked at each clause and statement and mentally rotated it to see where it could go wrong. He was trying to conjure up events that could leave me unprotected and spot risks that weren't specifically called out. He was drawing on his experience with how the world works to anticipate what could go wrong. You don't find that in law books.[25]

For experts, explicit and tacit knowledge are so tightly interwoven that "we are usually oblivious to the tacit knowledge we use in applying our explicit knowledge of facts, rules, and procedures."[26]

The study attorneys, like Klein's business attorney, combine their technical legal expertise with profound practical judgment. They seamlessly integrate explicit knowledge and tacit knowledge, evaluating the evidence in its legal and practical dimensions and understanding jury decision making in its normative and actual forms:

---

[24]Klein, Gary. (2009). *Streetlights and shadows* (p. 32). Cambridge, Massachusetts: MIT Press.
[25]*Id.* at 34–35.
[26]*Id.* at 35.

- I've learned over time the important thing is to take what I know and [mentally] put it in front of a judge or jury. This is different from a legal analysis. I have to look at how they will appear to a judge or jury ... Based on the facts I know, how would they look? I ask them [clients], "What is the other side like?" My opinion is never based on just the legal issues.
- One thing that occurs to me is many attorneys fail to recognize how their client will evoke a particular reaction by the jury. They are not looking at who the person is, what the jury's reaction will be. They are just looking at objective factors, which is what most attorneys are talking about when they evaluate a case.
- Quite often evaluation is about intangible things. You get a feel for it.
- Normally what happens is the law is fairly clear. If it's an unsettled area of law, the court can decide the issue. The most important factor is the witnesses. Most cases turn on the testimony of witnesses – the witness lies or is not credible.
- Jurors can have some strong feelings about employers and you don't always know, even if you ask. After one trial, we all went out to a restaurant and some of the jurors were there too. One juror came up to me after a while and said, "You asked [during voir dire] about whether I had ever had a problem with a boss. I said 'No' because I didn't think it was any of your business."

Asked whether she had always been able to discern intangible factors that might influence the jury, a defense attorney replied, "I've always been competent with that, I must say. A lot of people say that an attorney has to have good people skills. I'm extraordinarily intuitive. I connect with people very well. It just flows."

5.7 Peripheral Vision

Novice drivers keep their eyes straight ahead and their legs rigid as they strive to maintain a constant speed in their lane. Their goal is simple: move forward and avoid hitting the car ahead. As a driver gains experience and confidence, she develops peripheral vision – the skill of controlling the automobile while being aware of traffic ahead of her, behind her and on the sides. She anticipates threats to her safety from a car merging onto the freeway, the distracted driver she observes in the rear view mirror and the oncoming car that is recklessly passing another vehicle. She strains to see the highway maintenance vehicle far ahead that, she worries, might suddenly stop trimming grass, raise the boom mower and speed across all lanes to start cutting grass in the median. At the same time, she is aware when she becomes tired, has been distracted by her passengers and is losing steering feedback as the rainfall increases.

Like expert drivers, expert attorneys and business leaders develop keen peripheral vision. Professors George Day and Paul Schoemaker, co-authors of *Peripheral Vision: Detecting the Weak Signals That Will Make or Break Your Company*, have identified seven key elements of peripheral vision to assist individuals and organizations that are still looking straight ahead in their own lanes. The seven steps to "bridge the vigilance gap," Day and Schoemaker write, are: (1) scoping [where and how widely to look and what issues to address]; (2) scanning [how to look actively and open-mindedly]; (3) interpreting [how to make sense of what is found]; (4) probing [what to explore more closely]; (5) acting [whether and how to act on signals from the periphery]; (6) organizing [how to develop a flexible and inquisitive culture that detects and shares obscure and weak signals]; and (7) leading [showing people how to balance peripheral and focal vision]. Peripheral vision, they conclude, requires "practice, dedication and seasoned judgment."[27]

Peripheral vision is an attitude more than a technique; it "is more about anticipation and alertness than prediction."[28] Because it enables individuals and organizations to prepare for unforeseen problems and act rapidly under uncertainty, it requires a great tolerance for ambiguity. Images on the periphery inevitably are discernible but imprecise, and weak signals are faint and blurred.[29] "By the time a clear prediction or forecast can be made," Day and Schoemaker assert, "it is probably too late." When applied directly to the practice of law, peripheral vision enables lawyers "to look at problems from many perspectives, to think across doctrinal categories, to spot threat or opportunity originating from outside what seems to be the boundaries of a problem."[30]

Although the study attorneys did not use the term "peripheral vision," they constantly search and scan the environment for weaknesses in their cases – issues they may have overlooked, emotional reactions they might have underestimated, societal norms or problems they did not associate with the case or an adversary's trial skills of which they were uninformed. The underlying motivation for their peripheral vision is a relentless sense of curiosity about what the other side knows that they haven't yet anticipated, discovered and discredited. The attorneys recognize the importance and value of this relentless scanning and note that their attitude of alertness and anticipation encompasses jurors who have not yet been selected, judges who have not yet ruled and appeals after trials that have not yet started:

- There are extraneous factors always. It's not only your job to know them but to seek them out.
- At an early stage you have a good idea of the case. You've taken some depositions. You see their [opponent's] paper and his ability to persuade. I then start asking, "Why is my position more likely to be accurate?" The other guy's paper is important because you have to think about an appeal early in the game. Look at the past rulings of the judge and the likelihood of being overturned. Judges

---

[27]Day, George S., & Schoemaker, Paul J.H. (2006). *Peripheral vision: Detecting the weak signals that will make or break your company* (pp. 5, 7). Boston, Massachusetts: Harvard Business Press.

[28]*Id.* at 168.

[29]*Id.* at 168.

[30]Payton, Sallyanne. (1985). Is thinking like a lawyer enough? *University of Michigan Journal of Law Reform, 18,* 241. Quoted in Krieger & Neumann, *supra* note 3 at 38.

make mistakes, and some cases you start to realize you could lose at trial. So you need to know, "Is this a judge that often makes rulings that are overturned on appeal?"

- In one case an experienced plaintiffs' attorney brought up an issue – the lack of a backup surgeon – that simply was not part of the standard of care or a causation issue. When we talked to the jurors afterwards, a couple of them said they would have wanted a backup surgeon there if it had been them. I've learned from these types of experiences to anticipate what the jurors might be thinking, even if it's not technically legally relevant. I think about peripheral issues – like whether the doctor was gruff, had to be called four times or was unresponsive, even if the doctor met the standard of care.

- Being a good lawyer is like a chess player. You're looking not just at your move but the other side's next move.

"A core part of my being," states a defense attorney who frequently serves as a temporary judge, "is being someone who looks at all angles of things – in my personal life and in my professional life."

Clients and attorneys who lack peripheral vision often get clobbered at trial. One of the most lethal competitors is the attorney who "doesn't look like a trial attorney" or does not display the icons of status and power that identify "the ones you have to worry about." Like other individuals operating in competitive enterprises, attorneys frequently are blindsided by tomorrow's competitors because they do not have the resources, strategies, appearance and mannerisms of today's competitors. The underestimated, overlooked attorneys benefit from their opponents' myopia in two major respects. First, their adversaries do not allocate sufficient resources or approve a litigation budget adequate to scrutinize and eviscerate their claims before trial. Not perceived as serious threats, minimized attorneys benefit from their relative obscurity. Second, the opposition law firm often assigns attorneys with low levels of legal experience to their case because the level of perceived threat is commensurately low. The inexperienced attorney to whom the case is assigned perpetuates the received wisdom by also assuming the case is relatively insignificant – otherwise it would not have been assigned to him. The junior attorney then evaluates the pre-trial proceedings and opponents with the stipulated degree of insignificance. When disconfirming evidence later materializes through discovery, the associate may feel that, if conveyed to the responsible partner, this newfound concern will be seen as inexperience and timidity. Pre-trial discovery that otherwise might be flagged as potentially damaging is instead disregarded, misconstrued or downplayed. When a senior attorney picks up the file months later to prepare for trial and realizes, like Dorothy arriving in Oz, "we're not in Kansas any more," it may be too late to save the client's assets at trial.

Three cases handled by the study attorneys illustrate how misevaluations can be built on stereotypes, misconceptions, and complacency – mindsets that could have been corrected with peripheral vision. In one case, the study attorney was an associate attorney at the time he represented the plaintiff. The defendant's case was handled by a law firm's associate attorney until shortly before trial, at which time it was taken over by a more senior trial attorney. After the jury returned a verdict, which was more than 30 times the amount of the defendant's offer, the defendant's attorney told him, "I did not think this was an important case to your firm because you were not a partner." Thinking about how that case was handled on the defense side, the study attorney observes, "In most cases an associate does all the work-up. In this case, the associate was not sophisticated enough to realize the impact of the witnesses." In another case where a study attorney represented the plaintiff, the defendant's settlement offer was less than 2% of the ultimate jury award. Asked why he thought attorneys sometimes misevaluate cases, the study attorney commented:

> Some of it is fee-driven, churning. Some of it is a misunderstanding of law. Some of it is arrogance. Some is internal scuttlebutt at the defense firm, thinking they can kick my butt. Maybe they think I don't know how to do it.

Another study attorney, whose case was seriously misevaluated by an adversary, seems to have become accustomed to being marginalized and uses an adversary's lack of peripheral vision to her client's advantage: "You can tell when they have lost their objectivity and then you pounce. They make judgments based on whether you're a woman, whether you look like a success in their world, how you dress, what car you drive. I don't play on it; I prey on it."

Chapter 6
Connectedness

Beyond legal expertise, mastery of the case facts and persuasive communication skills lies another characteristic of effective lawyers – connectedness. This is the quality of understanding and being linked to people and the ways in which they work, learn, socialize, play, celebrate, observe, love and rest. The quality of connectedness underpins our judgments about a person's credibility, trustworthiness, maturity, charisma and judgment and is expressed in common terms like "grounded," "centered," "worldly," "plugged in" and "real." People who lack connectedness may be considered clever but never wise and are denigrated in expressions like "clueless," "head in the clouds," and "never worked a day in his life." Although connectedness may strike some people as a vague or metaphysical concept, it is a distinct, palpable skill that enables some attorneys to know how jurors will see and react to their clients' cases and leaves other attorneys stunned and surprised by a verdict.

Understanding jurors is an unnatural state for many attorneys and requires an extraordinary investment of time to achieve. Attorneys generally live in a social stratum quite different from an ordinary juror's experiences and, to understand jurors, have to make deliberate efforts to overcome their personal experiences and connect with jurors. Jury consultant Patricia Steele asserts that attorneys "have no frame of reference" for understanding and connecting to jurors and explains how easily lawyers disassociate from jurors:

> The vast majority of civil cases settle before trial, and few litigators ever serve on juries or watch mock jurors deliberate. In addition, lawyers typically have little in common, either socially or economically, with the average juror. Most lawyers spend their time with colleagues or friends who, like them, tend to be affluent, well educated and privileged. In other words, lawyers aren't like regular people. In fact, by design they don't even think like regular people.[1]

---

[1]Steele, Patricia. (2006, Summer). To deal better with juries, stop thinking like a lawyer! *Defense Comment, 21*(2).

R. Kiser, *How Leading Lawyers Think*,
DOI 10.1007/978-3-642-20484-5_6, © Springer-Verlag Berlin Heidelberg 2011

The bottom line, Steele contends, "is that in many ways legal training hinders your ability to understand, persuade and communicate with juries."

To surmount that trained incapacity, this chapter shows how the study attorneys view connectedness and how they continually update their understanding of the world to stay connected.

6.1 Sense of Connectedness

Connectedness is both a body of knowledge about how the world works and an ongoing effort to update, supplement and modify that knowledge. Attorneys may be connected with jurors at some point in their careers, but they do not remain connected unless their view of the world is continually updated. The social awareness that precedes connectedness must be continual, comprehensive and sensitive to nuance, depth of sentiment and the velocity of change. Because jurors' attitudes and views invariably evolve, attorneys who do not see those shifts are evaluating cases based on juries that no longer exist:

> Talking about experience, I'm reminded of one of my colleagues who can be said to have a tremendous amount of experience – tried 200 cases – but I would not trust their judgment on case evaluation because it's easy to fall into a routine that is a rut. Evaluating the jury is an evolving art. It requires an understanding of our own culture, our political trends. It's a dynamic process, but some attorneys are stuck in a rut, essentially blind to changes.

When attorneys are dumbstruck by a jury's verdict, it may reflect their own failure to update their view of the world more than the jurors' incomprehension or wrongheadedness. As a relatively young plaintiffs' attorney observes, "I try to stay real, and so many attorneys think from a different plane, not what the real world is thinking, not what jurors are going to be thinking." Another attorney, whose practice is balanced between plaintiff and defendant representation, referred to attorneys who "live in a bubble." When asked what that meant, he said, "He does not get out and does not know what people think. In my cases I will get a couple of those people. What they lack is connectivity."

6.1.1 Social and Economic Context

The study attorneys placed great emphasis on the social and economic context in which a case is being tried and the importance of understanding how that context affects jurors' predispositions toward their clients and the conservativeness or liberality of their verdicts:

- At the end of the day, the client's injuries and the economic climate and the lawyers and the trend in the mindsets of jurors are the most important. It seems to me all of those things combine in a way to make a perfect storm or a perfect disaster. The perfect disaster should be settled, and the perfect storm should be taken to trial.

- Post 9–11 everything changed. The jury pools changed, in my experience, in the five boroughs and throughout New York state. Juries are much more conservative, less likely to give plaintiffs the benefit of the doubt. It's more of a CSI world. Jurors are expecting evidence to be clear and convincing instead of more probable than not. You have to know that. You need strong, solid cases – strong on medicine and strong on damages.
- But starting with Ronald Reagan there has been a constant drum roll about greedy lawyers and a flawed tort system. This has had an impact on juries. They are tougher on plaintiffs than they were before. You have to be realistic. Some courts that used to be good for plaintiffs have changed. You have to know these changes.
- The economy has a major effect on damages in the last two years. People who don't have a job don't have much sympathy for pain and suffering.
- Pain and suffering is now a dirty word. Pain and suffering is now a code word for a meritless claim. They [insurance companies] have made it impossible to make a settlement out of those cases.
- We're in a time of flux. I don't know how the current economic situation affects trial outcomes. My sense is that more claims are probably more likely to be pushed into mediation in this economy. I'm very concerned about how jurors will consider plaintiffs' claims in this economic climate. I'm also concerned about how the Internet affects them. They're instructed not to look at evidence outside the trial but they've become accustomed to investigating and checking things on the Internet.

"We're all trying to get a sense of where we are in 2010," states a New York defense attorney. "We are all trying to prognosticate about what is the effect of the economy."

6.1.2   Personal Background and Experience

Where do the study attorneys get their sense of connectedness to jurors and the world in which they live? When asked, "How does an attorney acquire the skill to see a case through jurors' eyes?" or "How do you know how jurors will react to your client?" the study attorneys often cited the importance of experience and their own personal backgrounds:

- I came from the real world and I always thought that was a big plus for me, but now I'm less connected than I was. I'm still a good trial attorney but not the great one I was 10 years ago. Some lawyers have that connection with the world and some don't. I grew up in [small East Coast city] a blue collar, no bullshit town. I know who is going to sell.

- To evaluate cases you have to be socially in tune with the file clerk as well as the senior partner in your firm as well as the minority employees in your office. You need a jambalaya of experiences to understand people and be able to relate to them.
- I try to bring everything I have learned in life to the table. I get into the shoes of the adversary and learn what they want. I had 40 years of growing up before I tried my first case. I had 10 years of experience in the business before I got my ticket [bar admission].
- Some attorneys are clueless, socially aphasic. I sometimes wonder how they meet people, how they talk to people. Other people are naturally curious and able to read people. That comes from life experiences and being observant.
- I went through a lot of pain. Also, I'm a Holocaust survivor's kid. My father had a good beam on people. He could just smell you. I think he passed that on.

When asked "What about attorneys who haven't had the life experiences to learn what you call common sense?" a defense attorney who has tried more than 80 cases to verdict responded tersely: "They're fucked. Get out of your office – talk to people, study Buddhism, read a book on physics or a book on cross-exam."

To understand how an attorney applies a sense of connectedness to actual case evaluation, listen to this veteran of 120 trials:

> After I've met with all the defendants, I put zero to ten by their name in my notes, based on how a jury will receive them. I meet five or six times with all the witnesses before trial, and each time I look at that number again, and it's always changing based on what I see. The first witnesses have the biggest impact, so you have to be strategic in deciding who to put on at the beginning. The same is true on the reverse side. Plaintiffs take into account the same things.
>
> I'm comfortable with my rankings of the witnesses. I worked at a gas station from [age] 12 to 24. In those days, you met the customer. You pumped their gas and checked their oil – and the air in their tires. I have dealt with a number of people over my life. In those days you talked to a number of customers. Some of them were SOBs, but you could still sell a tire to them.
>
> I've been exposed to some good people and some not so good people. You get a good cross-section. It's important to have that exposure. Sales is probably the most important.

He stresses the value of experience but notes that, unless an attorney is open-minded, experience is worthless: "If you're biased, you don't learn from experience. You're stuck in a position despite numerous years of experience – stuck in the mud."

6.2 Sources of Connectedness

For attorneys enjoying relatively affluent lifestyles and socializing with other successful, well-educated people, staying connected is difficult. A special skill of the study attorneys is their deliberate use of multiple sources to maintain connectedness and test their opinions many times before trial. These sources include scheduled meetings and extemporaneous conversations with colleagues, discussions with friends and family members, focus groups, periodic reviews of jury verdict data and reports and general reading. These inputs are neither incidental nor accidental; they are an integral part of the attorneys' practice of testing and revising their assessments and avoiding the biases of overconfidence, selective perception and defensive misconception.

6.2.1 Colleagues

In the Goodman-Delahunty study of attorneys' predictions about case outcomes, discussed in Chap. 2, the researchers considered the somewhat disconcerting results and concluded that attorneys should elicit their colleagues' opinions:

> One implication of the present findings is that lawyer performance can be improved by implementing case management strategies that take into account the potential overconfidence biases of the litigators. Case consultations with legal peers can take place informally. For example, in many legal firms, regular meetings are held where cases are periodically reviewed so that the partners can manage the caseload efficiently and ethically. These meetings provide ideal opportunities to obtain objective opinions from other legal professionals in the form of third-party feedback about the strengths and weaknesses of a case and the likelihood that the stated goals can be achieved. Many of the most overconfident lawyers will be the senior partners who may not typically obtain third-party review or feedback in the course of their practice. Law firms should take affirmative steps to incorporate third-party feedback for the more experienced or senior litigators in their case management systems.[2]

For the study attorneys, this suggestion already has been incorporated into their practices, possibly explaining why they do not exhibit the overconfidence biases detected in the Goodman-Delahunty survey of 481 attorneys.

The study attorneys' interactions with colleagues take a variety of forms, ranging from informal chats in the hall to regular roundtable meetings with partners, associates and claims representatives. The types of meetings and the benefits derived from those meetings are illustrated by these remarks:

- I grew up in a large firm and as I walked through the hallway, I got the opinion and inputs from senior partners. They were there to guide me, assist me, to lend me their advice. Plaintiff attorneys who open their own practice right from the start don't have this access and it's hard for them to get this advice.
- We sit down after work and talk about everything under the sun, including cases. There's no ego. My partner is a brilliant strategist.
- I might get a feel for it [after discussions] in the attorneys' room in Brooklyn.

---

[2]Goodman-Delahunty, Jane, *et al.* (2010). Insightful or wishful: Lawyers' ability to predict case outcomes. *Psychology, Public Policy, and Law, 16*(2), 152.

- Especially on more difficult cases, I'll talk among ourselves. My partners and I go into each other's offices. Another person I rely on a lot is my wife. She doesn't like me to go on and on a lot and sometimes just says, "Get to the point." But I have to lay everything out. She was a court reporter, so she's used to attorneys, as she says, "droning on and on." I respect my wife's opinion.
- We have roundtables here all the time. We throw it on the table – four or five of us sit around at lunch and kick around the numbers.
- You get input from other attorneys in the field, see things you might not see that other attorneys do. It is absolutely essential to bounce ideas off them. I was a team leader 15 years into this. After digesting cases we'd discuss the pluses and minuses. With four or five attorneys under me, I always had a bank under me. Some attorneys never go through that process. It can be an informal discussion, doesn't need to be a scheduled meeting. It's very helpful.
- When I wonder if the other side is crazy, I pick up the phone and ask colleagues in other firms, "What am I missing?"
- We're always talking with each other and looking at verdicts [reported in legal publications] and asking, "Where did people miss the boat?"
- People [in this firm] come up with a fairly fixed range. We all have 20–50 jury trials and 6–16 years of experience. We also do roundtables with claims people, and we have informal meetings and discussions with them. I circulate my report before sending it to the insurance company, and I run it by my wife. The more you do that, the greater the chance of knowing how a jury would respond. That's why I think the mock jury can be valuable.

"Sometimes when I have other counsel on a case I'll ask what they think," states Robert Gilliland. "If they're aligned counsel, I'm always seeking their input. I'm an information guy – information is power."

The value of these types of interactions has been demonstrated statistically by trial consultant Jonas Jacobson and his colleagues. In their study of experienced trial attorneys, who were given brief descriptions of actual cases tried to verdict and then asked to estimate the verdict amount, they found that the accuracy of the estimates improved when attorneys consulted with each other: "The fastest, cheapest, and likely the most common method to supplement an attorney's personal estimate is simply to solicit the opinions of other attorneys."[3] When attorneys obtained a second opinion from another attorney, their estimates showed a higher level of accuracy; and when they were required to discuss the case with another attorney *and* agree upon a single estimate, their estimates showed "significant accuracy gain."[4] Although the attorneys were "experts" by most definitions – they had an average of 27 years of civil trial experience and each attorney had

---

[3]Jacobson, J., Minson, J., Dobbs-Marsh, J., & Liberman, V. (2010). Predicting civil jury verdicts: How attorneys use (and misuse) a second opinion. Paper given at the Cornell Institute for Social Sciences Judgment by the Numbers Conference. Submitted for publication.

[4]*Id.* at 20.

tried an average of 52 civil trials – their collective wisdom was superior to their individual judgment; their average estimate of the verdict amount was far more accurate than the vast majority of single estimates.[5]

6.2.2   Non-attorneys

The study attorneys also sought input from non-attorneys, both within and outside their law offices. Some attorneys discussed their cases with friends and family members, and many attorneys felt that non-attorneys' opinions were more valuable than attorneys' opinions:

- Attorneys don't seem to see things the way jurors do. I try to run cases by non-lawyers to get their gut.
- Sometimes I like to ask someone who doesn't know anything about law – people who will be like the people in the jury, bookkeepers, firemen, cops. It's not going to be us making that decision.
- With scar cases, we take the photos and show them to the attorneys and secretaries in the office to see what they think. With death cases we talk that around the office, too. It's very hard to value someone's life.
- I test it. I bring the whole office in – lawyers, some of whom are intelligent, secretaries, everybody. So I've got them all in the room – Hispanics, a Polish guy, a Waspy guy. I listen very closely to what they say.
- I had my family over and asked them what they thought about a case.
- Good lawyers talk to family, friends, and other attorneys to see, "How do other people look at this?" ... Really effective lawyers look at how my case will be seen by others, not themselves.
- More than anything else I spend my time talking to people who are not lawyers. I have a lot of friends who are not lawyers. I try to be objective in describing the facts to them. It's more useful to get reactions of people who are not lawyers.
- The most important thing is to talk with everyone about your case, not just attorneys because they're not the people who will make that call. The attorneys across the street, they're just jaded. Any ordinary person could listen to the case and say, "Gee, that's tragic." The attorneys across the street may say, "Oh, they're faking it."

One managing partner narrows the array of opinions to a single factor: "I assume my Mom is going to be on the jury – that's how I see the client through the jurors' eyes. I consider her to be Middle America – pretty conservative, a reasonable barometer. So really, I understand."

---

[5]Palmer, Michael. (2010, Fall). Which is better? The deal or the ordeal? *The Vermont Bar Journal*, p. 6, fn. 29.

Attorneys' surveys of non-attorneys can be tightened up a bit to yield more dependable responses. Michael Palmer, founder of the litigation strategy firm, *Win Before Trial*, suggests that attorneys prepare a synopsis of the case in less than 150 words, commit its substance to memory, share the synopsis with friends and acquaintances and compile the responses. The informal survey, he explains, "will tap into the shared sense of justice in your community and will sometimes indicate the relative degree of outrage (or lack of it) that your respondents feel."[6]

6.2.3 Focus Groups

In addition to eliciting the opinions of colleagues, other attorneys, employees, friends, and family members, many of the study attorneys rely on focus groups. Although the term "focus group" may conjure up an image of large rooms with one-way glass windows and electrodes taped to fingertips, focus groups actually range from informal, small group discussions to multiple deliberation panels of focus-jurors recruited from jury, voter registration and driver's license lists. David Ball, a leading trial consultant, defines a focus group as "pretrial research in which information about a case is given to a group of laypeople selected to represent the jury-eligible population of the trial venue. Discussions, written questionnaires, mock deliberations, or some combination of all three are used to gather the opinions of the laypeople about the case."[7] Focus groups can be conducted by jury consultants, ADR providers or attorneys, and Ball suggests that in small cases, attorneys can "trade favors" and get another attorney to make the case presentations and conduct the focus group.

The purpose of a focus group is to preview jurors' reactions to a case and provide an opportunity to learn about their questions, predispositions, doubts and reactions to specific witnesses and items of evidence. Focus groups also inform attorneys about how prospective jurors talk about the case and the themes and analogies they see in the cases. Although many attorneys are reluctant to use focus groups, Ball thinks this reluctance is unjustified:

> Some attorneys still believe they do not need focus groups. These attorneys are dangerously and mistakenly reliant on their ability to project themselves into the minds of various kinds of laypeople. When you are as close to a project as you are to your own case, and when you have spent years in law school and in practice, you no longer think about a case the way a layperson does. Even if you could, you could not project yourself into the multiple minds of a jury or the dynamics of its deliberations. In fact, the longer most attorneys practice, the less they tend to see things the way jurors do.[8]

---

[6]*Id.* at 4.

[7]Ball, David. (2001). *How to do your own focus groups* (p. xiii). Louisville, Colorado: National Institute of Trial Advocacy.

[8]*Id.* at xvii.

When attorneys use focus groups, they often think of them as a one-shot event. But Ball believes multiple focus groups, staggered weeks apart, are preferable: "This gives you time to use what you learn in one to refine and reposition your case for the next one, thus testing your improvements."[9]

The study attorneys who use focus groups express a high level of satisfaction with the results, but also are aware of their limitations:

- Focus groups are extremely helpful in understanding how juries think. We've probably learned more from focus groups than anything else we do. Things that turn lawyers on don't turn jurors on. And things that turn jurors on do not affect attorneys.
- Some attorneys are better than others in evaluating cases. Experience, in my view – jury trial experience, I mean – is the main thing that makes an attorney a better case evaluator. Also, focus group experience is very important. I would take an attorney who's done 20 focus groups instead of 20 jury trials. I would probably take an attorney who has done 20 focus groups and no trials.
- In one case we used a focus group and, by watching the videotaped deliberations, found out what people think of school districts. I learned a lot about what people expect. The tape shows jurors hold school districts to a higher standard of care. When they drop their kid off at school they expect to see them in the same shape – no harm done – at the end of the day.
- You learn more about being a good trial lawyer by watching a focus group deliberate about a case you're presenting. This teaches you more than talking with jurors afterwards.
- Focus groups are very helpful, but some attorneys misuse focus groups. If the jury does not like the client, just as an example, they may think they can just change how the client is presented. Sometimes you can change strategy so you minimize the client's role in the case – maybe make this case about the defendant, not the plaintiff. But sometimes you cannot change the basic fact that the jury probably will not like the client. Attorneys have to be careful about overestimating how much they can change.

A few study attorneys were adamant about not using focus groups and jury consultants, regarding them as unnecessary or an unjustifiable use of the client's money. One defense attorney expressed a moderate view: "I've never hired a jury consultant. I respect what they do, but I'm saving the client $5,000 minimum."

6.2.4   Research

To test their case assessments, many study attorneys search verdict reports to find verdicts and settlements in similar cases. Other attorneys read verdict reports

---

[9]*Id*. at 6.

regularly and often discuss specific reported cases in their area of specialization at weekly or monthly meetings. As one attorney notes, "You can't just use your personal opinion. You have to look at history and statistics." The study attorneys' use of verdict reports ranged from strong reliance to willful neglect. Attorneys who regularly relied on verdict reports stated:

- You need to read what are juries doing. You can get this from *VerdictSearch* or *Verdictum*. You have to take all this into consideration.
- Jury verdicts are the only true measure of valuation.
- Another factor is regularly reading the verdict reports. When I started we got a two-page mimeograph report on the cases. The verdict reports are a good guide that keeps you tethered. That's how we know juries have gotten tighter with money. We share this information with the younger attorneys, teaching them how to be an evaluator.
- Watch jury sheets. Have an idea of what different juries are doing in different cases.
- Another thing I do is a lot of research into my adversaries. In my experience, plaintiff attorneys like to report their verdicts in *VerdictSearch*. I see what they settle similar cases for.
- I use *DepoConnect*. You can get transcripts in some cases. I will read them for valuation purposes. Those are very valuable.

When asked, "Where do other attorneys get their opinions about the value of cases?" an attorney replied, "From personal experience and close colleagues they respect. When all else fails, they look at reported verdicts."

Some attorneys expressed reservations about verdict reports, while others ignored them altogether:

- *VerdictSearch* is helpful, especially for mediators or to show the other side for settlement. But it's hard to apply it across the board to cases because each one is different, the facts and injuries are just different in almost every case, at least to a certain extent.
- I look at verdict reports. But I'm not heavily swayed because it's another lawyer. They may not try the case the way I would or get the results I get.
- Generally, I'm not all that impressed with verdict reports. I develop my own sense of what a case is valued at.
- I don't abide by *VerdictSearch* – never used that as a guideline.
- I'm less inclined to place much value on jury verdict reports. I do not find those to be trustworthy.

Expressing his concerns about attorneys who rely upon previously reported cases to assess their own cases, a defense attorney muses, "People are like snowflakes. No two people are alike."

6.2.5 Reading

To stay connected with jurors' priorities and values, the study attorneys also spend a large portion of their lives reading books and newspapers (print and online), studying public sentiments on the Internet and watching television news. They consider this to be an essential part of their work:

- I spend a lot of time reading newspapers. They help me to understand what the public is thinking and how sensitivities and values are changing. People's opinions about privacy, for example, have changed. My wife chides me for spending so much time reading newspapers. She goes and comes back later and says, "Are you still reading the newspaper?" But it really is part of my job.
- I really do believe if you don't read a lot of magazines, newspapers like the L.A. Times and the New York Times, and don't watch CNN, don't take in information, you cannot possibly have the power of information to see how other people see the world.
- I'll also go on the computer and see how a particular issue plays out on the public.
- Read newspapers and find out what jurors are reading. I read three to four newspapers daily. I want to know what jurors are thinking and really reading. It also teaches you how to write.

Constantly broadening and enhancing their frames of reference, so that their case assessments reflect jurors' views rather than their own, the study attorneys deliberately seek out external sources of information. They seem to recognize the limitations of their personal lives and professional opinions and continually compensate for those limitations by searching for, scanning and absorbing multiple depictions of contemporary life. They are connected.

Part III
Feelings and Traits

Chapter 7
Emotional Intelligence

In Part III of this book, we move from the mental frameworks and social connectedness discussed in Part II to the personal traits that support and drive superior performance. Those traits include curiosity, interest, adaptability, humility, maturity, pride, empathy, realism, competitiveness, discipline, resiliency and the sheer enjoyment of overcoming challenges and excelling.[1] Those traits are grouped roughly into three categories: emotional intelligence (Chap. 7), perpetual learning (Chap. 8), and survivor skills (Chap. 9). In this first chapter of Part III, the importance of emotional intelligence and the law's historical antipathy toward emotions are discussed.

7.1 Law and the Emotions

The law and emotions have an uneasy if not antagonistic relationship. In an extreme view, emotions are antithetical to the rule of law – human frailties that pose a constant threat to the orderly and impartial dispensation of justice. The central purpose of a statute or legal principle, in this view, is to ensure that emotions like empathy, anger and revenge do not poison the objective analysis of facts and the uniform application of rules. The rule of law and the progression of society "from status to contract" are intended to elevate the judicial system above personal pique and favoritism, displacing emotions with uniformity and predictability.[2] The sign that a law student has evolved from a naïve scholar to an incipient lawyer is the belief, as expressed by one student, that a lawyer's work is "like a mathematical

---

[1]Csikszentmihalyi, Mihaly, *et al.* Flow. In Elliot, Andrew J., and Dweck, Carol S. (2007). *Handbook of competence and motivation* (p. 599). New York: The Guilford Press.

[2]Maine, Sir Henry. (1861). *Ancient Law*, Chapter V.

R. Kiser, *How Leading Lawyers Think*,
DOI 10.1007/978-3-642-20484-5_7, © Springer-Verlag Berlin Heidelberg 2011

problem to be solved" and, for that reason, "I don't get too emotionally involved in what I'm doing."[3]

Although the law may denigrate the role of emotions, the successful practice of law requires a high level of emotional intelligence. In a study of 2,000 attorneys and law students, law professor Marjorie Shultz and psychology professor Sheldon Zedeck found that successful lawyers demonstrate strong competencies in "networking, building relationships, practical judgment, ability to see the world through the eyes of others, and commitment to community service."[4] These traits are predominantly emotional, and their importance and development are neglected in the traditional law school curriculum. These traits, moreover, are "negatively associated" with high academic performance – meaning that law students with high grades do not frequently exhibit these traits. Thus, academic success is unlikely to ensure emotional development.

The importance of a comprehensive skill set – integrating substantive legal knowledge with emotional intelligence – is again shown in the American Bar Association's MacCrate Report, which ranks the skill of "problem solving" above legal analysis and legal research.[5] That report also identifies communication, counseling, negotiation, advising a client, and the ability to recognize and resolve ethical dilemmas as "fundamental lawyering skills." These fundamental skills necessarily require a blend of human judgment, technical proficiency and emotional maturity. The MacCrate Report's concerns about the narrowness of attorney education are reiterated by The Carnegie Foundation for the Advancement of Teaching: "The difficulty, as we see it, lies in the relentless focus, in many law school courses, on the procedural and formal qualities of legal thinking. This focus is sometimes to the deliberate exclusion of the moral and social dimensions and often abstracted from the fuller contexts of actual legal practice."[6]

Both legal education and law practice are "aggressively rational, linear, and goal oriented," and lawyers tend to be unaware of the "wishes, fears, beliefs and defenses that motivate our actions," according to Professor Melissa Nelken, Faculty Chair of the Hastings Center for Negotiation and Dispute Resolution. She notes that lawyers deliberately divorce emotional issues from client cases, seeing emotions as impediments to intelligent, rational problem solving:

---

[3]Tan, Seow Hon. (2010, December). Birthing the lawyer: The impact of three years of law school on law students in the National University of Singapore. *Singapore Journal of Legal Studies*, 417. See Mertz, Elizabeth. (2007). *The language of law school.* New York: Oxford University Press.

[4]Henderson, William D. (2009, July). The bursting of the pedigree bubble. *NALP Bulletin, 21*(7), 14.

[5]American Bar Association, Section of Legal Education and Admissions to the Bar. (1992, July). *Legal education and professional development – an educational continuum.* Report of the task force on law schools and the profession: Narrowing the gap. Chicago: American Bar Association.

[6]Sullivan, William M., *et al.* (2007). *Educating lawyers: Preparation for the profession of law* (p. 145). San Francisco, California: Jossey-Bass.

Law, many lawyers say, is based on facts, not feelings; it is logical; and success is measured by whether you win or lose in court or by the dollar amount of settlements. Lawyers must act on behalf of their clients, and there is a premium on reaching sound decisions quickly. In law school, students are taught that how they feel about the cases they read is irrelevant; what matters is the soundness of their logic. Unlike medicine, for example, law is still taught largely as an exercise in abstraction, based on case reports and analysis of judicial opinions. Resistance to the human dimension of the lawyer's work is built into most law training.[7]

Professor Nelken contends that actual practice "inevitably involves the lawyer deeply in the hopes, fears and conflicts of her clients" and that lawyers' conflict resolution capabilities are enhanced by emotional skills like self-observation and awareness of the "assumptions, anxieties and conflicts that are part of who one is."[8] Her law students, nevertheless, resist thinking about how their emotions and personal backgrounds affect their conflict resolution styles and goals. As one student said to her, "If I'd wanted to learn about feelings, I wouldn't have gone to law school."[9]

Joe Jamail, a Texas trial attorney famous for representing Pennzoil in its lawsuit against Texaco and winning a $10.53 billion verdict in 1985 (reduced on appeal to $8.53 billion), criticizes law school instruction that ignores the role of emotions: "Today's law schools teach students how not to get emotionally involved in their cases," he says. "That's bullshit. If you are not emotionally involved, your client is not getting your best effort."[10] A similar controversy about the role of emotions has emerged in medical schools where the curriculum "creates doctors who lack humanity, who see patients as diseases rather than as whole people and who have what the medical literature calls 'ethical erosion' – a loss of idealism, empathy, morality."[11] In light of research indicating that personal traits like openness, agreeableness, extraversion and conscientiousness may be more predictive of success in clinical practice than test scores, some medical schools now introduce students to real patients on the first day of class and emphasize "relationship" skills like listening and building trust.[12] Dr. Abraham Verghese, one of the leaders in bridging the gap between the art and science of medicine, says, "I've never bought this idea of taking a therapeutic distance. If I see a student or house staff cry, I take great faith in that. That's a great person, they're going to be a great doctor."[13]

---

[7]Nelken, Melissa L. (1996). Negotiation and psychoanalysis: If I'd wanted to learn about feelings, I wouldn't have gone to law school. *Journal of Legal Education, 46*(3), 421–422.

[8]*Id.* at 422, 425.

[9]*Id.* at 422.

[10]Curriden, Mark. (2009, March). Lions of the trial bar. *ABA Journal,* p. 34.

[11]Hartocollis, Anemona. (2010, September 3). In medical school shift, meeting patients on day 1. *New York Times,* p. A15.

[12]See Comrey, Shen H. (1997, September). Predicting medical students' academic performances by their cognitive abilities and personality characteristics. *Academic Medicine, 72*(9), 781–786. Lievens, Filip, *et al.* (2009, November). Personality scale validities increase throughout medical school. *Journal of Applied Psychology, 94*(6), 1514–1535.

[13]Grady, Denise. (2010, October 12). Physician revives a dying art: The physical. *New York Times,* p. D1.

7.2   Emotional Intelligence

Shortly after the study interviews started, it was evident that many of the attorneys were deeply emotional yet highly objective about their clients and cases. In discussing case evaluation, the attorneys displayed a broad range of emotional skills balanced by technical expertise and astute strategies. Words like "empathy," "emotions," "personal," "intangible," "ego," "sympathetic," and "subjective" appeared in word counts as frequently as words like "case," "research," "argument," "verdict," "courts," "rules," and "venue." The attorneys' comments, distilled below, focus on the relative importance of legal and emotional issues, the role of emotion in case evaluation, and the necessity of self-awareness.

7.2.1   Legal and Emotional Issues

When asked whether other attorneys' errors in case evaluation are attributable to errors about the law or intangible factors like witness appeal and credibility, the attorneys generally point to subjective judgments as being the culprit:

- [O]f course you have to know the law. But when lawyers fail, it's the subjective that they do not take into account. The law is not as critical as the guts that go into the jury's deliberations.
- They don't see the soft facts and don't appreciate the art of advocacy. The vast majority of cases that I've gotten large awards in had de minimis offers. They misunderstood the art of advocacy.
- The emotional component that a good plaintiff's case has is something that is not considered by defendants because they get more attuned to the medicine. There is an emotional component that some defendants lose sight of as it relates to a juror's sympathy. When defendants in med mal cases get bad results at trial, it's not because they get it wrong as much as it's because it's more of a medical judgment issue to them as opposed to how people are going to respond.
- They don't understand how these personal factors, the intangible factors, will evolve through the process, how the facts will unfold. It comes full circle.
- We never know the truth; we know the perception. The law is the simplest part of it.

An attorney who spent decades practicing on the defense side and then became a plaintiffs' attorney noted that attorneys were technically competent but often unaware of the complexities and dynamics of jury trials: "They know what they're doing as lawyers, but not as trial attorneys and trial evaluators. They get lost in the maelstrom."[14]

----

[14]The study attorneys' perception that their colleagues are technically proficient but occasionally insensitive to other issues is buttressed by Fulbright & Jaworski's annual survey of corporate

7.2.2 Emotions and Judgment

When asked whether emotions interfere with case evaluation and, specifically, whether emotions promote or hinder sound judgment and effective trial advocacy, the attorneys made some critical distinctions and highlighted the ongoing tension between emotional commitment and professional objectivity. Referring to the role of emotions in case evaluation, some attorneys remarked:

- A lot of attorneys can't take the emotion out of it. That can be a good thing but you have to be able to stand back. After the depos are done, I start to visualize in my own mind how the trial will play out. If I think the plaintiff is likely to be sympathetic, or my client is not credible, that's a bad combination.
- Some types of clients I may visit in their homes. It gives me a better feeling for who they are and how their family relates to them. There are times when you definitely need to be emotionally involved, but you have to keep that to a minimum. It's really important to stay detached.
- There are times when you need to be emotional. There are times when you have to use some emotions to decide what to do. I'm probably more emotional than my male partners, but I think that's to my advantage.
- There are cases that benefit from a more passionate approach, some from a dispassionate approach. Whatever approach you take, you still have to be very professional.
- Emotions only sustain you for so long. But it is also a damaging tool. I've seen an attorney get too emotional – gets sidetracked, loses concentration. I think emotion is a blinder.

"If I really like my client," comments a plaintiffs' attorney, "I have to be in a position to say, 'Whoa, we need to step back. Am I being affected by the fact I like this client and want to win for him?'"

Reflecting on the relationship between emotion and trial advocacy, the study attorneys noted that some degree of emotional involvement or sensitivity is critical:

- It's a combination. You have to have some inner man to know if you're connecting with the jury.
- Some attorneys never connect with their clients. At times this is good because it makes you objective. But other times you have to have that missionary zeal to connect with the jury. Some attorneys are just flat, too dry, too dead. The middle

---

counsel. "The good news is that only a small minority of respondents cited incompetence among their law firms as problem areas," report Fulbright partners Helen Duncan and Peter Matson. "The real issues were unpredictable costs, poor communication and inadequate preparation on case matters." Consistent with the emphasis on delivering results, discussed in Chapter 2, corporate counsel informed Fulbright that "law firms should refocus their efforts and that law firms can best serve their litigation clients as true service providers, not merely specialists in the law." Duncan, Helen, & Mason, Peter H. (2004, September 27). In-house counsel offer their advice to law-firm litigators. *San Francisco Daily Journal*, p. 5.

ground is tough to find. Out of 1,000 cases I handled on the defense side, only three plaintiff attorneys took the time to find family and friends [who would testify regarding how the accident changed the plaintiff]. If you get the jury emotionally involved you will always win.

- There has to be a fire in the guts for the attorney and the client.
- If I get emotional about evaluating the case, I'm probably on the losing end. But in looking at what happens at trial, I have to be emotional. My forte is closing argument. Juries are primarily emotional. ... I have to understand what that emotion is going to be when I get to trial. So I try to understand that emotion that's going to come out. If a woman has scars on her arm, I cannot argue she should wear blouses with sleeves. My time to get emotional is the night before closing argument. It's a gut instinct, it's ego. You decide what that feeling will be in your closing argument.

Another attorney, who had changed his career from a defense practice to a plaintiffs' practice, noted that an attorney has to understand his own emotions very well. "You should know where your emotions are and how to stop that emotional train," he commented. Asked whether he was emotionally more mature now than when he started practicing law, he responded immediately, "Undoubtedly. I know myself better. You learn things about yourself, if you're paying attention."

7.2.3 Emotions and Clients

Apart from knowing how emotions could affect their own judgment and advocacy, the attorneys repeatedly pointed to the importance of understanding how emotions affect clients and adversaries, especially in settlement negotiations:

- When I started representing plaintiffs, my first case settled for $900,000. That's a case I would have paid $75,000 for if we represented the defendant. Everybody is afraid – plaintiffs and defendants laying out all of this money. You have to manipulate the other side's fear and have none yourself. Fear equals the perception of risk – not even risk, but the perception of risk.
- Doctors' belief that they did nothing wrong interferes with settlement. For their part, it's an emotional issue. They believe deep down they did nothing wrong. But even if they believe they did nothing wrong, there's a business decision [to settle or try a case] that has to be made.
- People do not realize the emotional effect litigation has on clients. Young attorneys do not realize the damage that is done by having to relive the trauma of an emotionally devastating event like wrongful death. Humans have a capacity to mend, to recover over time, and litigation reopens memories that people are trying to recover from. They do not realize the damage they will do to their own clients even if they win. They [clients] have to relive all the painful events they are trying to put behind them. Most attorneys do not realize that winning is resolving a case earlier rather than winning at trial.

- I see non-money issues popping up all the time. In the case you mentioned in your letter, my client wanted the relationship to continue more than the judgment. In defendant's obstinacy and anger – just being a dickhead – he refused to continue the business relationship he was contractually bound to. As a businessman, my client wanted to earn his money. He did not just want a settlement payment. They [defendants] just wouldn't do it. We just wanted them to buy [product] from us. Even post-judgment they could have resolved this by resuming the relationship. But since the defendant wouldn't do that, we went on and also got attorneys' fees and court costs. Sometimes there is a disconnect. People are caught up in agendas – "I did nothing wrong."

In discussing the emotional impact of litigation, the study attorneys also emphasized the tremendous value of apologies:

- At the beginning, the client says, "I want a full confession, I want a full apology." Defendants stupidly refuse to do it. They could get out of most cases for a few cents on the dollar if they would just apologize. It's not just about the dollars and cents. It's the huge human desire to make people fess up and the defendants' desire not to fess up.
- I go with the presumption that everyone in that seat [points to client's chair in his office] has in their own mind a big problem. For most clients, the driving principle is "he never even said he was sorry."
- Even after a case has been settled and the settlement agreement is being signed, I've had clients object to the "no admission of liability" clause. Clients want a confession – "I was wrong." All defendants could just say that and you take the wind out of the plaintiff's sails. He goes from being a world crusader to thinking, "this guy's not so bad."

The attorneys' belief that apologies would facilitate the resolution of many disputes is supported by extensive research. Jennifer Robbennolt, a law professor at the University of Illinois College of Law, has conducted numerous simulated negotiations in which all case facts remain the same except the type of apology offered by the offending party. In one experiment, for example, she found that, when no apology was offered, only 52% of the injured parties would "definitely" or "probably" accept the settlement offer. But when the settlement offer was accompanied by a full apology, 73% of the injured parties would definitely or probably accept the offer. Ironically, a partial apology had a worse effect than no apology; when settlement offers were made with a partial apology "only 35% of the respondents were inclined to accept the offer."[15] Apologies not only affected the outcome of the settlement negotiations but also changed the injured party's perceptions of the offending party. Offenders who made full apologies were seen

---

[15]Robbennolt, Jennifer K. (2003). Apologies and legal settlement: An empirical examination. *Michigan Law Review*, *102*, 460, 486. See Robbennolt, Jennifer K. (2008). Attorneys, apologies, and settlement negotiation. *Harvard Negotiation Law Review*, *13*(2), 349.

as "experiencing more regret, as more moral, and as more likely to be careful in the future than one offering a partial or no apology."[16] Injured parties, moreover, expressed "greater sympathy and less anger" at parties who made a full apology and "indicated the settlement offer would better make up for their injuries when they had received a full apology than when they had received either a partial or no apology."[17]

7.2.4 Jurors and Claims Representatives

The study attorneys also considered the impact of subjective factors on jurors and insurance company claims representatives. In many cases, intangible features of a case were considered as important as "hard" facts:

- The soft stuff is important – the charismatic nature of the client, the attractiveness of the client. I've had adjusters say they will tender the limits after they met an attractive client.
- If I have a motorcyclist with a tattoo for a client, helping a grandmother cross a street, and he's hit by a drunk driver, that case is still worth less than a Boy Scout helping her across the street. A large part is based on subjective human behavior.
- For jurors a big question is, "Is the plaintiff a nice person?"
- [Y]ou have to evaluate the overall case; this includes the likeability and unlikeability of the plaintiff and the defendants. We always look very carefully at the personal factors and have to ask, "Is there anything about the defendant that would offend anyone?", because that will change the evaluation.
- Personality is the most important factor in case evaluation. It's a people skill. If you don't have a feel for people you won't make it. . . . This has so many facets it's like a symphony. The tuba may not sound very good by itself, but when you put the tubas with the French horns and get them all together in the right way the sound is great.
- In a wrongful death case, I have to be very mindful of how to address the representative. I can't address them like I would a regular plaintiff, even if I think they're exaggerating. I have to watch my tone, my words. In one case they put their granddaughter on the stand, and I had to decide whether to cross-examine her. I said to myself, "I'll earn my points somewhere else." I'm not that stupid.
- If the plaintiff makes a sympathetic appearance, you have to take that into consideration. Conversely, if your client makes a poor witness – even if the medicine is on your side – it doesn't matter. In another case I had, the jury said they had problems with my client and the doctor's office manager's credibility. The jurors' perceptions of the parties go to the liability side.

---

[16]Robbennolt (2003) *supra* note 15 at 487.
[17]Robbennolt (2003) *supra* note 15 at 488.

Integrating all case factors – subjective and objective – into a composite evaluation is a major challenge for even the most savvy trial lawyers. "You have to become somewhat of a psychiatrist and a psychologist and relate to people and have them relate to you," remarks a renowned plaintiffs' attorney.

7.2.5   Self-Awareness

The study attorneys display a deep sense of their own skills, biases, shortcomings and limitations. Many have developed empathy by experiencing failure and rejection in their own lives, and some have overcome alcoholism, childhood abuse, debilitating illness and other personal tragedies. An attorney famous for his ability to connect with jurors describes a setback early in his career:

> I think I see how people really are and how they come across. I also know what it's like to be ignored. When I graduated from law school there was nothing I wanted more than to be a plaintiffs' attorney in the San Francisco Bay Area. I got there and found it was a buyers' market, and I could not even get an interview at [two San Francisco personal injury firms]. I showed up three times and tried to talk the receptionist into letting me talk with a lawyer at [law firm]. I couldn't even get past the receptionist. Back then I hadn't had a decent haircut in years and didn't have these [points to lower teeth] because they had been knocked out in a fight. I spent weeks trying to get a job before heading to [city] where I had said I would never live.

For every study attorney who enjoyed a comfortable childhood, another study attorney seemed to have lived a hardscrabble existence as a youth. To varying degrees, the attorneys have fought to fulfill their own sense of accomplishment and meet their personal standards of integrity and professional commitment to clients. Whatever their individual circumstances have been, the study attorneys exhibit a high level of self-awareness and deliberateness about their practices.

The self-awareness exhibited by the study attorneys is a frequently overlooked element of expertise. Expert performers like the study attorneys distinguish themselves by continually completing a self-regulatory cycle of forethought (task analysis and self-motivation), performance (self-control and self-observation), and self-reflection (self-judgment and self-reaction).[18] Although non-experts also attempt to improve their performance in some way, experts accelerate their improvement by setting higher goals for themselves, recalling more pertinent and substantial information about their performance and attributing errors to sources over which they have control.[19]

---

[18]Zimmerman, Barry. Development and adaptation of expertise: The role of self-regulatory processes and beliefs. In Ericsson, K. Anders, *et al*. (Eds.). (2006). *The Cambridge handbook of expertise and expert performance* (p. 708). New York: Cambridge University Press.

[19]*Id*. at 711, 712.

Self-awareness is as important in the legal field as it is in any other professional endeavor where lives, reputations and assets are at stake. When lawyers lack self-awareness and emotional intelligence, they unwittingly overlook key factors in case evaluation, mismanage pre-trial preparation and fail to achieve optimal trial results. This lack of personal awareness directly harms case strategies, as law professors Stefan Krieger and Richard Neumann explain: "Most lawyers have some personality trait that, if left uncontrolled, will in one way or another obstruct strategy."[20]

The fact that some attorneys may be unaware of their emotions and how their personalities affect people is discussed by one of the study attorneys:

> Case evaluation is like body consciousness. Do you know what that means? We had a guy in this office who had no body consciousness – could not walk around without hitting something. He had a big blustery voice but no sense of how he impacted people and how he moved around the office. Many lawyers are personally brilliant but oblivious to where they are in the world. They do not see how they come off to people. They are not honed in their thinking. They might be book smart, but they are not people smart.

"Book smart but not people smart" suggests that attorney self-awareness has changed little since 1955, when Erwin Griswold, the Dean of Harvard Law School, said, "Many lawyers never do seem to understand that they are dealing with people and not solely with the impersonal law."[21]

Interacting with people and understanding the personal implications of legal decisions, the attorneys exhibit many of the core competencies that constitute emotional intelligence: self-awareness, self-assessment, consciousness, self-control, trustworthiness, conscientiousness and adaptability.[22] They are self-critical and continually monitor themselves for maladaptive behavior. In describing the interplay between emotions and law practice, they made these observations about themselves and other attorneys:

- Lawyers are ego driven, egocentric driven, especially trial lawyers. They start to believe they are invincible, they can do anything, like it's just a matter of personality. Lawyers are guilty of being too egocentric. You have the leading role, you're on center stage, you're the producer and the director. There's a danger in that. Trial work has a lot of stress; it attracts you when you're young and you have a lot of testosterone, but there's a price to pay. Sometimes it's your judgment.
- How do I know when I'm getting too emotional? When I can't see everything – when you can't see – when you start to believe your own bullshit.

[20]Krieger, Stefan H., & Neumann, Richard K. (2007). *Essential lawyering skills* (p. 39). New York: Aspen Publishers.

[21]Reilly, Peter. (2010). Mindfulness, emotions, and mental models: Theory that leads to more effective dispute resolution. *Nevada Law Journal, 10*, 433.

[22]Goleman, Daniel. (2000). *Working with emotional intelligence*. New York: Bantam. Goleman, Daniel. (1995). *Emotional intelligence*. New York: Bantam.

- In the old days, I was more emotional, one way or the other, about each case. I got better over time with controlling my emotions, more analytical, but I still feel like crying sometimes in closing argument. I let my voice crack. That's as far I can go with the jury, even if I feel like crying.
- It's my personality – I want to fight everything. I know now to pick my wars.
- It's hard to know when the jury thinks you're beating up on a plaintiff. I consider myself to be pretty sensitive, but in one case I misread the jury. Maybe I didn't think to ask myself, "Will this bother the jury?" Maybe I wasn't paying enough attention. You have to carefully assess the impact of your words – not just not getting angry but not being sarcastic.
- Some partners are very detail-oriented but have had some very bad results at trial because they lack that emotional sense.

As indicated by these remarks, the line between constructive and detrimental emotional involvement is opaque, and it is a perpetual challenge to exploit the benefits of emotional commitment and enthusiasm while avoiding the damage of emotional biases and extremism. What seems to distinguish the study attorneys from some of their colleagues is not that they avoid this conundrum altogether but that they are thinking about it regularly.

The role of emotion in case evaluation and the importance of emotional commitment in trial representation are synthesized in this email to the author from a study attorney:

> I wanted to add a couple points after thinking about our discussion.
>
> Maintaining a professional distance is important to accurate evaluation, as I said. But a lawyer really serves two roles: that of an advocate, putting the client's best case forward to the outside world, and, on the other hand, serving as a neutral (this is the real point for evaluation) advisor about the likely outcome of the case. I am not sure many lawyers appreciate this distinction or realize that they have these two roles that must be separated.
>
> In the advocate's role, feeling the emotion of the case, even for a defendant who will not pay a dime if the case is lost, is important to the best advocacy. Letting oneself feel the emotion, without being overcome by it, helps trial advocacy. During almost every trial, I end up crying sometime, away from court, not because of unhappiness or fear of loss, but just from the overwhelming emotion I feel during trial. I don't know if I am unique in this respect. I do think some lawyers lose this as they age—a sort of cynicism can creep in. I consider myself lucky that I can genuinely feel the emotion in every case.
>
> This is probably beyond your topic of interest, but your inquiry prompted me to have these thoughts that I felt I should share with you.

Chapter 8
Perpetual Learning

A few years after completing their formal education, most professionals exhibit a modicum of competence and are practicing their profession with little or no supervision by another professional. "At that time," observes psychology professor K. Anders Ericsson, "most professionals reach a stable, average level of performance, and then they maintain this pedestrian level for the rest of their careers. In contrast, some continue to improve and eventually reach the highest levels of professional mastery."[1]

The traditional explanation for the difference between average and expert performers is innate talent – the "some people have it, some don't" explanation for advancement. That explanation assumes that one's abilities and capacities are set like a thermostat and regulate the level of accomplishment throughout one's life.[2] The modern theory of expert performance, however, focuses more on "deliberate practice" than innate talent. In the modern view, performance is extraordinarily malleable and dependent on a person's commitment to "seeking excellence" and setting increasingly difficult performance standards. Deliberate practice requires performers to set goals beyond their immediate abilities and refine their performance through repeated practice, concentration and regular feedback.[3]

---

[1]Ericsson, K. Anders. The influence of experience and deliberate practice on the development of superior expert performance. In Ericsson, K. Anders, *et al*. (Eds.). (2006). *The Cambridge handbook of expertise and expert performance* (p. 683). New York: Cambridge University Press.

[2]According to psychology professor Carol Dweck, the belief in modifiable ability is part of the "incremental" theory of intelligence, while the emphasis on "innate" ability fits into the "fixed" theory of intelligence. She contends that people who adopt the incremental theory are more receptive to failure and learning from failure, while those who adhere to the fixed theory fear failure because it reflects negatively on their "innate" abilities. See Elliot, A. J., & Dweck, C. S. (Eds.). (2005). *Handbook of competence and motivation*. New York: Guilford Press.

[3]Ericsson *supra* note 1 at 692–693. See Simonton, Dean Keith. (2001). Totally made, not at all born [Review of the book *The psychology of high abilities*]. *Contemporary Psychology, 46*, 176–179.

Average performers, in short, accumulate experience through rote effort, while experts improve performance through deliberate practice.

Because deliberate practice requires a continuous cycle of effort, self-assessment and improvement, experts are perpetual learners. When they stop learning and rely on old mental models to solve new challenges, they cease being experts. "Some experts will at some point in their career give up their commitment to seeking excellence and thus terminate regular engagement in deliberate practice to further improve performance, which results in premature automation of their performance," notes Ericsson. But experts committed to perpetual learning and improvement develop "increasingly complex mental representations to attain higher levels of control of their performance."[4]

The study attorneys have developed the habit of perpetual learning. Although the attorneys had practiced law for 29 years, on average, they displayed the curiosity and flexibility of the "beginner's mind" – an attitude of enthusiasm, humility, receptiveness and interest. They did not allow their experience to get in the way of learning. To show how the attorneys engage in and benefit from perpetual learning, this chapter highlights five traits and attitudes conducive to continual learning: (1) reliance on "developed" talents instead of "innate" abilities; (2) openness to improvement and change; (3) humility, modesty and caution; (4) a belief that performance can be improved through effort and self-evaluation; and (5) active solicitation of feedback and criticism.

8.1 Developed Talents and Innate Abilities

Among the 78 study attorneys, only seven stand out as "naturals" – attorneys who felt confident and comfortable in the courtroom from the very beginning of their career. One of the seven attorneys said, "I had it from the beginning. I had that sense. I walked into a courthouse the first time and was not afraid and actually started enjoying it." The seven attorneys may have had "innate" trial skills, but at least for some of them, their abilities were augmented by family background or previous employment. At least one was a son of an attorney, and two had extensive experience in a related business like insurance before bar admission. The remaining 71 attorneys started their legal careers with varying degrees of ease in the court-room and facility in relating to clients, judges and juries. Their development as trial attorneys also proceeded at uneven rates and in different, sometimes nonlinear directions. Few, if any, of the study attorneys coasted on their innate, fixed abilities or considered their careers to be a succession of victories strung together by their

---

[4]Ericsson *supra* note 1 at 685.

natural talent. Instead, they developed expertise in case evaluation and trial representation in a conventional manner – long hours, intense scrutiny of documents, fastidious investigation, arduous trial preparation, occasional losses and setbacks, observation of other attorneys and a sense that they could always do a better job with more diligence, experience and practice.[5] To people who believe success is just a matter of luck and genetic endowment, the study attorneys would be a major disappointment.

Many of the study attorneys got off to a rocky start in the courtroom and were forced to perform far beyond their personal comfort zones:

- I sometimes wonder what happened to the law student who was uncomfortable speaking in class. I told one of my professors, "I'd prefer not to be called on." He asked me, "What are you going to do after you graduate and become a lawyer?" I told him, "I don't know. I just prefer not to be called on."
- When you first start out you're more nervous. I'm more confident now. I used to go to the wrong courtroom – got confused between divisions and departments. Back when we had municipal courts and superior courts, I'd be in the wrong courtroom, the wrong place. I just sat down at any table in the courtroom, didn't pay attention to where plaintiff and defense counsel were supposed to sit.
- I tried my first case – not second chair, but on my own – a month after admission. Sure I had terrible diarrhea during the whole trial and my voice was trembling all the time, but I got through it.
- During my first year I didn't know where to stand in the courtroom. I went to the city attorney's office when I graduated. There was no turning back – we had to try a case a week.
- Sometimes I wonder how I became a trial attorney. When I was a kid, my mother asked me to phone the department store to find out when they opened. I was too shy to pick up the phone and make that call, just couldn't do it.

Acknowledging the unsettling lack of proficiency that troubles conscientious attorneys early in their career, a plaintiffs' attorney said, "You're walking malpractice when you come out of law school. You may be an attorney but you cannot be considered a litigator or a trial attorney for at least 10 years." For some study attorneys that sense of unease never goes away. "I'm still nervous before every trial," comments a defense attorney. "I can hear the cracks in my voice when the trial starts." She adds: "You have to learn to fake it. I don't touch a piece of paper at the beginning of a trial because the jury will see the paper shaking."

---

[5]In this respect, the attorneys' training is roughly similar to the military's "Eight P's: Proper prior planning and preparation prevents piss-poor performance." Ripley, Amanda. (2008). *The unthinkable: Who survives when disaster strikes and why* (p. 206). New York: Three Rivers Press.

8.2   Open-Mindedness

Because few of the study attorneys felt comfortable and confident right from the beginning of their careers, they developed the habit of building competence through inquiry, learning, preparation, accomplishment and reflection. A prerequisite to their development is open-mindedness, a state often commended but rarely embraced. Lord Thomas Dewar is well known for his aphorism, "Minds are like parachutes, they only function when they're open." But if minds are indeed like parachutes, we also should remember that they are usually tightly packed, kept away from direct sunlight, unopenable absent a countervailing force and used only to avert catastrophic impacts. For most people, open-mindedness necessarily carries a risk of dissonance and self-doubt, as gaps invariably exist between our self-perceptions and actual performance. The study attorneys accept this risk and regard candor, receptiveness and flexibility as essential to professional improvement. In representing clients, they are non-defensive learners, stressing the importance of open-mindedness:

- You have to have an open mind. This is not to say you will always change your mind, but you have to be open to it. You also need to have as much information as is available, to complete your discovery, to make a legitimate decision.
- There are attorneys who say this is a slam-dunk and then change their opinion right before trial. I only change my opinion when I have a basis for changing my opinion. But it could change at any time. It's like a judge said after ruling on motions in limine: "These are my rulings and I don't want any further argument. But they are set in marshmallow." What he was saying is, "Don't give me any more of the same arguments, but if there's something new I could change my mind." That's the way I am with case evaluation.
- I will abandon my beliefs in a heartbeat if necessary. Most people think that's a weakness – like when they tried to portray Gore as a flip-flopper. But I think it's a strength – it's what you have to do when the evidence changes. If you don't change your mind, you go from being wrong to stupid.
- I listen a lot more than talk. When you listen it makes you more directed and effective. My approach over time has moved more to listening, learning, watching.

A defense attorney thought that enthusiasm was an essential part of being a conscientious, open-minded attorney. In explaining why some attorneys do not improve with experience, he states, "Enthusiasm is the other factor I mentioned. If they're not enthusiastic, not a go-getter, they will not change their minds because you just don't give a damn."

8.3   Humility, Modesty and Caution

Contrary to some caricatures of successful attorneys as being arrogant, pretentious and dominating, most of the study attorneys were models of grace, dignity and self-assurance. They were confident but not imperious. This profile is consistent with expert performance. Jim Collins and his staff of 22 research associates studied 1,435 Fortune 500 companies and found only 11 that achieved Level 5, the highest level of performance, based on numerous quantitative and qualitative standards "essential to take a company from good to great." The key feature of Level 5 company leaders is "an individual who blends extreme personal humility with intense professional will." Leaders who demonstrate this "paradoxical combination of traits," writes Collins, "are catalysts for the statistically rare event of transforming a good company into a great one." They are what Collins calls a "study in duality" – modest and willful. When assigning responsibility for poor results, they "look in the mirror," and when apportioning credit, they "look out the window." Collins summarizes the characteristics of Level 5 leaders: "compelling modesty," "never boastful," "acts with quiet, calm determination" and "never blaming other people, external factors or bad luck." Interviewed by Collins, one of the Level 5 chief executive officers said, "I never stopped trying to be qualified for the job."[6]

The study attorneys exhibit the "humility and fierce resolve" identified by Collins in Level 5 leaders. Their strong sense of responsibility – "looking in the mirror" – was featured in Chap. 2, as it presages the traits described in the subsequent chapters. Joined with their sense of responsibility is a humble, modest and cautious attitude:

- The moment you think you're the best, you'd better get out because there's always someone better than you.
- If you have good attorneys on both sides, they cancel each other out. I tell clients, "Just because I'm a good lawyer doesn't mean I can change the case."
- From an experience point of view I know I'm a much better trial attorney. But that doesn't mean I'm more sure about what a jury will do.
- I've had many mentors here. Everything I've accomplished, all of my success, I've learned from other attorneys here.
- In every case, I've learned from the best. All the great lawyers just learned it from someone who had learned it from somebody else. There's nothing wrong with this. I try to teach humility to my sons. The only thing wrong with taking somebody else's techniques is when you act like they're your own.

With some of the other study attorneys, an apparent lack of modesty may mask a realistic self-assessment. One plaintiffs' attorney, for instance, said, "A case for settlement purposes is worth more for me than another attorney. There aren't that many that can consistently hit in the stratosphere." Based on his track record and reputation, that appraisal may be conservative.

When asked, "What do you do to prevent yourself from becoming over-confident?" the study attorneys responded with characteristic modesty:

---

[6]Collins, Jim. (2005, July-August). Level 5 leadership: The triumph of humility and fierce resolve. *Harvard Business Review*, 138. In his study of creative individuals, Mihaly Csikszentmihalyi reports that they, too, are "remarkably humble and proud at the same time." Csikszentmihalyi, Mihaly. (1996). *Creativity* (p. 68). New York: Harper Collins.

- I don't think I ever suffered from over-confidence. ... I have not had to do anything to prevent over-confidence because I'm just not self-confident. I've just never felt completely comfortable. I'm always asking myself, "Why do I think that? Why do I believe that?"
- Well, I've thought about this myself. My cases fall into two categories. One, cases I was expected to lose by the other attorneys in this firm and, two, trials that anyone could try. So I never developed any big ideas of what I could do.
- No, no, I really try to temper that. One of the attorneys I worked with said, "You're never as good an attorney as you think you are after you win a case, and you're never as bad an attorney as you think you are after you lose."

Another attorney responded succinctly, "I can't get complacent or cocky because the moment you do that you get hammered."

Keeping their egos in check, some study attorneys noted that experience had actually decreased their confidence and increased their sense of caution. As they gain more experience, they sometimes see more risks:

> I'm probably more scared now, more intimidated, more fearful. You're more arrogant when you're young before you see some rogue jurors and realize what could happen. A few months ago, I talked with two or three jurors that did not vote for me, and I was appalled – not appalled, just surprised – to hear what they said. One juror said she was scared of me. She said my cross-exam of a witness was so aggressive it scared her. I spent a lot of time talking with another juror – connected with him at a social level but could not get him to open up even a little about how his view of the case just wasn't consistent with what the evidence showed. As you become more experienced you see more things happening.

A defense attorney echoed this sentiment: "When I was younger, I would think there's not a chance in hell I could lose this case. Now I know that's wrong."

8.4 Improvement Through Effort and Self-Evaluation

Starting with open-minded and humble attitudes, the study attorneys enhanced their performance through inquiry and self-evaluation. For some study attorneys, these methods of self-development had proven to be worthwhile even before they started practicing law. An attorney who worked as an insurance company claims manager before studying law describes his claims evaluation system as a mixture of inquisitiveness and humbleness:

> I had a lot of responsibility dumped on me. I would call a guy like Bruce Walkup [well-known San Francisco plaintiffs' attorney, now deceased] and ask – this was 30 years ago – and just say, "What do I have to tell my superiors to show my superiors how stupid they are?" What worked for me at the beginning is I didn't know much, and I had no problem letting people know that. If you ask enough questions, you reduce your risk factor. Your approach has to be more behavioral than actuarial. ... I fessed up to the fact I didn't know. This was dialing for dollars, and if you can convince me, you get dollars.

For many attorneys in the early phases of their careers, questions imply weakness; inquiries connote ignorance; and asking for further explanation suggests denseness.

A study attorney, however, takes a different view: "But the thing a young lawyer can have is the confidence to ask and be candid about your questions. You have to have some courage to be open about what you don't know and what you need to know."

In addition to using the power of inquiry, the study attorneys closely examine their own performance – especially their defeats, mistakes and near misses – to improve their skills. They are candid in acknowledging their own shortcomings:

- It's really important to learn from experience, and it makes me a better role model for my employees. I want to be a model and the only way is to learn from mistakes.
- I actually lost my first case representing a plaintiff. Your mindset as a defendant, as opposed to a plaintiff, is completely different. . . . You don't have a burden of proof [when you represent a defendant]. You just sit back and take potshots at the plaintiff's case. That was a lesson I learned – one you have to think of all the time. You have to prove every element of your case. Once I got into the swing of cases representing plaintiffs, I was fine.
- I got burned in one of my cases here. .... After the trial was over, the judge said to me, "You try one hell of a case, but you have to pay attention to who you're putting on the jury and how you're presenting yourself." . . . What I took away from that – whether it's a man or a woman – is that I had to learn how not to be a threat to them. This applies to everything you do in the courtroom.
- On one case I tried a few years ago, three jurors voted in favor of liability. My initial thought was they did not understand the evidence. But as I gave it more thought and looked back on the case, I thought more about my performance and realized I was not passionate about the client. It is extremely important for an attorney to be passionate, to have an unwavering belief in the client.
- I believe in volition. We can all learn. I learned a few years ago you really cannot put on a case if you need an interpreter. The interpreter becomes the client in the jury's eyes and the jury cannot hear the melody of the personality of my client. This is an example of what experience teaches you. Technically, it should work but it doesn't. I've tried to keep my ears open and keep my eyes open to hone my skills.

Reflecting on the value of learning from mistakes, a plaintiffs' attorney who frequently serves as a temporary judge, muses, "I have lost cases I should have won and won cases I should have lost. If you're getting kicked around but you're learning, it's tough; but if you're getting kicked around and not learning, it's worse."

When asked whether there was any educational value in the cases that did not turn out the way they had expected, or whether they disregard those cases as being aberrational, the study attorneys were uniformly adamant:

- Oh, my God, no. You have to learn from every case. You cannot leave any case behind you as though it never happened.
- Absolutely, because you always second-guess your losses – "What should I have done?" I can tell you in great detail every case that went bad for me. I remember

my failures, my losses, much more than my wins. I don't question the wins. With the wins you're just glad it's over and say, "Thank God. I dodged a bullet."

- You learn more from your losses than your wins. The best closing arguments I do are the ones I deliver in my car after I've lost a case.
- You have to take it on the chin every once in a while. You remember the cases that didn't work out much more than the ones that did. Michael Jordan said what motivated him was not the victory but the fear of losing.
- There is educational value in the sideways cases. Juries evaluate witnesses differently. In one case, I was sure the plaintiff's treating physician was a jerk, an arrogant guy who the jury would dislike. I was wrong.
- I spend a lot of time thinking about the losses, working through all the aspects.

The study attorneys do not just mull over defeats and surprises; they study them to avoid making similar mistakes and ensure that their future performance will improve. The victories seem to receive less attention. "The great thing about winning," says a study attorney's partner, "is there's so much less to explain."

8.5 Soliciting Feedback and Criticism

Deliberate practice is dependent on timely and accurate feedback and criticism. In litigation, accurate feedback is difficult to obtain because responsibility is diffuse. Case outcomes can be attributed to multiple actors and factors, and the motivations for deflecting responsibility for bad outcomes are sufficiently strong to ensure both a proliferation of theories and a multiplicity of suspects. The study attorneys attempt to overcome the inherent noisiness of litigation feedback by directly soliciting jurors' opinions in all cases, whether won or lost:

- The most fascinating part of the trial is being able to interview jurors afterwards. I seize the opportunity. They tell me things like, "The old guys talked too much. They just droned on." This is an MTV generation. We have gone digital. We use Elmos. You have to do your best to keep the jury interested. Their attention is elective.
- I've been before many juries throughout the state. If you're in Suffolk County, the jurors are conservative, hardworking. I take my most conservative suit and tie. How do I know to do this? From my experience. Years ago, the jury said, "You're too slick."
- My criterion has changed after losing as many cases as I have. That's because when I talk to jurors after trials, the criteria is the jury did not like my client.
- After a case is over, I ask jurors, "Who would you like to be your doctor [the defendant, another physician, or an expert witness]?" I ask, "What about my presentation – was I too hard on this witness?"

Another study attorney solicits an associate's input to understand how he might change his oral argument style: "I discuss the cases with my associate and ask for advice on problems I'm having – like I do better in front of male judges than female judges. It's something about my way of arguing that works with male judges but doesn't work with female judges."

After a case has been tried, one study attorney reviews all the trial pleadings and exhibits. "I don't just throw them in the box after a trial," he says. "I look at everything and ask, 'How did that go?'" For "practical" lawyers, this may seem like a useless exercise because the trial is over and an attorney cannot bill for introspection and reflection. For an attorney committed to excellence and improvement, however, retrospection is essential. Ironically, many attorneys who employ military metaphors to describe litigation and pride themselves on "fighting," "ambushing," and "taking no prisoners" seem to be unaware that, in the military, after action reviews and reports (AARs) have been mandatory for more than 50 years.[7] Military operations, like trials, are too hazardous and consequential to escape strict scrutiny after the premises, predictions and promises have clashed with reality.

---

[7]Fletcher, J.D. The value of expertise and expert performance: A review of evidence from the military. In Ericsson, K. Anders (Ed.). (2009). *Development of professional expertise* (pp. 464–466). New York: Cambridge University Press. See Zsambok, Caroline E., & Klein, Gary (Eds.). (1996). *Naturalistic decision making* (pp. 54, 79). Mahwah, New Jersey: Lawrence Erlbaum Associates. In another context, Klein notes that "outcome feedback – knowledge of results – doesn't improve our performance as much as process feedback, which helps us to understand how to correct flaws." Klein, Gary. (2009). *Streetlights and shadows* (p. 166). Cambridge, Massachusetts: MIT Press.

Chapter 9
Survivor Personality Traits

Surviving a plane crash in the Andes and winning a trial in Brooklyn seem to be unrelated experiences. But when we compare the adaptive characteristics of effective attorneys with the traits that enable survivors to recover from accidents that leave hundreds, sometimes thousands, of people dead, a few similarities emerge. These similarities should not be a surprise because both effective attorneys and survivors surmount antagonistic conditions that overwhelm other people. They both grapple with unanticipated tragedies, struggle to understand accidents with indeterminate or multiple causes, confront hostile adversaries and obstacles intended to halt their progress, find that options have been eliminated by conditions over which they have no control and encounter risks that, at times, result from their own overconfidence or errors in judgment. They also know the fear and frustration of discovering that old views, skills and habits will not lift them out of an impending disaster and may, in fact, embed them in it.

The study of survivors and disasters has captivated researchers and intrigued armchair adventurers. From cyclones to earthquakes, from building collapses to plane crashes, from outbreaks of malaria to widespread famine, all catastrophes pose an inevitable question: "Would I be among the survivors or the dead if this happened to me?" To answer this question, researchers like Laurence Gonzales (*Deep Survival: Who Lives, Who Dies and Why*), Amanda Ripley (*The Unthinkable: Who Survives When Disaster Strikes*) and Al Siebert (*The Survivor Personality*) have identified the traits that virtually assure death and have highlighted the traits that distinguish survivors. Many of their conclusions defy our preconceptions.

In catastrophic disasters, the "Rambo" types are often the first fatalities.[1] "Humility can keep you out of trouble," Gonzales observes. "If you go busting into the wilderness with the attitude that you know what's going on, you're liable to miss important cues."[2] Gonzales finds that the people that seem most physically

---

[1] Siebert, Al. (1996). *The survivor personality* (p. 5). New York: Penguin Group.

[2] Blake, John. (2008, September 8). Miraculous survivors: Why they live while others die. CNN. Available at http://www.cnn.com/2008/US/09/08/survive/index.html.

prepared for disasters – those with the most physical strength and experience – die first because they are careless and overconfident. In contrast, "weaker" people survive because they "know when to rest, when they shouldn't try something beyond their capabilities, when it's wise to be afraid."[3] Disasters are not so much Darwinian struggles for survival among the fittest but practical efforts to stay alive among the most adaptive.

In their rich studies of survivor personalities, Gonzales, Ripley and Siebert pinpoint at least nine survivor traits that extricate people from "that boundary region between life and death."[4] The reason he calls it a "boundary region," Gonzales explains, "is that not everyone can do it. Some fail. Some die." The people who escape the boundary region and live on as survivors are amalgams of flexibility, adaptability, resiliency, realism, inquisitiveness, creativity, tolerance for ambiguity, independence and intuition. These survivor traits – and the study attorneys' application of these traits to litigation – are the subject of this chapter.

9.1   Realism

Survivors are painfully realistic. They do not rely on optimistic visions to overcome setbacks; they are coldly analytical in assessing their circumstances and how close they are to dying. Although most people are stunned and start to shut down after accidents, survivors move rapidly to assess their condition and take action:

> The first rule is: Face Reality. Good survivors aren't immune to fear. They know what's happening, and it does "scare the living shit out of" them. It's all a question of what you do next.[5]

Survivors do not waste time blaming others for their predicament or bemoaning their fate. Instead, they exhibit an "automatic openness to absorb new information."[6] Their attitude has three key elements, according to Siebert: (1) "quickly absorb information about what is happening;" (2) "expect that something can be done to influence events in a way that leads to a good outcome;" and (3) "be willing to consider *any* possible action or reaction." The trait of open-mindedness, discussed in the previous chapter, is essential to survival: "This open-brainedness is a mental orientation that does not impose preexisting patterns on new information, but rather allows new information to reshape a person's mental maps."[7]

---

[3]*Id.*

[4]Gonzales, Laurence. (2003). *Deep survival: Who lives, who dies and why* (p. 25). New York: W.W. Norton and Company.

[5]*Id.* at 27.

[6]Siebert *supra* note 1 at 186.

[7]Siebert *supra* note 1 at 190.

Although realism may seem to be a logical and ordinary response to a catastrophic event, only 10% - 20% of victims can pull themselves together to plan their
recovery.[8] Many people "go numb" and wander around in a daze. Others delay,
procrastinate, retreat to a state of denial and become lethargic. Rather rapidly
they become resigned, disintegrate psychologically, tidily arrange their personal
belongings and lie down to die quietly or, if at sea, slip over the side of an inflatable
boat, saying "I'll be back in a few."[9]

While resignation and lethargy characterize many victims' reactions, others are
cognitively damaged by overstimulation. Under extreme stress, their bodies are
flooded with norepinephrine, epinephrine and cortisol, and their vision, hearing
and depth perception decline dramatically. They lose peripheral vision and, overwhelmed by stress and the resultant "task saturation," may experience amnesia or a
functional loss of consciousness.[10] A helicopter pilot responding to an emergency,
for instance, intended to turn off the radio but instead shut down one of the engines.
As Ripley explains, stress causes tunnel vision in all occupations, and as stress
increases, people tend to become "mentally obsessed with one data point to the
exclusion of others."[11]

Survivors see the same catastrophe that renders others inert or panic-stricken.
Instead of senselessly arranging boughs for their bed or impulsively pressing the
wrong control button, however, they exhibit the characteristic of "active-passive-
ness" – accepting one's situation without giving in to it.[12] They are afraid, but their
fear does not eclipse their assessment of where they are and what will be necessary
to survive. They proceed cautiously, calculatedly and deliberately, absorbing new
information and modifying their plans to avert new dangers. Neither cheerleaders
nor doomsayers, survivors "discover the flow of the expert performer, in whom
emotion and thought balance each other in producing action."[13]

Balancing emotion and thought, the study attorneys demonstrate the survivors'
skill of intense realism. They continually stress the attorneys' duty to maintain
objectivity and combat the tendency to see a case in the best light. Their skill
in representing clients is not founded on the ability to contort a few facts into a
positive narrative but rather the power to comprehend all facts and build a persuasive, legally cognizable plan for recovery or defense. They see no advantage in
overlooking bad facts; experience tells them that tactic is a disservice to clients,
may be seen as an affront to jurors and fosters a habit of professional self-deception:

---

[8]Gonzales *supra* note 4 at 24.

[9]Gonzales *supra* note 4 at 167, 168, 196, 212. Ripley, Amanda (2008). *The unthinkable: Who
survives when disaster strikes* (pp. 8, 16). New York: Three Rivers Press.

[10]Ripley *supra* note 9 at 64, 74, 78.

[11]Ripley *supra* note 9 at 71–72.

[12]Gonzales *supra* note 4 at 218.

[13]Gonzales *supra* note 4 at 289.

- When you're looking at the facts of the case, you cannot see things the way you want them to be. As a young lawyer, I thought if I tried hard enough, I could change the facts of the case. But you can't change the facts. I have to look at who did what, when, how, where. You have to be very objective and be a devil's advocate and ask very clear questions.
- Your strategy changes with the type of case. In med mal, you have to realize the general presumption that doctors are competent. No one wants to believe their doctor makes mistakes. It scares the piss out of people.
- You cannot change someone's fundamental belief system. You can try to get them [jurors] to carve out an exception for your client.
- I've met hundreds of lawyers whose cases get better every day. I have associates who have never had a bad depo. If you read their reports to carriers, everything is going their way. This can't happen. I ask them, "What are you overlooking? Step back, you're overlooking something." You have to step back and be objective. When you're young it's easy to be emotional and passionate, but our job is to be more objective.
- Don't fight reality. In every trial, witnesses see things differently. In closing arguments, I tell the jury that it's less credible to have a case where everybody says exactly the same thing. There will always be contradictions in how different witnesses remember and see things. Different perceptions are to be expected. It is human nature.
- When you're young, you want to help your client so badly you tell yourself, "There's really not an elephant in the room, there's really not a big gray elephant over there with a pink ribbon on it" – especially if you think you found a case that you think says, "There's no elephant in the room." As you get older, you tell your client, "There's an elephant in the room" – and they need to deal with it.

"You have to ask yourself what would the other side look like," advises an attorney who represents both plaintiffs and defendants in commercial cases. "Around here, we have an expression, 'Unless you can be a wicked devil's advocate, you have no business being an advocate.'"

9.2 Flexibility, Adaptability and Resiliency

"When I ask survivors if there is any quality or trait that contributes most to being a survivor," Siebert writes, "they usually answer without hesitation either flexibility or adaptability."[14] People who have developed the trait of resiliency, another type of flexibility and adaptability, learn more from catastrophic events and respond more constructively to them, explains Ripley:

---

[14]Siebert *supra* note 1 at 30.

Resilience is a precious skill. People who have it tend to also have three underlying advantages: a belief that they can influence life events; a tendency to find meaningful purpose in life's turmoil; and a conviction that they can learn from both positive and negative experiences. These beliefs act as a sort of buffer, cushioning the blow of any given disaster. Danger seems more manageable to these people, and they perform better as a result.[15]

Gonzales also stresses the importance of flexibility, noting that "rigid people are dangerous people" and "you must hold onto the plan with a gentle grip and be willing to let it go."[16] For survivors, flexibility not only means openness to change but also tolerance of uncertainty and ambiguity. People who lack mental agility and whose sense of security is derived from predictability, definition and control degrade quickly.

The study attorneys consistently exhibit a high level of flexibility, adaptability and resiliency. Although the interview questions did not include the bald inquiry, "Are you flexible?", the attorneys' description of their case evaluation methods, negotiation techniques and trial strategies indicate that they regard versatility and receptiveness to change as key components of superior performance. Their insights reflect general litigation strategies as well as specific tactics. Turning first to overall strategies, they remark:

- Being an attorney means you have to adopt different personalities – you don't hit every problem with the same hammer. Being a lawyer is not always being a tough guy.
- Tort litigation is like exploratory surgery. You don't know exactly what you've got until you cut in and start looking around. Before you start, you look up the law and see the remedy. But once you've gotten into the case, you see there may be a liability but it is something different from the one they [clients] thought they had.
- You have to adapt. Being willing and able to adapt is paramount, especially because you might find out [during the trial] why the other side is offering so little or demanding so much for the first time. Case valuation evolves at all times. What if the judge says, "You can't do that." What if you can't get some evidence in? You have to be prepared for everything.
- It's not about the kicks and the punches. It's about redirecting the energy. You don't take the hits – you control and redirect the other party's attack.
- You always have enough information and you never have enough information. You should have enough information from the start to have an opinion. But this opinion can change at any time – right up to the trial or during the trial. It's a dynamic process – I treat it that way.

Epitomizing the study attorneys' flexibility and adaptability, a managing partner remarks, "I always have a gut feel about a case, but I'm receptive to new information."

---

[15]Ripley *supra* note 9 at 91.

[16]Gonzales *supra* note 4 at 280.

Shifting their focus from general litigation strategies to trial tactics, the attorneys continue to emphasize the value of flexibility and adaptability:

- You have to learn to be flexible. Even though you may be very anxious, you have to let things go. You can feel when there's a shift in the courtroom, not always but most of the time. When the testimony is different from what you expected, you deal with it directly. Ask the doctor to explain, "Tell us what you meant by that?" I stay very flexible, let things take their course.
- The same case will be tried differently with a judge or a jury. Your demeanor has to change with the witnesses, too. If they're credible, why in the world would you attack them? The only time you can get into an aggressive cross exam is if they have earned it.
- In war, your battle plans only last until you've met the army on the other side. In trial there are always [problems] that happen you don't expect. Even though mistakes are made, you can win a case.
- Certain things you don't know until the motions in limine are decided. Some judges let everything in; some don't let anything in. These factors determine whether a case will be settled right before trial.
- I try to counter what I see as potential arguments that will be proffered by the other side. It's like a chess game; you don't want them to take your king. Some evidence does come in you don't expect; someone testifies differently from what they said before or maybe the other side's witness has something you didn't know about. You can't let the jury see you react. You have to act like it's nothing [flicks finger over his coat lapel as though propelling a speck of dust into the air].

"Having a variety of available responses is crucial when handling variable, unpredictable, chaotic, or changing conditions," asserts Siebert. "Successful people in any profession know that it is better to have many possible responses than to be limited to a few."[17]

Continually anticipating problems and considering possible responses, the study attorneys deal directly with any weaknesses in their cases. They are neither hopeful that opposing counsel will overlook the deficiencies nor confident that jurors will minimize them. When cases have gaping holes, the study attorneys display them and show the judge or jury how to walk around them:

- If there's something negative in your case you should address it in a motion in limine [to exclude or limit evidence at trial]. You can't leave it to your adversary

---

[17]Siebert *supra* note 1 at 33. See Tucker, John C. (2003). *Trial and error: The education of a courtroom lawyer* (p. 148). New York: Carroll & Graf Publishers. ("Of all the mistakes made even by experienced trial lawyers the most common is failure to adjust to changing circumstances in the heat of battle. Time and again, lawyers plow ahead with questions they had planned to ask on cross-examination even though a witness's previous answer has rendered the planned questions unnecessary, or even dangerous. Concentrating on their planned attack, it is as though they had been rendered blind and deaf.")

because they will spin it in a way that makes it even worse. So you have to take the initiative and deal with it head on.

- Every case has problems. It's a question of how you deal with them. If you think positively about the problems, you can come up with a way of dealing with it. If you worry about it and let your ego get in the way, you settle.
- You have to say something. You cannot ignore it. I don't always know exactly how I'm going to deal with a problem until I'm in trial. Sometimes it's just an epiphany – and the other attorney says, "Where the fuck did you come up with that?" Usually the answer is, "In the shower."

Being flexible, adaptive and resilient requires not only an awareness that clients, witnesses, judges, jurors and adversaries act unexpectedly but also the foresight to reduce the risk of damage from the unexpected. Most people, however, neither anticipate the unexpected nor attempt to mitigate its consequences. As Don Norman, a Northwestern University professor, points out, "We know two things about unexpected events: first, they always occur; and second, when they do occur, they are always unexpected."[18] As indicated by the attorneys' comments, they anticipate problems and devise ways to surmount them. In addition to directly addressing weaknesses in their cases, the study attorneys anticipate that jurors may not limit their deliberations to the evidence presented at trial and may engage in the usual panoply of juror misconduct – visiting the accident site, talking to family and friends about the case, and using the Internet to supplement their knowledge. "If you don't think jurors check you out online, you're mistaken," David Ball writes.[19] His warning is echoed by a study attorney: "Jurors will look at your website and the accident site. They're not supposed to, but you have to know they might do that."

9.3 Creativity, Inquisitiveness, and Tolerance for Ambiguity

Although creativity and inquisitiveness are distinct characteristics, it is almost impossible for survivors to generate creative solutions without continually seeking new information. "Creativity comes from the ability to see unusual connections, find unusual ways to combine things, and make remote associations," observes Siebert.[20] People who lack creativity don't see those connections, combinations and associations; they have a dogmatic view of the world that eviscerates curiosity and obscures reality. Psychologists call this "premature perceptual closure," a condition

[18]Norman, Donald. (2007). *The design of future things* (p. 13). New York: Basic Books.
[19]Ball, David. (2005). *David Ball on damages* (p. 364). Louisville, Colorado: National Institute of Trial Advocacy.
[20]Siebert *supra* note 1 at 78.

correlated with "intolerance of ambiguity."[21] People who exhibit premature perceptual closure evaluate people and situations hastily, react impulsively and make their minds up quickly.[22] Conversely, people who resist premature perceptual closure tend to tolerate contradictions, exercise independent judgment, counter group pressures and integrate intuitive and non-rational aspects of their thinking.[23]

To be genuinely inquisitive and tolerant of ambiguity requires a high degree of modesty, self-control and, at times, discomfort. Siebert finds that "life's best survivors ask lots of questions," but these inquisitive people risk embarrassment and some loss of ego: "Getting smarter comes from asking questions and searching for answers, from experimenting with life, and from even being willing to look foolish and make mistakes."[24] Inquisitive people risk looking like idiots when they are striving to become experts. Inquisitive and creative people also experience the awkwardness of not always knowing the answers and the agitation of having to seek their own solutions. In describing the benefits of open-mindedness, tolerance for ambiguity and an absence of preconceptions, psychiatry professor Nancy Andreasen also depicts the downside:

> This flexibility permits them to perceive things in a fresh and novel way, which is an important basis for creativity. But it also means that their inner world is complex, ambiguous, and filled with shades of gray rather than black and white. It is a world filled with many questions and few easy answers. While less creative people can quickly respond to situations based on what they have been told by people in authority – parents, teachers, pastors, rabbis, or priests – the creative person lives in a more fluid and nebulous world.[25]

Dean Simonton, a psychology professor who has studied creativity and genius extensively, reiterates the importance of autonomy in formulating innovative solutions: "Highly creative individuals are independent, autonomous, unconventional and perhaps even iconoclastic. As a consequence, they will impose fewer a priori constraints on the scope of what they are willing to consider."[26]

Although creative people may live in a more uncertain world, their independence, awareness and deliberateness lead them to a safer world. Sixty-nine people who survived the World Trade Center attack, for example, disregarded what they had been "told by people in authority" – the announcement that "their building was secure and to return to their offices." Reflecting the survival trait of independent judgment, one person who ignored the announcement and proceeded down the

---

[21]See Smock, Charles. (1957, March). The relationship between "intolerance of ambiguity," generalization and speed of perceptual closure. *Child Development*, 28(1), 27–36. Levitt, Eugene E. (1953, September-December). Studies in intolerance of ambiguity: I. The decision-location test with grade school children. *Child Development 24*, (3/4), 263–268.

[22]Siebert *supra* note 1 at 79.

[23]See Eiduson, Bernice T., & Beckman, Linda (Eds.). (1973). *Science as a career choice: Theoretical and empirical studies* (pp. 244–245). New York: Russell Sage Foundation.

[24]Siebert *supra* note 1 at 20.

[25]Andreasen, Nancy C. (2006). *The creative brain* (p. 101). New York: Penguin Group.

[26]Simonton, Dean Keith. (1999). *Origins of genius* (p. 92). New York: Oxford University Press.

stairs said, "I was thinking that there is a real difference of opinion here about what my eyes are seeing and what the announcement was saying."[27] In contrast, an employee who heeded the announcement spoke to his father by phone shortly before his death: "Why did I listen to them – I shouldn't have."[28]

Although the study attorneys are not making life or death survival decisions, they are handling cases of enormous complexity and consequence. In fulfilling that responsibility, they employ the survivors' traits of inquisitiveness, creativity and tolerance of ambiguity to evaluate and resolve those cases. Their comments regarding inquisitiveness reflect a belief that curiosity and humility always trump egotism and vanity:

- Use the process to ask a lot of questions and learn. Don't be afraid to use the "Columbo" approach. Say, "I'm new at this – tell me why." Information is where it all is, that's the power. You get more information when you're open about your inexperience.
- When I first started practicing, a classmate was married to a partner of a noted firm, and I asked to get a half an hour of his time whenever I had a new case. I'd show him the police report, medical records and he would know who the attorneys were and the carriers. He'd tell me what the case is worth, what's going to happen. This is how I learned.
- Don't be afraid to say you don't know the answer.
- Lawyers want to impress doctors with their knowledge, and they spend time trying to get the pronunciation of medical terms right. They want to convince the doctor how smart they are. I say, "Don't do that – do the opposite. Don't worry about what they'll think of you. If there's something you don't understand, ask them to explain it again. Make sure you get it, and if you still don't get it, keep asking them to explain it again. Ask those questions, get that information."
- It's easy to see and just react. But the question is, "What really happened?" I read an associate's draft letter to the carrier about a pre-trial scheduling conference he attended. It says the attorney appeared at the hearing and the judge set the trial for x date. And of course all of that's true. But what I want to know is, "Was the judge friendly with plaintiffs' counsel? What did the judge do before he was on the bench? Why was the trial date set so soon?" Then when you ask these questions and do some investigation it turns out, "Oh, the judge was a former plaintiffs' attorney." That's important. He seems to have some respect for the other attorney, and it looks like they set an early trial date because they're trying to put pressure to settle it. You have to walk into the trees first before you talk about the forest.

---

[27]Proulx, G., & Fahy, R.F. (2004). Account analysis of WTC survivors. *Proceedings of the Third International Symposium on Human Behaviour in Fire, Belfast, UK*, September 01–03, 2004, pp. 203–214, (NRCC-47309).

[28]Gonzales *supra* note 4 at 174.

Questioning, challenging, asking, probing, doubting – these are the tools of the inquisitive lawyer. And the process is incessant. "I'm always in self-analysis, asking myself questions until the case is over," relates an attorney with more than 40 years of trial experience. "I keep asking myself the question, 'Why?'" states another veteran trial lawyer.

The attorneys' inquisitiveness facilitates their creativity in developing case themes, countering damaging evidence and devising an overall strategy to protect their client. Although the law is often perceived as a very traditional field, the study attorneys are inventive, creative and innovative:

- You have to listen. Don't formulize, don't turn everything into a formula. No matter how mundane the case seems, start over and look at the burdens a case presents. Ask yourself, "What are the client goals and your own ambition and what is realistic?" That can be hard for a kid because they haven't seen much of life.
- Be inventive. Don't stick with what the book says. Be creative – be different from what the other side can do.
- You have to be able to bob and weave, be inventive.
- Sometimes taking a legal approach is not even the best way of solving a problem. Sometimes they [lawyers] overlook a telephone call. You have to ask yourself, "If I was trying to solve this problem for someone I really care about, what would I do?" A lot of times you decide that a phone call might be better than filing a complaint.
- Most swords have two edges. You just have to find the edge that works for you. When the other side is referring to your client as an illegal immigrant, you tell the jury they considered him good, cheap, hard-working labor, not an illegal immigrant, until he got injured. You take something they think is an asset, and you turn it into your asset. For some people, there's nothing in the refrigerator. I learned to cook from my mother. There's always enough in the refrigerator. Even if it's only two eggs you find a few more things around and you've got a great meal.

The study attorneys' creativity dispels the myth that creativity is "an innate and mysterious personality trait possessed only by artists and others like them." As law professors Krieger and Neumann explain, "Creativity is the process of solving problems through insights that you arrive at on your own. Everyone is creative to some extent, although some are more creative than others."[29]

Despite the critical importance of creativity in client representation, some attorneys still think of creativity as a trait that is exercised in the margins, at the edge of cases, and does not affect substantive outcomes. They think of creativity as the clever juxtaposition of conflicting evidence in a cross-examination or a rhetorical flourish at the end of an argument. In reality, creativity is displayed broadly and

---

[29]Krieger, Stefan H., & Neumann, Richard K. (2007). *Essential lawyering skills*, (p. 31). New York: Aspen Publishers.

goes directly to the bottom line. In one case, for instance, a defense attorney's creativity saved the client from an enormous financial loss:

> I've had cases where the plaintiffs were from Hollywood Central. You know how a jury will feel about them, so you have to be strategic instead of taking them head-on. Sometimes that means finding a weakness or – like I did in one case – settling and educating their attorney about who else they should have sued. In one case, I knew the verdict would come in between 5.6 and 5.8 [million], and the verdict was 5.8. But they didn't get this out of my client because we had settled; they got this out of [a different party] that I not only pointed them to but told them how to make the case.

If this attorney had been combative instead of creative, he might never have noticed the missing defendant.

9.4 Independence

Survivors are leaders, not followers, and if they can't find any followers, they strike out on their own. They do not suffer from "the good kid" handicap and will bend or break the rules when necessary to stay alive. They "do what bad kids do" – fight, get angry, question authority, fail to cooperate, and sass back.[30] As author Laura Hillenbrand describes Louis Zamperini, a survivor of World War II POW camps and the subject of her book, *Unbroken*:

> Defiance defines Louie. As a boy he was a hell-raiser. He refused to be corralled. When someone pushed him he pushed back. That made him an impossible kid but an unbreakable man.[31]

"People raised to be good and not bad can be emotionally handicapped outside the structured environment they were raised in," asserts Siebert. "They are trapped into only good ways of acting and paralyzed from bad ways of acting, even if one of those perceived bad actions could save their life."[32] Referring to the passengers who stayed near the wreck of their airplane in the Peruvian jungle instead of walking downhill to find water, Gonzales says, "They were rule followers, and it killed them."[33]

Because the subject of personal independence was not broached directly during the study interviews, it is difficult to assess whether the study attorneys possess this survivor trait. Perhaps the best evidence of the attorneys' independence, however, may be their own careers. The majority of the study attorneys in group practices were founding or managing partners of their own firms. A defense attorney said he resolved to have his own firm early in his career: "Shortly after I started practicing,

---

[30]Siebert *supra* note 1 at 95–99. Gonzales *supra* note 4 at 85.

[31]Oney, Stephen. (2010, November 12). The defiant ones. *The Wall Street Journal*, p. D1.

[32]Siebert *supra* note 1 at 98.

[33]Gonzales *supra* note 4 at 174.

I wrote a note to myself – 'I want to have my own firm and have my name on it.' I made seeing clients my Number One goal." Many of the attorneys had well-established careers before practicing law and took the risk of abandoning stable, remunerative jobs in favor of an uncertain, new career in law. Other attorneys spent decades in a defense practice and in mid-career joined a plaintiffs' practice. A few attorneys referred to clashes with judges that came close to contempt citations: "I tried the case; it was one of the most harrowing experiences of my lifetime. The judge threatened to put me in jail. I'm a mouth."

Robert MacDonnell, a New York plaintiffs' attorney, explains the importance of independence and describes how law firms can strip attorneys of their independence and individuality and how young attorneys must struggle to maintain their identities:

> Young lawyers are put into a system. They're told what to do and trained how to do it. A lot of them lose their personality, their style. Their sense of self becomes lost. A good trial lawyer has to be comfortable with how you are, who you are, how you do things. You can't be someone else. But the system pushes attorneys to handle cases a certain way – even the trial notebooks all look the same. . . . It's the business; it's the necessity to advance, not fall by the wayside. That's what you do or you're left behind. In law school, they talk about the greatness of the law. But then you get out there and it just grinds you down unless you can stand apart.

Again emphasizing the importance of independence, other attorneys referred to some colleagues as "robots" with "checklist" mentalities, moving passively "from verdict to another trial, from that trial to the next trial."

9.5 Intuition

Intuitive thinking, states psychologist and Nobel Prize winner Daniel Kahneman, is "perception-like, rapid, effortless."[34] Asserting that intuition is a survival skill, Siebert describes it as "knowledge gained without rational thought" or, stated differently, "the ability to be receptive to information coming through one's subconscious mind."[35] Gonzales explains the critical importance of intuition in his analysis of four Mount Hood climbers who cascaded down a 1,000-foot ridge. They were tied together by a rope at 35-foot intervals and could not arrest their fall after one climber's axe "went through the ice like it was a slush puppy."[36] Noting that peer pressure may have been a cause of the accident, Gonzales writes, "None of the climbers wanted to be the one to say, 'I can't handle this' and force everyone to belay and delay." If there was a doubt, no one paid attention to it or voiced it:

---

[34]Myers, David (2004). *Intuition: Its powers and perils* (p. 1). New Haven, Connecticut: Yale University Press.

[35]Siebert *supra* note 1 at 66.

[36]Gonzales *supra* note 4 at 122.

A true survivor would be attuned to those subtle cues, the whisper of intuition, which might have been saying, *I don't feel quite safe here. Why is that so?* But since most of us are not conscious of those processes, we have nothing to draw our attention to what's happening to us. We don't have what psychologists call meta-knowledge: the ability to assess the quality of our own knowledge.[37]

When we cannot listen to ourselves or heed knowledge masked as subliminal unease, our accidents unfold as highly predictable events – a synergistic succession of conditions, acts and judgments.[38]

Intuition plays a serious role in the study attorneys' evaluations and decision making. Describing his approach to cases, a plaintiffs' attorney says, "I use a word – the intuition for the law. It's an all-encompassing thing. Nothing I learned in law school gives you the intuition for the law." Another plaintiffs' attorney was preoccupied with a case: "There's a case I have now. Something about the case has got the hackles in my neck standing up. I'm trying to find out why my gut is unhappy with this file." Others referred to cases that they settled in mid-trial because "I had a feeling about this case." In those cases, the other parties aligned with their client – co-plaintiffs or co-defendants – proceeded with the trials and were gravely disappointed by the verdicts. "It's instinct," says a defense attorney with more than 40 years of experience. "It's probably all instinct."

The attorneys rely on intuition in evaluating clients, selecting jurors and even predicting what a judge will do. When asked, "Does intuition play a role?" an attorney responds:

It does for me. It plays a big role in everything. I'm asking, "What can I get away with? How prepared is my opponent?" I rely on intuition to tell me these things. In one trial, I told my associate during a break, "I'm going to get the judge to instruct this witness to answer the question." She said, "How do you know that?" I said, "I don't know. I just know it's going to happen." The judge actually was not paying much attention to the testimony. But after the recess, I started asking a series of questions and interrupting the witness with another question. After a few of these, the judge told the witness, "You have to answer Mr. [name]'s question. If you keep giving evasive answers, I'll strike your answer."

Another attorney, asked about the role of intuition, integrates intuitive and deliberative thinking: "Sometimes I've gone out on a limb to ask a question, but I had an objective reason to ask that question. I had a fallback position."

In evaluating facts, clients and jurors, the attorneys frequently referred to "intuition," "feel," "instinct" and "guts:"

- I go with my heart wrong or right. I try to read people, and I'm pretty good at it.
- The more you do it, the better the feel you have for it. You get a feel for what can work.
- I'm much less mechanical. I've learned to listen to my gut. I do the calculations, but if the numbers don't feel right I'll go back and do them over. It's got to rest with my gut. It's better than my analytical ability. I don't think most lawyers do

---

[37]Gonzales *supra* note 4 at 124.

[38]Gonzales *supra* note 4 at 123.

that – especially defense lawyers. The biggest single change I have made is I
have become vastly less mechanical, more intuitive.

- There's a skill in cherry-picking cases for trial. You have that instinct that you
have more upside than downside.
- I combine intuition and assess witness potential and assess the opponent's
demeanor and hopefully you know what will happen. A lot of it is intuitive,
sometimes all of it.
- By the time of trial, the attorney has synthesized everything and in their gut they
have a strong conviction of how this case will be decided. It's got objective
components and subjective components like witness credibility. You do have an
intuition regarding the defensibility of the case.

One attorney's intuition, however, may be another attorney's common sense. When
asked whether he relies on intuition, a business trial attorney replied, "Generally
you have an idea. If your prominent witness shows up as an asshole, I would not say
it's intuition to say you're going to have a problem."

Part IV
Techniques and Strategies

Chapter 10
Case Evaluation

In Part IV of this book, "Techniques and Strategies," the study attorneys outline the key factors in case evaluation; discuss client interviewing and counseling practices; demonstrate how they relate to opposing counsel, mediators and judges; describe the effects of insurance and insurers; show how they negotiate settlements; and impart their methods of jury selection. This first chapter in Part IV provides a context for analyzing the study attorneys' techniques and strategies by defining the skill generally known as case evaluation and identifying the information and sensibilities required for accurate case evaluation. It then explains the ever-increasing importance of sound case evaluation and examines whether attorneys and clients, in general, evaluate cases and predict trial outcomes accurately.

10.1 Meaning, Scope and Purpose of Case Evaluation

When clients seek legal advice, they expect something more than a complete and accurate description of the applicable law. In addition to an explanation of the controlling statutes, regulations and judicial decisions, they want an assessment of the likely outcome of the dispute. Clients recognize that judicial systems fall short of their formal guarantees, and gaps invariably exist between apparent rights and actual remedies. For that reason, clients want to know not only what they're entitled to but also what they will receive. This additional, predictive component of legal advice – whether called "the voice of experience," "how things work in the real world," or "a dose of reality" – is at the core of the skill generally described as case evaluation.

Case evaluation in general civil litigation is the ongoing process of estimating the monetary value of a legal claim and determining the costs and consequences of realizing that value. It necessarily requires the identification and assessment of all case factors influencing the claim's probable outcome. These factors, narrowly viewed, are the applicable law and the admissible evidence. Viewed more expansively, however, the salient factors encompass tangible and intangible considerations ranging from the efficacy of a summary judgment motion to the credibility of a client, from the skeptical tone of a judge's question during oral argument to the tension on a witness' face, from the applicability of a legal defense to the effect of a client's appearance. As one prominent Los Angeles trial attorney notes, "One quivering lower lip and it's over. That's how you lose your money. In a moment everything can go."

Case evaluation is vastly more complex than legal analysis and fact selection. It extends far beyond the five basic skills taught in law school (clarifying facts, applying legal principles to facts, clarifying the law, parsing the effects of legal procedure, and discussing policy or social implications of legal decisions).[1] Some attorneys never develop reliable case evaluation skills after law school graduation; some seem to be adept, visceral evaluators even before they enter law school; and most refine this skill in an idiosyncratic manner through close calls or defeats at trial, clients that balk at paying for arguably ineffective legal services, or jurors' candid discussions with them after trial.

An effective case evaluator is able to anticipate how an adverse party, insurance claims representative, mediator, judge, or jury will react to a case and can accurately predict the range of case outcomes. To fully anticipate and accurately predict, an attorney relies on experience and judgment, perception and sensing, explicit knowledge and tacit knowledge, and historical verdict data and contemporary sensibilities. "As an attorney, you're evaluating really at two levels," explains an attorney whose practice emphasizes cutting-edge legal issues. "One is your case, the facts and the law. The other is understanding how jurors have changed and will react to the case – why a particular fact situation that arises today could result in a particularly different result than would have occurred five years ago."

Despite many attorneys' conviction that intangible, subjective and seemingly amorphous factors should not be allowed to infect case evaluation and the judicial system, the courts expressly invite and oftentimes require juries to consider such factors. Jurors' personal judgments, beliefs, common sense, experience and values are an integral part of the American judicial system, placing a premium on case evaluators' ability to discern both objective and subjective factors affecting case outcomes. For those attorneys convinced that the practice of law is a detached exercise in applying laws to discrete facts, it may be helpful to remember that one of the first instructions a trial court judge gives to jurors authorizes them to rely on their own personal judgment:

> As far as the law is concerned, it makes no difference whether evidence is direct or indirect. You may choose to believe or disbelieve either kind. Whether it is direct or indirect, you should give every piece of evidence whatever weight you think it deserves.[2]

---

[1]Mertz, Elizabeth. (2007). *The language of law school* (p. 65). New York: Oxford University Press.

[2]CACI No. 202. Judicial Council of California Civil Jury Instructions (2010).

Jurors are further instructed that, in deciding a witness's credibility, they may consider: How did the witness look, act and speak while testifying? Did the witness have any reason to say something that was not true? What was the witness' attitude toward this case or about giving testimony?[3]

In both the consideration of testimony and the ultimate determination of liability and damages, jurors are authorized to rely upon their own opinions of credibility, reasonableness and consistency. After listening to opinion testimony of a lay witness, the jury "may disregard all or any part of an opinion that you find unbelievable, unreasonable or unsupported by the evidence."[4] Even after a court has ruled that a witness is qualified to testify as an expert, the court instructs, "it is up to you to decide whether you believe the expert's testimony and choose to use it as a basis for your decision."[5] The jury's ultimate determination of physical pain, mental suffering and emotional distress damages also is a personal, essentially subjective opinion: "No fixed standard exists for deciding the amount of these noneconomic damages. You must use your judgment to decide a reasonable amount based on the evidence and your common sense."[6] The burden of proof itself is an ostensibly objective standard superimposed over a subjective test of persuasion, requiring an individual juror to compare and weigh evidence that cannot be quantified: "A party must persuade you, by the evidence presented in court, that what he or she is required to prove is more likely to be true than not true."[7]

Attorneys practicing commercial law sometimes believe that, unlike personal injury cases, breach of contract cases are decided by hard facts. Commercial litigators tend to believe that issues like contract interpretation and breach of contract damages are relatively cut and dry compared to the emotional tenor of tort cases. In reality, jurors' awards of damages in breach of contract cases are affected by concepts of fairness that may override narrow legal factors. Studies indicate, for instance, that jurors "view breach as a moral harm" and "breaches to engorge gain are perceived to be more immoral than breaches to avoid loss."[8] An identical breach thus may result in different damage awards depending on whether the breach was committed for the purpose of gaining a higher profit or avoiding further losses on a deal that had become economically infeasible.

---

[3]CACI No. 107. Judicial Council of California Civil Jury Instructions (2010).

[4]CACI No. 223. Judicial Council of California Civil Jury Instructions (2010).

[5]CACI No. 219. Judicial Council of California Civil Jury Instructions (2010).

[6]CACI No. 3905A. Judicial Council of California Civil Jury Instructions (2010).

[7]CACI No. 200. Judicial Council of California Civil Jury Instructions (2010).

[8]Wilkinson-Ryan, Tess and Hoffman, David A. (2010). Breach is for suckers. *Vanderbilt Law Review*, *63*, 1003. Temple University Legal Studies Research Paper No. 2009–33. Available at SSRN: http://ssrn.com/abstract=1451123. Experiments also indicate that breach is "less morally problematic" when a contract has been assigned to a third party. Wilkinson-Ryan, Tess. (2010, October). Psychology of assigned contracts. University of Pennsylvania, Institute for Law & Economics Research Paper No. 10–14; 5th Annual Conference on Empirical Legal Studies Paper. Available at SSRN: http://ssrn.com/abstract=1636802.

Because the facts in commercial cases often seem dull and the context of the disputes may be unfamiliar to jurors, the development of coherent narratives and compelling themes is even more important in commercial cases than tort claims. "In a personal injury case," explains jury consultant Susan J. Macpherson, "the plaintiff's story usually evokes the jurors' experiences with pain and recovery or permanent loss."[9] In commercial cases, however, jurors' experiences may not provide an adequate background for understanding the parties' motivations and actions. For that reason, Macpherson elaborates, the effect of narratives "is even greater in commercial cases where esoteric subject matter makes it more difficult for jurors to construct the narrative on their own." California Superior Court Judge Gregory Alarcon reiterates the serious challenges commercial litigators face in presenting their cases: "Jurors understand why they're there on a criminal case, but when a case involves money, lawyers have to work even harder to not waste the jurors' time, to make it interesting to them, and to not keep them waiting."[10]

10.2   The Emerging Importance of Case Evaluation

During the last 50 years, as litigation practice has shifted from trials to settlements, accurate case evaluation has become an essential skill for attorneys. Because about 95% of cases are now resolved without a trial, an attorney's ability to accurately assess the strengths and weaknesses and the likely outcome of a case has become the foundation of client decisions to commence, defend, underwrite and ultimately settle cases.[11] "Settlement rather than trial has emerged as the dominant endgame of civil litigation," explains Vanderbilt University law professor Richard Nagareda.[12] When cases were tried to verdict, the attorney's case evaluation skills were less important, as a jury or judge determined the actual value of a case. Even if the attorney was a lousy case evaluator, it made little difference because the true value was not affected by the attorney's opinion but rather was determined by a jury or a judge. The frequency of trials also affected the cases that were settled because attorneys had sufficient experience with jury trials to ascertain the likely trial

---

[9]Macpherson, Susan J. (2000). How to hook jurors in commercial cases. *Trial, 36,* 56.

[10]George, Evan. (2010, July 9). Lively & loose. *San Francisco Daily Journal,* p. 2.

[11]Eisenberg, Theodore and Lanvers, Charlotte. (2008, November 21). What is the settlement rate and why should we care?. Cornell Legal Studies Research Paper No. 08–30. Available at SSRN: http://ssrn.com/abstract=1276383.

[12]Nagareda, Richard A., (2010, March 10). 1938 all over again? Pre-Trial as trial in complex litigation. Vanderbilt Public Law Research Paper No. 10–12; DePaul Law Review, *60* (forthcoming 2011). Available at SSRN: http://ssrn.com/abstract=1568127.

outcome.[13] Trials were a reference point for settlement valuation, not a worst-case scenario if mediation failed.

In contemporary litigation, juries and judges rarely determine the merits and value of cases, and cases usually are resolved through pre-trial settlements reflecting attorneys' case evaluations. This preference for settlements may reflect the necessity more than the efficacy of consensual resolution, some professors suggesting that "the prominence of settlement has so profoundly eroded young lawyers' skills as litigators that they are functionally incapable of bringing cases to trial, with the self-perpetuating result that even cases warranting trials wind up being settled."[14] Despite this dramatic shift from third-party adjudication to consensual settlement – decried or applauded as the "vanishing civil trial"[15] – case evaluation skills receive scant attention in law schools and uneven scrutiny in law firms. "Many attorneys do not appreciate the importance of case evaluation," observes a founding partner, "and most of the information on the subject is just one attorney's opinion in an article he writes. Case evaluation is a very difficult skill to learn."

Attorneys who learn the skill of case evaluation hold an overwhelming advantage in negotiations and trials. Whether resolved by a pre-settlement or a trial, a claim ultimately will be reduced to a specific sum stated in a settlement agreement or a judgment. Accurately predicting that outcome is the expert case evaluator's monopoly. That prediction ultimately drives the parties' assessment of a reasonable resolution of that case and determines whether a case will be settled or tried. For a plaintiff, accurate case evaluation can result in a fair, expeditious settlement of a difficult claim, and it can propel a strong case past an inadequate settlement offer and into a courtroom, permanently changing a client's business or personal life with a favorable verdict. For a defendant, accurate case evaluation has the power to divert a potentially devastating liability onto a moderate settlement track or extinguish a seemingly extortionate settlement demand with a financially advantageous verdict.

10.3   Attorneys and Clients as Case Evaluators

If attorneys and clients were already functioning as accurate case evaluators and effective negotiators, this book would be unnecessary. Extensive research during the last 50 years, however, indicates that many attorneys and clients may be biased

---

[13]Most civil cases have been resolved by settlements for many decades. See Galanter, Marc. (1985). "... A settlement judge, not a trial judge:" Judicial mediation in the United States. *Journal of Law and Society, 12*(1), 1. Galanter, Marc. (1988). The quality of settlements. *Journal of Dispute Resolution*, 55–84.

[14]Moffitt, Michael. (2010, Spring). Which is better, food or water? The rule of law or ADR? *Dispute Resolution Magazine*, p. 12.

[15]Galanter, Marc. (2004). The vanishing trial: An examination of trials and related matters in federal and state courts. *Journal of Empirical Legal Studies, 1*(3), 459–570.

case evaluators and ineffective settlement negotiators.[16] Because their case evaluation skills may be inadequately developed, plaintiffs and defendants frequently
obtain suboptimal results for both settled and adjudicated cases. Plaintiffs may
settle cases for amounts less than adversaries would pay or less than juries would
award, even after adjusting for the costs of a trial. Defendants, for their part, may
pay larger amounts to settle cases than plaintiffs are willing to accept or juries
would have awarded, even after considering the costs of defense. In the cases that
are not settled and proceed to trial, many plaintiffs and defendants find that the trial
outcome is financially inferior to the result they could have achieved by accepting
an adversary's pre-trial settlement proposal. At the core of these suboptimal results
– whether administered through negotiated settlements or contested trials – is a case
evaluation problem.

Deficiencies in case evaluation are acknowledged by attorneys and substantiated
by studies. In a 2007 LexisNexis study of attorneys in mid-size and large law
firms, 64% of attorneys reported that "time is the greatest barrier to performing
effective early case assessment," and 66% of the attorneys recognized that "they
could enhance their case assessment skills."[17] Although the attorneys surveyed by
LexisNexis "put a premium on being able to clearly gather, organize and review the
facts of a case" and believed that early case assessment resulted in favorable
outcomes and reduced litigation costs, 87% of the attorneys reported their case
assessments were performed "on an informal basis rather than utilizing a specific
methodology or set of tools." The absence of evaluative methodologies and tools is
consistent with professors J. Edward Russo and Paul Schoemaker's caution that
"professionals should rethink their roles." Although professionals' intuitive skills
are suitable for framing questions, assembling facts and identifying issues, they

---

[16]Rosenthal, Douglas E. (1976). Evaluating the competence of lawyers. *Law & Society Review, 11,*
257. Wissler, Roselle L., Hart, Allen J., & Saks, Michael J. (1999). Decision making about general
damages: a comparison of jurors, judges and lawyers. *Michigan Law Review, 98,* 751. Rosenthal,
Douglas E. (1974). *Lawyer and client: Who's in charge?* (p. 59). New York: Russell Sage
Foundation. Loftus, Elizabeth F., & Wagenaar, Willem A. (1988, Summer). Lawyers' predictions
of success. *Jurimetrics, 28,* 437. Goodman-Delahunty, J., Granhag, P.A. & Loftus, E.F. (1998).
How well can lawyers predict their chances of success? Unpublished manuscript. University of
Washington. Cited in Koehler, Derek J., Brenner, Lyle, & Griffin, Dale. (2002). The calibration of
expert judgment: Heuristics and biases beyond the laboratory. In Gilovich, Thomas, Griffin, Dale,
& Kahneman, Daniel (Eds.). (2002). *Heuristics and biases: The psychology of intuitive judgment*
(pp. 705, 706). Cambridge: The Press Syndicate of the University of Cambridge. For a study of law
students' overconfidence see Eigen, Zev J. and Listokin, Yair. (2010, July 14). Do lawyers really
believe their own hype and should they?: A natural experiment. Yale Law & Economics Research
Paper No. 412. Available at SSRN: http://ssrn.com/abstract=1640062.
[17]Survey: Early case assessment results in favorable outcomes in 76% of cases and reduced . . .
Business Wire, May 16, 2007. LexisNexis. (2007, May 17). Survey: Early case assessment results
in favorable outcomes in 76% of cases and reduced litigation costs in 50% of cases. [Press
Release].

warn, "shooting from the hip when many data points are involved is simply unprofessional."[18]

Recent studies of litigation outcomes also suggest that case evaluation often is idiosyncratic, and the systematic development and implementation of case evaluation skills has been neglected. In her 2010 article, "Insightful or Wishful: Lawyers' Ability to Predict Case Outcomes," Professor Jane Goodman-Delahunty and her colleagues report the results from a survey of 481 attorneys practicing in 44 states.[19] The attorneys were asked to identify a case that had not yet been resolved and then to answer the question, "What would be a win situation in terms of your minimum goal for the outcome of this case?" They also answered the question, "From 0 to 100%, what is the probability that you will achieve this outcome or something better?" After the cases were resolved by settlement negotiations, dismissal, or trial, the researchers checked in with the attorneys to determine how the attorneys' minimum goals compared with the ultimate results. The attorneys reported that "44% of the outcomes were less satisfactory than the minimum goals set by the lawyers." Among the remaining cases, 32% "matched the goal set by the lawyers," and 24% "exceeded the lawyers' minimum goals."[20]

The researchers analyzed the specific effects of gender, age, and confidence. Female attorneys, they concluded, were "slightly better calibrated" than their male counterparts. With respect to experience levels, "the data provided no support for the hypothesis that lawyers with more practical experience are better calibrated than lawyers with less experience."[21] Ironically, the lawyers who were highly confident about achieving their goals were less likely to achieve them: "In general, the higher the expressed level of confidence, the greater the overconfidence."[22]

Perhaps the most important finding, for purposes of understanding why attorneys may not try hard enough to improve their own case evaluation skills, is the absence of a mental connection between attorney responsibility and case outcomes. The sense of regret and disappointment that might normally precede self-evaluation and self-improvement simply did not exist among the attorneys who fell short of their minimum goals. "Fewer than one fifth of the lawyers (18%) were very disappointed or somewhat disappointed with the case outcomes," states Goodman-Delahunty, "although more than twice as many (43%) actually failed to achieve their stated minimum goal. Of the group of lawyers who did not achieve their minimum goal ($n = 208$), two thirds reported that they were somewhat pleased or very pleased

---

[18]Russo, J. Edward & Schoemaker, Paul J.H. (2002). *Winning decisions* (p. 158). New York: Doubleday.

[19]Goodman-Delahunty, Jane, *et al.* (2010). Insightful or wishful: Lawyers' ability to predict case outcomes. *Psychology, Public Policy, and Law, 16*(2), 133–157.

[20]Goodman-Delahunty (2010) *supra* note 19 at 140–141. Fifty-nine percent of the cases were resolved by settlement, 31% were tried to verdict, and 10% were dismissed or resolved by motion practice.

[21]Goodman-Delahunty *supra* note 19 at 144.

[22]Goodman-Delahunty *supra* note 19 at 141.

with the actual outcome."[23] These attorneys, in short, reported high levels of subjective satisfaction for themselves despite poor results for clients.

Summarizing the results of the study and its implications for lawyers, clients and the judicial system, Goodman-Delahunty states:

> Clients of lawyers who are susceptible to an overconfidence bias may detrimentally rely on the advice of these legal professionals when making decisions about whether to litigate, they may choose litigation over settlement, or they may allocate valuable resources without securing anticipated objectives. These clients are likely to experience disappointment, frustration, or anger if the outcomes they were led to expect are not achieved. Client dissatisfaction may increase public antipathy toward lawyers and diminish public confidence in the legal system. Lawyers who have had several experiences with dissatisfied clients are likely to adopt a risk-averse strategy in managing client relationships to avoid a negative outcome by deliberately lowering all client expectations so that subsequent disappointment is avoided.[24]

Inaccurate case evaluation, therefore, can take at least two forms. In the over-confidence model, it results in overoptimistic assessments of the case, the expenditure of resources to achieve an unrealistic objective and an outcome that deviates markedly from expectations, aspirations, reserves and requirements. In the under-confidence model, it manifests as an unreasonably low estimate of a plaintiff's likely recovery or a dangerously pessimistic assessment of a defendant's defenses to a claim. It can result in a plaintiff declining to underwrite a case that in reality would be remunerative, compromising a claim for an unreasonably low amount or deciding to forgo it altogether, or a defendant paying large amounts to settle a claim of dubious validity. In either model – overconfidence and underconfidence – the client is vulnerable to a serious financial loss and a host of reputational risks.

The LexisNexis survey reported attorney self-assessments of their case evaluation skills, and the Goodman-Delahunty study focused on attorneys' minimum litigation goals. When studies shift from analyzing attorneys' self-assessments and minimum goals to scrutinizing the actual financial results of rejecting settlement proposals and proceeding to trials, the findings are even more troubling. It appears that many attorneys and clients, when choosing trial over settlement, inaccurately predict trial outcomes and the financial consequences. Five studies by three independent research teams indicate that (1) plaintiffs consistently achieve worse financial results at trial than they would have achieved by accepting a defendant's settlement offer, but the cost of these settlement decision errors is relatively small; and (2) defendants make settlement decision errors less frequently than plaintiffs but sustain larger monetary losses than plaintiffs when they misevaluate cases.

In the first major study comparing rejected pre-trial settlement proposals with ultimate trial awards, University of Michigan law professors Samuel Gross and Kent Syverud (now Dean, Washington University in St. Louis School of Law)

---

[23]Goodman-Delahunty *supra* note 19 at 147.

[24]Goodman-Delahunty *supra* note 19 at 151.

examined 529 California cases adjudicated between June 1985 and June 1986.[25] They analyzed the settlement proposals and awards in those cases because "the real question, for any party, is whether it would have been better off if it had not gone to trial." According to Gross and Syverud, "any plaintiff who was offered as much as the verdict or more, and any defendant who could have settled for as much as the verdict or less, has lost."[26] They found that plaintiffs obtained a worse result at trial than was available through a pre-trial settlement in 61% of the cases; and defendants obtained an inferior financial result in 25% of the cases. Only 14% of the trials could be considered "win-win" outcomes, i.e., both the plaintiff and the defendant obtained a better result at trial than they would have realized by accepting the other side's settlement proposal. Gross and Syverud later expanded their dataset by adding a sample of 359 cases reported between 1990 and 1991. The new cases, as reported in their second study, displayed a similar pattern when the pre-trial settlement offers were compared with the actual trial awards: plaintiffs were "clear losers" in 65% of the cases and defendants were "clear losers" in 26% of the cases.[27]

In the third major study of litigation decisions, Cornell Law School professor Jeffrey Rachlinski compared parties' settlement offers with jury awards in 656 cases adjudicated between 1981 and 1988.[28] He classified the results of the comparison as either a "Plaintiff Error" (the jury award was lower than the defendant's settlement offer) or a "Defendant Error" (the jury award was greater than the plaintiff's settlement offer). His data showed a Plaintiff Error in 56.1% of the cases and a Defendant Error in 23% of the cases. Although Plaintiff Error was more frequent than Defendant Error, Rachlinski discovered that the average cost of Plaintiff Error ($27,687) was dramatically smaller than the average cost of Defendant Error ($354,900). The aggregate effect, he states, is that "defendants paid a huge price for failing to settle with the plaintiffs," and the defendants' losses "were even more striking among the corporate litigants."[29] Synthesizing his results, Rachlinski states, "The fact that defendants, as a class, lost money demonstrates that they were unable to distinguish those cases in which they would win from those in which they would lose."[30]

The overall results of the Gross and Syverud and Rachlinski studies were corroborated in 2008 by a new study of 4,532 actual cases. Co-authored by Randall Kiser (DecisionSet®), Martin Asher (The Wharton School) and Blakeley McShane (Northwestern University), the study reported that 61% of plaintiffs and 24% of

---

[25]Gross, Samuel, & Syverud, Kent. (1991). Getting to no: A study of settlement negotiations and the selection of cases for trial. *Michigan Law Review, 90,* 319.

[26]Gross, Samuel, & Syverud, Kent. (1996). Don't try: Civil jury verdicts in a system geared to settlement. *UCLA Law Review, 44,* 1, 42–43.

[27]*Id.*

[28]Rachlinski, Jeffrey. (1996). Gains, losses and the psychology of litigation. *Southern California Law Review, 70,* 113.

[29]*Id.* at 158–159.

[30]*Id.* at fn. 156, 158.

defendants obtained a result at trial between 2002 and 2005 that was the same as or worse than the result that could have been obtained through a pre-trial settlement.[31] The average cost of these adverse outcomes was $43,100 for plaintiffs and $1,140,000 for defendants. Interestingly, for purposes of understanding case evaluation skills, the study found that clients who were represented by attorneys with mediation training experienced a lower incidence of adverse outcomes. Although the data was only suggestive, it appeared that mediator training and experience – inculcating the ability to see both sides of a dispute – reduced the frequency of adverse trial outcomes.

The dataset used in the Kiser, Asher and McShane study was expanded and updated in 2010 with the publication of Kiser's book, *Beyond Right and Wrong: The Power of Effective Decision Making for Attorneys and Clients.*[32] Despite the addition of 1,224 cases to the datasets, the frequency of adverse outcomes remained constant: 60% for plaintiffs and 25% for defendants. The average cost of these adverse outcomes escalated from $43,100 to $73,400 for plaintiffs and from $1,140,000 to $1,403,654 for defendants, and the disparity between the average plaintiff and defendant cost of error persisted. To determine whether these results would obtain in the "high-end" cases, where the clients may be more experienced in handling litigation claims and their attorneys may be more adept case evaluators, the study isolated and analyzed cases in which the plaintiff's demand was between $1,000,000 and $50,000,000. In those high-end cases, plaintiffs displayed a slightly lower error rate (58%), and defendants exhibited a slightly higher error rate (28%). The mean cost of error for plaintiffs was $327,158, while defendants' mean cost of error was $5,325,785.

The persistent patterns of decision-making error shown in these empirical studies are consistent with judges' opinions about cases that proceed to trial. When asked to identify the most likely reason why cases are resolved through trial rather than settlement, a majority of judges participating in a recent survey "attributed the parties' failure to settle to the fact that one of the litigants exaggerated the likelihood of his prevailing at trial."[33] Sixty-six percent of federal district court judges and 59% of state trial court judges thought cases were tried because "One side has an unrealistic assessment of its chances for success on the merits."[34] Only 29% of federal district court judges and 31% of state trial court judges selected "Each side has approximately the same likelihood of prevailing on the merits" as the most likely reason cases are tried.[35]

---

[31]Kiser, Randall, *et al.* (2008). Let's not make a deal: An empirical study of decision making in unsuccessful settlement negotiations. *Journal of Empirical Legal Studies*, 5(3), 551–591.

[32]Kiser, Randall. (2010). *Beyond right and wrong: The power of effective decision making for attorneys and clients* (pp. 42–46). New York: Springer Science + Business Media.

[33]Posner, Richard A., & Yoon, Albert H. (2011). What judges think of the quality of legal representation. *Stanford Law Review*, 63, 337.

[34]*Id.*

[35]*Id.*

Because adverse outcomes at trial are common and costly and the opportunities to try cases and learn how jurors react to clients and claims are diminishing rapidly, it is imperative for attorneys to develop sound case evaluation skills. Attorneys seeking to improve their case evaluation skills could read the 7,000 verdict reports analyzed by Gross, Syverud, Rachlinski, Kiser, Asher and McShane; work as clerks or attorneys for stellar judges and outstanding trial attorneys; seek employment in a district attorney or public defender's office where they are more likely to try cases; or read practice books written by exceptionally talented attorneys. Any of these options would entail weeks if not months of effort and could cause attorneys to view cases through the narrow prism of one trial attorney's experiences or the small pane of a single practice area. A faster and more expansive alternative is to extract, from the following chapters, the study attorneys' techniques and strategies.

Chapter 11
Evaluation Factors

The study attorneys identified more than 50 factors affecting case evaluation. These factors ranged from prosaic variables like case type to more esoteric considerations like client appearance. Once the attorneys' evaluation advanced beyond the basic, tangible issues of liability, damages, venue and insurance, they assessed somewhat intangible factors like witness credibility, client likeability, expert witness authoritativeness, injury severity and juror predispositions. The less tangible factors are critical but inherently subjective. When, for instance, does a witness change from being knowledgeable to arrogant, from confident to conceited, from attractive to vain? The study attorneys conceded that they were not always accurate evaluators of these impalpable factors. One attorney, for example, thought that his client's "princess" appearance would recede during a long trial, and the jury would begin to see a fuller person behind the "she's attractive and she knows it" exterior. "My competitive juices got flowing enough that I said, 'OK, I'm going to win this case,'" he recalls. "But what I could not overcome was her princess demeanor."

Many study attorneys expressed concerns about how other attorneys evaluated cases and indicated that other attorneys lacked adequate evaluative skills as a result of inexperience or an inability to separate advocacy from evaluation. A seasoned defense attorney, who is often asked to serve as an arbitrator and mediator, describes this problem:

> As a mediator and arbitrator, I've had attorneys ask me, "How did you evaluate this case?" I say, "It's based on the evidence you gave me." They don't understand this. They think whatever they say is the value of the case.

Like some other study attorneys, he estimates that about 75% of attorneys are poorly calibrated evaluators. "I have settled $25,000 cases when the demand started at $250,000," he declares. "It is outrageous for an attorney to think his adversary is such an idiot he will pay ten times what a case is worth." The idiosyncratic nature of case evaluation is also demonstrated by another defense attorney's observation that case value ultimately cannot be higher than the plaintiff's demand: "It's not clear what a case is worth until you start dickering. I may believe it's a $700,000 case, but

R. Kiser, *How Leading Lawyers Think*,
DOI 10.1007/978-3-642-20484-5_11, © Springer-Verlag Berlin Heidelberg 2011

the plaintiff's attorney comes in with a $250,000 demand. So it's now worth less than $250,000."

This chapter shows how some study attorneys approach case evaluation in general and how they analyze specific factors that heighten or deflate case value. The following topics are addressed: overall evaluation; settlement and trial tracks; client objectives; applicable law; case type; client appearance, credibility and likeability; damages; statutory limitations on damages; expert witnesses; venue; and attorneys' evolution as case evaluators.

11.1   Overall Evaluation

"The settlement value of a case is what a reasoned jury would award at the time the evaluation is given," states an attorney whose evaluations are sought by other attorneys. He elaborates:

> I think it is difficult to forecast cases. I have a unique skill set to do that. I have a feel for values and judges and juries and how they will see a case. I'm probably called two to five times per month by other attorneys requesting my evaluation. I can see the arrogance of the client, the arrogance of the attorney, the judge's attitude. . . .
>
> Evaluation is fluid, it's dynamic. What a reasoned jury will award at any given time changes. In some cases the motions in limine are the most important factor, but you won't know what the rulings are until right before trial. If I win a motion in limine, the value could go from $1.5 million to $200,000. Unemployment is another factor. It's harder for plaintiffs to get a good verdict in this economy. Your lawyer needs to understand who they're selling to.

Commenting on the importance of understanding jurors' perceptions – "who they're selling to" – another attorney notes, "It's the thickness of the experience that teaches you how jurors see cases. This is what tells you what are the hooks in the case. You have to consider everything right down to what time of year is it – is it near the holiday season?" A third attorney interrupted his description of case evaluation techniques to offer a broad perspective: "It's hard to say who is a good case evaluator – they may be wrong on one case, right on another. And it could be the client who's directing everything. You never know who is doing what to whom."

Although attorneys weighted case factors differently, they generally started with an overall value and adjusted that value upward or downward based on objective and subjective factors. A plaintiffs' medical malpractice attorney describes this approach:

> I ask myself, "What is this case worth wringing wet?" It's a function of the client, the records, jury verdicts, and experience. If I hit this case on all cylinders, the jury will give the client, say, $150,000. I've tried over 100 trials. When I've decided on the number I'm confident about it – "Here's the number, pay me or play me." I ask, "If I try this case ten times, how many times do I win?" If liability's a problem, like med mal, you have to discount. The best odds I ever gave a case was 75% – this is experience, being realistic, not conservative. I have to discount for liability, so if there's a 50% chance of getting $150,000,

the number goes to $75,000, less costs. Now it's at $65,000. In some cases I have to discount for comparative negligence. The largest variation is in the starting number. The beginning variable is what can I hit it for. The gross number is rational and intuitive. Another factor is whether the jury will get pissed off at the doctor, or if it's a shitty client, he's going to make a shitty witness.

This "generalize and adjust" approach is reiterated by another plaintiffs' attorney: "It starts by being able to evaluate the range of potential verdicts. You start by being extremely honest with yourself about the pros and cons of the case. This is hard because most of the time you're trying to build up the case."

In generalizing and adjusting, the study attorneys consider a host of factors, many of which are missing from traditional legal analysis and education. Both plaintiffs' attorneys and defense counsel consistently emphasized the importance of a comprehensive approach to evaluation, combining a technical legal analysis with intangible considerations likely to affect a jury. When asked to identify the most important factors in case evaluation and describe how they evaluate cases, plaintiffs' attorneys responded:

- Liability, damages, witnesses, documents. I know what it takes at trial to win a case, and those are the ones I look at first. I always consider the objective and subjective facts – how will the witness come across? Most of the time it is not immediately apparent how good a witness will be. In 10% of the cases, the client does not tell their attorney everything and you find out later at a deposition or other situation. These clients are trying to sell you on the case initially and they leave out the bad facts.
- Sometimes a case has fantastic liability but no damages. I try to look at both. Can I prove liability? Then I feel comfortable going to the next step, damages. But not just damages – you have to understand what the net recovery will be for the client. Young lawyers make the mistake and don't realize the cost of litigation will equal or exceed any recovery.
- Most people tend to ignore or undervalue the non-quantifiable aspects of a case. I flipped through your [the author's] article and saw the tables and numbers. There's too much emphasis on statistics in case evaluation – they don't tell the full story.
- I've always thought there are four parts of cases: the plaintiff, facts, damages, and the lawyer. As a defense lawyer, if the plaintiff had three out of four, I worried. A jury can gloss over one, if all three are in place.
- The bottom line is how they will go over to a judge or jury. Are they here just to make a buck? Other factors are: How strong is liability? How egregious is the conduct of the defendant? How will the aspect of comparative fault be decided? Injuries – how will they compromise future functioning, earnings capability, potential for advance? This also is a moving target.
- My confidence level varies with empirical data, legal theories, factual and legal determinations. We become intimately familiar with the basis of our engineers and appraisers' opinions. We synthesize it and come up with an intuitive sense for what a case should settle for. Synthesizing, putting together, some are better

than others at this and can be more objective. Some express undue optimism, others undue pessimism.

"I pretty well know when I should lose and when I should win," comments a study attorney who represents both plaintiffs and defendants. "When push comes to shove, there is a value to everything. There are white hats and black hats."

Although some plaintiffs' attorneys criticized defense attorneys for disregarding the individual plaintiff and ignoring other subjective factors in their case evaluations and settlement offers, defense counsel uniformly described a broad range of factors that affect their evaluation:

- Size up the plaintiff, first. The most important thing is not how good the case is but how likeable the plaintiff is. If the plaintiff is attractive and speaks well and has good facts, they can take bad cases and make them better. Then I look at my own people. If it's a corporation, they already have one foot in the grave. Next is the facts. Then jury instructions – remind yourself as soon as possible what you will have to prove. Do not forget this is a crapshoot. There are so many wild cards.

- Three major factors can affect the outcome. One, does the jury like you [the physician defendant]? Do they believe you? Do you appear to be a caring and compassionate physician? Two, whether the jury likes me. Do they think I'm reliable? Do they think I am a strong advocate? Three, medical malpractice cases are driven by expert testimony – how the experts are viewed by the jury. These are not fungible cases. I ask, "What type of client do I have? How convincing will they be? How do I truly feel about this case?"

- We have a systematic method from the moment the file comes in, the case comes in, to expert disclosure. There are certain decision points and procedures along the way – records, witnesses, experts. This is combined with a good understanding of the law as it pertains to my area of specialty, applying the law to facts, as you know. Insurance companies require at least quarterly reevaluations of liability, so this also means we're constantly evaluating the case.

- There are two key evaluation factors. First, witness impression – it's always important. Second, damages are pretty quantifiable, but in the cases that have general damages like pain and suffering, that's the Blue Sky component. It's highly dependent on twelve jurors. If you have eleven accountants and my mother, who grew up in the Depression, you may get $2. If you have jurors from Berkeley, where they think everyone's a victim, you'll get a different result.

- One, appearance of the plaintiff. Two, appearance of the defendant. Three, what do the pictures show? Four, what is the backstory – is there a kid in the car, a mother upset? That sort of thing.

- I look at the facts and the medical records. I have a science background, and I understand how the body works. So I look at facts. The other components are the parties. Then I look at, one, are there things that will make a jury angry? Was the doctor blowing someone off? Is there something that will make the jury not pay attention to the evidence? Factually, what happened? Then I look at subjective issues. Who are the plaintiffs? When you meet them at depos, I want to be at the plaintiff's depo and my client's depo and the expert depos. Is the plaintiff sympathetic, over-exaggerating, lying? That's when you get the sense, "Is this witness credible?"

Very few defense attorneys used formal decision trees to evaluate cases. When asked about decision trees, some attorneys indicated they were "overused" or relied upon by insurance companies but not their attorneys. "No, I find these don't work for me, but I use them for clients to break down what could happen at trial and to show what compromises would have to be made to reach a settlement," comments a managing partner. "In my own mind, I'm making all those calculations anyway."

11.2   Settlement or Trial Track

For many study attorneys, a major factor in case evaluation is whether the case should be settled or tried and whether the adversary intends to try the case. Although numerous study attorneys adamantly declared that they do not accept a case unless they intend to take it to trial, other attorneys made a preliminary determination of whether the case should be on a settlement track or a trial track. For many cases, that determination may be more practical than legal, based more on the costs of litigation than the merits of the case. Some plaintiffs' attorneys describe how they decide whether to file a complaint or try a case and how an attorney's willingness to try a case affects evaluation and settlement negotiations:

- When you're evaluating cases as a plaintiffs' attorney, there are two ways. One, you're evaluating simply to settle and you have no intention of trying the case. Two, if you have a good intention of trying the case, it's different.
- My philosophy is if you prepare for trial, then the case will settle. Other attorneys assume cases will settle and they prepare for a settlement.
- No one is a trial lawyer anymore. They just settle cases, and that's why they don't look at the legal issues. They're settlement, not trial, attorneys. If you're a trial attorney, everything you do is different. They don't care about the facts. They're just going through the motions until settlement.
- I try not to get involved in the, "I've got to win, I've got to win" attitude. A good settlement is a good result in a lot of cases. I have to have a big white hat, and they have to have a big black hat, if the case is going to trial.
- Fender benders – insurance companies say, "take it to trial." They know plaintiff attorneys can't try them not just because of the economics – the time and the disruption to the attorney's practice – but it's because the jury is thinking you're wasting their time. It has to be something they care about.
- If the client doesn't pass my smell test but there are positive aspects, I don't ever want to file on that case. It might be a case we are more reticent about. I want to be able to feel comfortable with that client sitting next to me.

Discussing the difficulties of trying cases in a busy plaintiffs' personal injury practice, a study attorney comments, "For an office like mine, trials are really disruptive. They're draining – both mentally, physically, and financially."

Defense counsel note that an attorney's trial experience and willingness to try a case affect case evaluations for both plaintiffs and defendants:

- Some plaintiff firms spend all their time in mediation – two or three times per week with JAMS or ADR Services. Their counsel is disinclined to try the case, but for defense counsel we get paid to try cases. If they can get 75–80% of what they would get at trial, they'll take it. That influences plaintiffs' counsel and determines whether they will spend three weeks preparing for trial and five days in trial. It could stop the works in a one or two-attorney firm. I think that influences how they talk to the client about what the case should be settled for.
- Also sometimes the amount of the claim is so low, you know they [plaintiffs] can't afford to take it to trial. Sometimes on a small case, the plaintiff will take a low number. That number is not a case value that you can use in other cases. It's a grind down number. It's the settlement value for that case.
- We have attorneys here who have been practicing 14–20 years and have not gone to trial. When they go to mediation, they probably have a very different view of what will happen at trial than I do. They might focus on things that I would not. If you have been to trial, you learn there is no way in hell you can predict what will happen. You find out that some of your best evidence just goes right by them, and they reach a decision based on something entirely different from what I thought.

A defense attorney reduced the trial versus settlement decision to a simple formula: "If you have a stinky case, you have to settle it."

11.3 Client Objectives

Although a layperson might assume that an attorney's first priority would be ascertaining the client's objectives, this basic factor often is overlooked in the attorney-client relationship. As Thomas Jackson, general counsel for PH Glatfelter Company, observed at a law firm partners' retreat, attorneys may not ask clients the simple question, "What is an acceptable outcome in this matter?"[1] Other corporate counsel place a similar emphasis on client objectives, as indicated in their responses to Fulbright & Jaworski's annual survey of corporate law departments: "keep in mind our business needs, not just the law;" "understand business principles and match legal with business strategy;" "be mindful of the risk/benefit and cost

---

[1]DeGroote, John. (2010). Toward better client service: A few questions for outside counsel. Available at http://www.settlementperspectives.com/2010/03/toward-better-client-service-a-few-questions-for-outside-counsel/.

implications of suggested strategies;" and "realize that litigation has to be about economics and ways to resolve matter for least cost."[2] Many attorneys tend to assume that the client's primary objective is to prevail in the litigation and costs are a secondary concern when, in fact, the client may prefer to handle litigation like any other ancillary business matter – minimize total cost of non-core functions while concentrating capital and human resources on core functions that generate revenue and provide a long-term competitive advantage. Conversely, a client may prefer to allocate a seemingly unreasonable amount of time and money to a case that is relatively simple but has long-term consequences for impending claims or business development.

The importance of client objectives is demonstrated by this letter to the *New York Times* from the then-president and president-elect of the Defense Research Institute, responding to an article about one of the author's studies:

> As reported, the study presents a mechanistic picture of why it is economically advantageous to settle cases in lieu of less favorable monetary outcomes in court. Equally simplistic, the study underscores the economic incentives of lawyers to protract cases through trial.
>
> Such oversimplifications do not take into account the decision-making that actually governs in a predominant majority of instances. In fact, the decision to settle or not to settle often has nothing to do with the specific case itself. The overriding responsibility of the defense team is to see beyond the immediate effect of that single case and to calibrate litigation-related decisions to the long-term business interests of their clients.[3]

Some study attorneys voice related concerns about the implications of a single case, noting, for instance, "Organization defendants have other issues to address – branding, public image. Their evaluation can be driven by factors unrelated to the litigation and the specific merits of the claim." Collateral issues also affect individual physicians in medical malpractice cases because a single case may jeopardize hospital privileges and result in increased insurance premiums, the denial of malpractice insurance or the commencement of license revocation procedures.

Attorneys representing public entities also express reservations about settling a case without considering the long-term policy implications for similar claims. An attorney representing a public entity whose operations inevitably generate claims with similar issues states, "We know there are a number of cases where we know we could have gotten a better result at settlement. We believe that if we have to appeal to preserve the integrity of the issue, we will go and proceed." This attorney explains why the expediency of settling a single case is not a sufficient justification for disregarding larger policy considerations:

> I am endowed with the public trust. Sometimes a judge or an attorney wants us to pay something just to get it settled – just settle for nuisance value. That totally goes against what we're supposed to be doing here. I would be really violating the trust I have for the public monies.

---

[2]Duncan, Helen, & Mason, Peter H. (2004, September 27). In-house counsel offer their advice to law-firm litigators. *San Francisco Daily Journal*, p. 5.

[3]Settle or go to trial? Letters to the Editor, *New York Times*, August 17, 2008.

Another attorney who represents public entities noted that his recommendations to settle or try cases are submitted to the city council, and case results ultimately are scrutinized by the press. "I'm out on a limb if I make the wrong recommendation," he says. "Always in the back of my mind is that the local newspaper will be all over us if we're wrong."

11.4 Applicable Law

When asked to identify the most important case evaluation factors, the study attorneys tended to emphasize factual and personal issues more than legal issues. They did not denigrate the importance of legal issues; they simply minimized them in most discussions of case evaluation. In responding to interview questions about case evaluation, for example, both plaintiffs and defense attorneys used the words "fact" and "facts" about three times more frequently than the word "law." Plaintiffs' attorneys referred to "damages" and "insurance" more than twice as often as they mentioned "legal," and defense attorneys cited "jurors" ten times more often than they said "legal."

This tendency to downplay legal issues may result from the fact that the cases being evaluated already met threshold legal requirements. Otherwise, the plaintiffs' attorneys would not have accepted the cases at the outset, and the defense attorneys would have disposed of them through pre-trial motions. In fact, "lack of liability" is the predominant reason attorneys decline cases, according to one study of plaintiffs' contingency fee lawyers.[4] The legal issues also may have been omitted because of their "obviousness," just as one is more likely to state "brush my teeth" than "breathe" when asked to describe the first thing done after awakening.

To the extent the attorneys mentioned the law as an evaluation factor, they explained that it was a very significant factor during the early phases of litigation and may be the predominant evaluative factor right up to the trial date:

- It appears that case evaluation is a very subjective matter, especially when you're in the pre-trial stage. It changes as the case evolves. Pre-depo we're in a totally subjective place. Mostly what's being argued are points of law. At that point, facts are undetermined. The depos of the parties and witnesses will change the tenor of the liabilities of the case.
- What are the odds that you're going to win if you go to trial? Some cases depend 90% on the law, 10% on the facts. In those cases, the issue turns on how the judge is going to decide. When it's facts, it's much harder. You don't know what your witness will be like on the stand or what the jurors will think.

---

[4]Kritzer, Herbert. (2004). *Risks, reputations, and rewards* (pp. 84–85). Stanford, California: Stanford University Press.

- Evaluation is very case dependent. Some cases present legal issues that have a great bearing on case value – they are uncertain, untested, and you cannot make an evaluation until you see who the judge is and base your prediction on that issue. In a simple case, say a PI case, I'll make an evaluation at the outset, right at the very beginning. But when there are no precedents, it's very difficult to make an evaluation. You need to know who the judge is. You may be waiting for a case on appeal to be decided, and even then it will depend on whether the case is published or unpublished.
- When I went into a case, number one, the law had to be on my side. In one case the client drove into a dumpster on the road at night. Everyone seemed to assume this was entirely his fault. I went to the City of [deleted] and asked if they had any laws about leaving dumpsters on the road. The clerk showed me some ordinances that made it clear the dumpster could not have been left there legally.
- You've got to have the basic building blocks of the case – the basic elements of the case – to explain why you should logically win the case. I do a lot of bench trials, and you have to be able to lay out in a very logical order the basis for your case. That's one reason I start looking at case [jury] instructions and researching the law right away in any case. I always try to research the law. As you know, a case can turn on a single reported decision. That's another thing I've learned over the years. Research the case right from the start.

Overall, the study attorneys' emphasis on facts and party characteristics over legal issues may reflect their belief that legal rules are more malleable than past events and adult personalities. As Justice Benjamin Cardozo observed, a rule of law is only a "provisional hypothesis" for future cases. Because every "regulation, standard, rule, and procedure is constantly under attack and subject to modification," the meaning of legal rules "is up for grabs in every case."[5]

11.5   Case Type

Plaintiff win rates vary significantly with the type of case. In their study of verdicts in 16 states, research professors Stephen Daniels and Joanne Martin found that plaintiffs prevailed in 62% of automobile personal injury cases, 39% of products liability cases and 30% of medical malpractice cases.[6] RAND author Erik Moller

---

[5]Graham, Duffy. (2005). *The consciousness of the litigator* (pp. 50, 90, 112). Ann Arbor, Michigan: University of Michigan Press. The legal scholar Karl Llewellyn expressed this concept somewhat differently: "rules guide, but they do not control decision. There is no precedent that the judge may not at his need either file down to razor thinness or expand into a bludgeon." Krieger, Stefan H., & Neumann, Jr., Richard K. (2007). *Essential lawyering skills* (p. 242). New York: Aspen Publishers.
[6]Daniels, Stephens, & Martin, Joanne. (1995). *Civil juries and the politics of reform* (pp. 78–81). Evanston, Illinois: Northwestern University Press.

studied verdicts in 15 jurisdictions in six states and reported similar variations in win rates.[7] He found that plaintiffs won 66% of the automobile personal injury cases, 44% of the product liability cases and 44% of the medical malpractice cases. High variability in win rates was demonstrated again in the author's study of California verdicts entered between 2002 and 2007. That study indicated that case type was among the most important variables in predicting win rates and that win rates varied from 73% in contract cases to 21% in medical malpractice cases.[8]

In evaluating cases, the study attorneys gave ample weight to case type and recognized that plaintiffs prevailed in few medical malpractice cases:

- Almost all my cases are med mal. . . . In the med mal area, one of two things happens. You either settle or you go to trial. If you go to trial, you usually lose.
- To be objective you have to see which cases win and which cases don't. So many cases that seem attractive don't actually result in a win at trial. Different types of cases have different win rates. You have to drill down. Medical malpractice cases, for example, are easier to defense because people want to like doctors. But you need to know the specific types of malpractice. If it's a technical error [rather] than an error of judgment, it's harder to defend. When a jury can understand there is a simple test that could have been done or a technical error that was made, their verdicts are not the same as other medical malpractice cases.
- It also depends on the type of case. Once a discrimination case turns into a harassment case, it's a whole different thing. Sex discrimination to sexual harassment, racial discrimination to racial harassment – these are very different cases, and my evaluation changes, too.
- I handle a lot of different types of files – commercial, class actions, wrongful deaths. I have a different approach to evaluation depending on the type of case. . . . It rests on the nature of the wrong and the harm, the manner in which the jurors will appreciate the exposure of the defendants. There are dozens and dozens of markers – you cannot substitute years of experience. In wrongful death cases, the plaintiff's life history is important but that's not so important in contract cases. The facts of how the injury occurred are important in some cases but not the major issue in other cases.
- Another factor is case type. Public entity cases are tough for the plaintiffs. Medical malpractice and slip and fall cases are another example of cases that are easier to defend.

The attorneys' awareness of the low win rates in medical malpractice actions and their attendant reluctance to accept medical malpractice cases are consistent with an

---

[7]Moller, Erik. (1996). *Trends in civil jury verdicts since 1985.* Santa Monica, California: RAND Institute for Civil Justice.

[8]Kiser, Randall. (2010). *Beyond right and wrong: The power of effective decision making for attorneys and clients* (p. 56). New York: Springer Science + Business Media.

earlier study of plaintiffs' contingency practices. In that study of three different law practices, law professor Herbert Kritzer found that "lawyers are extremely cautious in accepting medical malpractice cases," and experienced attorneys impose more stringent screening procedures. Law practices with extensive experience handling medical malpractice cases rejected more medical malpractice cases than practices "with little or no medical malpractice work."[9]

11.6   Client Appearance

A party's ability to evoke a juror's sense of sympathy generally increases the likelihood of a favorable verdict and, for plaintiffs, increases the amount of the damages award.[10] The degree of sympathy elicited depends on numerous factors including similarities between the observer and the sufferer; the likeability of the sufferer; the capacity to visualize an injury and sense another's pain; the unusualness of the accident causing the injury; the relative blameworthiness of the parties; the severity of the injury; and the parties' relative financial status.[11] In rendering "total justice," jurors attempt to "give each party what it deserves," and this judgment incorporates jurors' emotional responses to the parties:

> The parties are linked in a complementary relationship, so that to the extent one party is perceived to be the good guy, the other cannot be; if one attracts sympathy, the other warrants anger. [citation]. Jurors' liability decisions mirror their emotional squaring of accounts. Doing justice in the accident case, as in any other kind of case, becomes a morality play [citation] in which jurors seek a right result by adjusting the fates of the parties to correspond to what the jurors believe each party merits.[12]

To be identified as "the good guy," plaintiffs need to overcome jurors' perception that they are "greedy and complaining" and may have caused the accident or "had it coming." Jurors also may attribute greater fault to plaintiffs who are severely injured than plaintiffs who sustain minor injuries due to the "just world" presumption that bad things happen to bad people.[13] For corporate defendants, the

---

[9]Kritzer, Herbert. (2004). *Risks, reputations, and rewards* (pp. 87, 92). Stanford, California: Stanford University Press.

[10]Feigenson, Neal. (2000). *Legal blame: How jurors think and talk about accidents* (p. 100). Washington, D.C.: American Psychological Association. See Gunnell, Justin J., & Ceci, Stephen J. (2010). When emotionality trumps reason: A study of individual processing style and juror bias. *Behavioral Sciences and the Law, 28,* 850–877.

[11]Feigenson *supra* note 10 at 76–77, 100–103.

[12]Feigenson *supra* note 10 at 104.

[13]Feigenson *supra* note 10 at 100.

main obstacle to being perceived as the good guy may be jurors' belief that they "should be held to a higher standard than individual defendants, because corporate defendants have greater knowledge of the risk of various courses of action and can devote greater resources to learning about and managing those risks."[14]

In light of the extensive research showing the importance of sympathy and anger in legal decision making, the study attorneys' emphasis on a party's appearance, credibility, and likeability is well-founded. Some attorneys depict a client's appearance as being the most important factor in case evaluation, especially for plaintiffs:

- We have a debate here about which would you rather have – good facts or a good witness? Ideally you would have both; usually you have one stronger than the other. Most choose a good witness over good facts.
- On the defense side probably the most important factor is what kind of witness does the other side make? How does your client appear as a witness, by occupation, by physical presence? I know that jurors will even overlook flaws in your story, flaws in your attorney. They will try to help you, if they like the client. They will not punish the client for the attorney.
- Presentation is more important for plaintiffs. If both plaintiff and defendant are comparable, push pays the dealer. It's easier for a jury to say "No" than "Yes" – that's an affirmative step for the plaintiff. If you're the plaintiff, you have to push them over a threshold.
- Likeability, believability and sympathy – they're the triumvirate of things having the most effect.
- Sometimes plaintiffs themselves don't realize how important it is how they appear. The appearance of the client, whether they are likeable, is so important. If the client is a sweet, innocent new teacher, just using that as an example, there's a premium that will be paid. People underestimate the importance of appearance. Like the witness who was wearing sunglasses during her testimony, the jury is going to have a harder time believing that witness.
- One of my friends who represents the other side – and he was right and this is one thing I learned from my father, too – he said, "You can't underestimate the value of your client." The client is the most important part of the case – are they fair-minded, egotistical, overreaching? You need to understand and appreciate your client.
- Case evaluation from the plaintiff's side – the one evaluation feature I have come to look at first is my client's presentation. From my best verdicts to the worst verdicts, the best was the nicest client and the worst was the client with a chip on his shoulder. You can take away $200,000 from the client with a bad presentation. The guy with the tattoo doesn't get $500,000, he gets $100,000. The nice grandmother with cancer gets $500,000.

---

[14]Feigenson *supra* note 10 at 99.

A plaintiffs' attorney sums up the attitude of many study attorneys who place a high priority on client presentation: "A good client with a so-so case gives you a better shot than a bad client with a better case."

11.7   Client Credibility

An evaluation factor closely related to client appearance is client credibility. Although some attorneys may lump these factors together, the study attorneys regarded credibility as a distinct factor, indicating that some clients had a pleasant demeanor but lacked credibility. Lack of credibility seemed to be fatal, as a client's case could survive a negative countenance but not a deceptive answer:

- A common factor is the jury not believing a party, like when the client is on the stand. That's why I tell clients what is most important is whether the jury trusts you. In one case that we lost, both the other side and I thought the client would make a good impression. It was funny when the client got on the stand and kind of froze up – there's a feeling in the courtroom because you can see credibility disappear, you can see their faces.
- On cases where I got hammered, the problem was not being truthful. It's the little lies that kill you. I would say if you don't like your client, the jury won't either. That impression is made early in the case, and it's pretty much correct.
- Number One is lying – you get a person lying in deposition or at trial. This goes back to whether the jury likes you at trial. If they think you're lying, they will be turned off. That's why defense attorneys spend so much time trying to find something about the plaintiff. That's all they have to affect whether the case is worth $20,000 or $200,000.
- I would say, to start off, when I get a case I look at who the plaintiffs are. You can have the best case in the world but if your client is not trustworthy you won't prevail. The question I ask in each case is, "If I put this person in front of the trier of fact, how will they come across?"
- I've defensed a lot of rear-enders, which some people think is impossible. So many misrepresentations – that's where plaintiffs get hurt and the jury gets angry. If a jury is pissed off enough about the plaintiff's misrepresentations and greed, they'll give them nothing. This is when you make it easy for them in closing argument and say that if nine [jurors] vote and decide there's no liability, all you have to do is sign the verdict and there's no need to discuss damages. They don't want to waste their time on someone they don't like.

The study attorneys were adamant about the critical effect of credibility. A plaintiffs' attorney said, "Credibility is everything." Another attorney, who represents both plaintiffs and defendants, described how her role changes as a case progresses from settlement negotiations to trial: "Before trial, I'm a salesman. In a trial, I'm a purveyor of fact."

11.8 Client Likeability and Sympathy

The intensity of juror sympathy is determined, in large part, by a juror's ability to identify with a party – to see similarities between the juror and a party and to imagine that a party's plight could befall the juror.[15] "Whether you're the plaintiff or the defendant," observes a defense attorney, "it comes down to making the jury look at your client and think, 'There but for the grace of God go I.'" Another attorney, who represented defendants for about 20 years before joining a plaintiffs' firm, makes a direct link between his client and the jury: "I tell them they have to believe in the system because if it doesn't work for my client, someday it's not going to work for you." A client's ability to evoke a sense of identification – and to persuade the jury that the client is not only sympathetic but likeable – is paramount, according to the study attorneys:

- The jury has to like you and your client. To some degree it is a beauty contest. I hate to say it.
- Jurors react to impressions, witness impressions. If they like you, they want to help you. They want good things to happen to you.
- In many cases there is something else, another dynamic. In one case I thought was fairly weak on liability, the jury ... felt for the guy; he was a sympathetic guy. His brother helped out [with his medical care]. They did not want the hospital hounding him for the bill.
- Some of the factors I focus on are: Is there overreaching? Is there dishonesty? Did the doctor try his best? Was the doctor compassionate? Doctors may come across as assholes, but that's usually because they feel badly; they're upset about what happened. Isn't everyone like that?
- The type of client I like is understated. You don't want the ones who keep diaries and notes about everything. I'll give you an example. I represented a kid in an accident when his head snapped forward and cracked the windshield. On the stand, I asked him whether that hurt. He said, "No." The jury loved him.
- Number two [after "fairness"] is the likeability factor – the person who is open, humble, has a friendly demeanor. That was a huge factor in the case you found me in. The plaintiff was ... like everyone's grandfather. He had no guile. The other side did not see it – that's where they misevaluated it. In that case we had to meet a clear and convincing standard of proof, not just preponderance. That standard did not give them [the jury] any problem, I think, because of who the plaintiff was.

Because likeability may be a dispositive factor, a study attorney asks herself, "Who are the players and how will they play to normal people?" In answering that question, she discovers, "Sometimes your client may be the wronged party, but not the good guy."

---

[15]Feigenson *supra* note 10 at 76.

11.9   Deposition and Trial Testimony

One of the most common surprises is the client who presents well in the attorney's office – and sometimes at deposition as well – but falls apart at trial. This inability to withstand cross-examination can change a case evaluation quickly and significantly:

- Some clients have good cases, but you can't take them to trial. One client seemed fine in my office but had a panic attack at her deposition. You can act like you're going to trial, but the other side knows you probably won't. For me, it's who the people are, the plaintiffs and defendants.
- Clients who you think are likeable may not come across that way at trial. A jury trial is awkward for clients. Juries may not see the client. They see someone up there that may not be the client anyway—they're not themselves. You tell them to look at the jury, but they have stage fright.
- I find a lot of time in these cases the client's appearance in your office is different from how they act at deposition or trial. That's why you should see how they handle themselves under stress.
- Older clients may be difficult because they don't listen. Maybe I shouldn't say that. You can prepare them, but they frequently do things their own way.
- There is a difference between clients when they are six feet away from me and when they are 35 feet away.

On rare occasions, a party's performance improves at trial. "I've had cases where at depo a plaintiff appears as an idiot but at trial comes across just fine," a medical malpractice defense attorney remarks. "That's why I like to, if I can, like to wait until I'm in trial to settle. You cannot tell demeanor until the trial."

The idea that "you cannot tell demeanor until the trial" has particular relevance to some of the study attorneys. They had been surprised at trials when they were retained by clients shortly before the trial date and had not had the opportunity to observe an adverse party during a deposition or other pre-trial proceeding. A defense attorney describes one of these trials:

> I got involved late in one case and everyone said the other side's main witness was a real slime ball and would be terrible on the stand. I was not there for his deposition, so I had not seen him. It turns out at trial he was a very likeable witness – did well on direct and held up well on cross. Sometimes they do great on direct and fall apart on cross, but he was good all the way through – even cried at the right time.

Other attorneys noted that, when cases did not turn out the way they had expected, they were retained too late to make their own evaluations of the witnesses. "If I have not had the case from the beginning," comments a medical malpractice defense attorney, "I've had problems. If I have not sat through the client's or the expert depo because it was someone else's case, I've had problems where jurors did not believe them."

11.10   Damages

In discussing damages as an evaluative factor, the study attorneys emphasized (1) the difficulty of assessing damages, particularly non-economic damages like pain and suffering; (2) changes in the value of certain injuries and the amount of juries' verdicts; (3) the effect of ancillary awards for attorneys' fees; (4) future medical expenses and the timing of settlement negotiations; and (5) statutory limits on non-economic damages in medical malpractice cases.

11.10.1   Assessing Damages

The study attorneys indicate that predicting juries' damages awards is a difficult task and that the difficulty is heightened by the severity of the injury:

- As severity goes up, the damages award increases geometrically. It's a parabolic effect. You can't even evaluate some of the most harmful damages that cause people to disconnect from their families, their jobs.
- First, take the really good lawyers out of the picture. They know what they're doing. For the rest, a lot of lawyers don't appreciate the value of non-economic damages – it's a subjective analysis and it's an important part of the evaluation. They truly believe that their analysis is correct, but they don't consider how juries see non-economic damages.
- It is not something you can learn from a book. There's not a list of settlements for fractured hips, knees, arms – whatever's in your case. You have to study the medicine. You need to know enough medicine so when you're cross-examining the doctor, you know the degree of injury, what is a traumatic tear.
- You have to get into the demographics of your clients. A broken arm or knee is worth something if you're Kobe Bryant and something else if you're a lawyer or someone else with a sedentary life.
- This is the easy part [lost wages, union contract benefits]. You just crunch the numbers. The visceral part, the difficult part, is the pain and suffering.
- It depends on what was the injury. What is a reasonable range? In loss of vision, for example, or loss of extremities, sometimes I ask, "What would I take?"
- One thing you're never really good at is scarring. Unless it's a professional model, it's always hard to evaluate scarring. Age, gender make a difference, but it's still hard to know what a jury will award for scarring. Another example of a difficult case to evaluate is a quadriplegic who breaks a bone in two legs but did not have use of his legs before.

When asked whether jurors have become more skeptical of plaintiffs' damages claims during the last 50 years, a veteran trial attorney responded, "I don't think they are – not in the good cases. If you can demonstrate to a jury that the economic losses are not an award – you're just putting in their pockets what they lost, they're just getting even – the jury can accept that. I have told juries, 'If it takes $20 million to make this plaintiff even, then your job is to render that verdict.'"

11.10.2   Changes in Settlements and Awards

Many study attorneys noted that the amount of damages awards has changed and that the insurance industry has been successful in reducing awards for soft tissue injuries:

- In the old days the axiom was three times specials – in the 50's and 60's. The three times rule permeated the industry. The problem with it was you can't compare you sister's or aunt's recovery with yours – injuries are not the same.
- I used to tell clients you can't get more than five times specials, plus lost wages. Nowadays it's closer to two times. Years ago we would settle cases around four times specials. The insurance company would be at two times, and the plaintiff was around five or six times and the case settled at four times. All of that has changed. Like with the whiplash cases, the insurance companies just said, "We're not paying these anymore." And that was just about the end of it. When I tell clients what the companies will actually pay, this often interferes with their expectations.
- The market rate of cases has gone way down. Part of that is better medicine, quicker recoveries. A torn meniscus used to be $225,000. Now it could be $75,000 to $100,000. ... All the stars would have to be aligned to do better than that.

High unemployment rates and a depressed economy also were perceived to influence jurors' attitudes about damages awards.[16] Referring to a county with one of the highest unemployment rates in California, a study attorney remarked, "Here there is a lot of pessimism about pain and suffering. They have to really like the plaintiff to want to award a large amount."

11.10.3   Ancillary Damages

Defendants' exposure to ancillary damages like an attorneys' fee award in an employment discrimination case heavily influences case evaluation and settlement. The amount of ancillary damages can be greater than the general damages award:

---

[16]See Macpherson, Susan. (2009, September). Talking to jurors about damages in a down economy. *Trial*, pp. 28–31.

In some cases, it's more of a risk management issue that goes beyond the merits. In civil rights cases, you have exposure for attorneys' fees if you lose. That's huge. It could be tens of thousands, maybe a hundred thousand in fees. We have the same issue with employment cases. In FEHA [Fair Employment and Housing Act] employment cases the court can award attorneys fees. You have to consider more than just liability; the attorney fee exposure can be much larger than the plaintiff's damage claim.

Similar considerations apply in antitrust and intellectual property cases, where treble damages may be awarded, and contract and personal injury cases, where prejudgment interest may be recovered. In ERISA actions, moreover, the courts have rejected the argument that attorneys fee awards must be proportional to the amount recovered. In a recent Seventh Circuit Court of Appeals decision, for example, the court reversed the district court's ruling that expending "over $50,000.00 in attorney's fees to collect, at most, $5,000.00 cannot be justified."[17]

Generally omitted from the study attorneys' discussion of damages was a consideration of punitive damages. Although defendants often regard punitive damages claims as being meritless and in mediation may refuse to "dignify" a punitive damages claim by factoring it into their settlement evaluation, research suggests that punitive damages claims merit more serious consideration. Law professor Neil Vidmar and political science professor Mirya Holman recently studied punitive damages claims and awards in state courts, finding that punitive damages were alleged in 8.8% of all civil cases and awarded in nearly one-quarter (23%) of the cases in which they were alleged.[18] The incidence of punitive damage awards varied greatly by case type. Punitive damages were awarded in 50% of the slander, libel and defamation cases in which they were sought, 43% of the intentional tort cases, 13% of the motor vehicle tort cases, 7% of the medical malpractice cases and 5% of the premises liability cases.[19] Another study found that a punitive damage claim was a strong predictor of adverse outcomes for defendants and that the frequency of defendants' settlement decision-making errors (defined as a trial verdict that is higher than the amount for which a defendant could have settled the case) nearly doubled in cases alleging punitive damages.[20] That study,

[17]Thrall, Michael W. (2010, November 17). Attorney's fee awards under ERISA: Is the argument for proportionality dead? *DRI ERISA Report*, 4(2).

[18]Vidmar, Neil, & Holman, Mirya. (2010). The frequency, predictability, and proportionality of jury awards of punitive damages in state courts in 2005: A new audit. *Suffolk University Law Review*, *XLIII*, 855, 880. See Eisenberg, Theodore, et al. (2009, June 1). The decision to award punitive damages: An empirical study. Cornell Legal Studies Research Paper No. 09–011; CELS 2009 4th Annual Conference on Empirical Legal Studies Paper. Available at SSRN: http://ssrn.com/abstract=1412864. See also Eisenberg, Theodore, et al. The relation between punitive and compensatory awards: Combining extreme data with the mass of awards. In Bornstein, Brian H., et al., (Eds.). (2008). *Civil juries and civil justice* (pp. 105–115). New York: Springer Science + Business Media.

[19]Vidmar & Holman *supra* note 18 at 855, 864.

[20]Kiser, Randall, Asher, Martin, & McShane, Blakeley. (2008). Let's not make a deal: An empirical study of decision making in unsuccessful settlement negotiations. *Journal of Empirical Legal Studies*, 5(3), 583–584.

moreover, indicated that plaintiff win rates were higher in cases alleging punitive damages than cases without a punitive damage claim. Thus, although punitive damage claims are asserted in a small minority of cases, they are awarded with greater frequency than attorneys may estimate and are a predictor of case evaluation errors.

11.10.4 Future Medical Expenses and Timing of Demand

Future medical expenses are a frequently disputed element of plaintiffs' damages claims, and the study attorneys indicated that the timing of plaintiffs' settlement demand often affected the consideration of "future meds":

- The defense has a better chance of prevailing on future meds. If the trial is three years out [after the accident] and if the surgery has not been performed, it's just that – the future.
- If they are really injured, they want to move along with the chain of treatment. The insurance company can argue that future surgery is unnecessary, but if the client has proceeded with the course of treatment and had the surgery before the trial, it's hard to make the argument the future meds aren't needed. It also separates the strong claims because clients don't go through surgery unless they have to.
- Then as we go along, it [evaluation] has to be tempered with, how is the judge? Who is the carrier? And where the client is with treatment. The timing factor can be difficult. Timing wise you don't want it to mature too early or too late. Timing wise, is there hope for recovery? Will there be further surgery? How much is there still left to do? How much more will it cost? What will the doctors be recommending for treatment? These are all the things I have to be considering.
- They [insurance companies] have a good assessment, but you can catch them off guard. They're as bogged down as we are, and sometimes it takes them months to look at a file again. Part of it is knowing the right time to make a policy limits demand. If the demand is premature, because the future meds or something else is debatable, it doesn't have an effect and may get a low valuation that stays with it.

Stressing the importance of timing the settlement demand, a plaintiffs' attorney remarks, "You have to be sure your claim has ripened. You want to make sure you're getting a double or triple off that swing."

11.10.5 Statutory Limitations on Damages Awards

In some medical malpractice cases, the single most important evaluation factor is the statutory limitation on non-economic damages awards. A study attorney describes the limitations imposed by California's Medical Injury Compensation Reform Act (MICRA):

> My experience is in medical malpractice defense. An important factor in those cases is MICRA, which in 1975 put limits or caps to contain insurance costs. The limit for non-economic damages is $250,000 under MICRA. That does not include loss of consortium, negligent infliction of emotional distress. However bad or horrendous the injury is, the pain and suffering is limited to $250,000, but economic damages are not limited and could be 24-hour care, maintenance, medical treatment, psychological treatment, medical equipment, supplies – all subject to proof.

Both plaintiffs' and defense attorneys thought that MICRA had decreased the number of medical malpractice claims and the amount of awards when plaintiffs prevailed. A medical malpractice defense attorney's comment is illustrative: "MICRA has really protected physicians. The elite plaintiff attorneys only take strong cases. They want the trifecta [liability, damages, insurance]." This observation is substantiated by a survey of 965 plaintiff medical malpractice attorneys in 42 states, concluding that caps on non-economic damages "tend to discourage attorneys from representing clients even if their cases are meritorious."[21]

Plaintiffs' attorneys noted that MICRA not only reduced the number of cases they filed but also had the ironic effect of making case evaluation easier:

- Tens of thousands of meritorious cases are not filed because of MICRA caps. I take two out of 100 med mal cases. At least 90 have merit.
- The case has to be worth at least seven figures or have absolutely clear liability – like operation on the wrong kidney – or just take bad baby cases. Some [attorneys] take only bad baby cases. They can easily cost $100,000 - $200,000 [in costs advanced by the attorney for expert witnesses, court reporters, filing fees, travel]. You can't afford to lose or win them. But we try to not lose it.
- In evaluating cases, I would say in California we are in a difficult venue in the trial and evaluation of cases in California. Because we have caps on non-economic damages this limits our capability of obtaining an extraordinary verdict. In some ways, caps also make this an easier venue for case evaluation because it limits the range of possible verdicts.

Some study attorneys have found that plaintiffs' attorneys often are unaware of MICRA limitations and apparently file cases without consideration of the limitations. Noting that sometimes "you have to educate the other side," a defense attorney states, "experienced plaintiff attorneys are familiar with the special rules regarding damages in med mal cases. Other plaintiff attorneys don't understand the concepts."

---

[21]Garber, Steven, et al. (2009, December). Do noneconomic damages caps and attorney fee limits reduce access to justice for victims of medical negligence? *Journal of Empirical Legal Studies, 6* (4), 637, 640.

11.11 Expert Witnesses

The study attorneys expressed conflicting views about the impact of expert witnesses. Plaintiffs' attorneys were more likely to believe that "experts cancel each other out," while defense counsel seemed to place greater value on expert witness testimony. The range of opinions on expert witnesses is reflected in these comments:

- If I can do it without experts, it's better because the jury wants to see regular people.
- One issue is, the doctor can make or break your case – how he presents himself, whether he is an advocate or comes across as a real doctor. On the defense side, they all look like Dr. Welby, not the ethnic doctors the plaintiffs actually see.
- When a case is expert witness intensive, I have to carefully handpick my experts. You have to have a great expert team. Who the clients are you don't have much control over, but the experts you can choose.
- You need to know how to get to these experts and how to break them. The defense has doctors that make more than $1 million per year testifying for the defense. Jurors don't like this.
- Expert witnesses are very important. We always ask, "What are the weaknesses in our experts and their opinions?"

This range of opinions about expert testimony mirrors the range of research results regarding juror comprehension and evaluation of expert witness testimony. In some studies, jurors report that "expert testimony was important to their cases," and they were aware of "conscious and even unconscious biases of experts." Other studies find that jurors misunderstand expert testimony and "had a difficult time distinguishing between experts." Consistent with some attorneys' belief that the experts negate each other, another study concludes that "the clarity of one side's expert canceled out the expertise advantage of the other." Examining the impact of an expert's compensation, yet another study found that, when the expert testimony was simple, "pay had no impact; but when it was complicated the highest paid expert was rated the least trustworthy."[22]

11.12 Venue

The study attorneys – both plaintiffs' attorneys and defense counsel – frequently cited venue as a critical and immutable evaluation factor. Clients could improve their appearance, liability could be proven or disproven with better demonstrative

---

[22]The research findings in this paragraph are described in Vidmar, Neil, & Hans, Valerie P. (2007). *American juries* (pp. 178–180). Amherst, New York: Prometheus Books.

evidence, damages could be presented or disputed more persuasively – but the place of trial and hence the biases and socioeconomic characteristics of jurors could not be changed. For some study attorneys, venue largely determined the case outcome:

- The paramount thing that directs my evaluation is the venue. Is this trial in Orange County or downtown Los Angeles?
- I represent defendants in the five boroughs except Staten Island. In the Bronx and Brooklyn, the patients get a very fair trial. In other words, patients will win. In Manhattan, the doctor gets a fair trial.
- Where you're trying the case is the second most important factor [after considering the witnesses' appearance]. Why are they trying O.J. [Simpson] in downtown L.A. when the crime was committed in Brentwood? When Gil Garcetti [former district attorney] decided to try that case in downtown L.A., they decided to lose the case.
- Venue is important. In Marin County, it's either nothing or a million. Marin is tough. So is San Mateo. In Alameda and San Francisco, you can have a nothing case and do well because it's not their money. In Marin, everyone has property, pays taxes, has insurance.
- In Nassau [County], it's like walking into an igloo. They have no reason to listen to you. They have no patience for cases like yours.

A defense attorney also noted that whether the case was being tried in a state court or a federal court is an important factor for many clients. "Some national clients are convinced they'll be hometowned in state court, and they'll get fairer consideration in federal court," he states. "For some defendants, there's a greater sense of being in jeopardy if they're in state court instead of federal court."

This emphasis on venue may be excessive, caution some study attorneys. They note that preconceptions about certain venues are based on stereotypes that at times prove to be inaccurate. A plaintiffs' attorney voices this concern:

> Venue is important, but it can be overdone. I tried a case [in which] liability was conceded. The plaintiff had significant fractures to the forearms and scarring from the shoulder down. According to the defense attorney and the judge, "You won't see a big verdict in this case. The jurors are conservative here." The defendant's offer was [less than $200,000], and the judge said, "I think I can get him to $350,000." We ended up trying the case, and the jury awarded [low seven figures]. Attorneys get caught up in venue – it works both ways. In the Bronx, it's a plaintiff-friendly environment. But you have to be careful. You have to have the right case. Venue is an aspect, but you have to be careful.

The effect of venue also may be less important than client characteristics. Noting that "Brooklyn juries give higher verdicts than Nassau County," a defense attorney warns attorneys, "You can't just make assumptions about the jurisdiction without considering the parties. I've seen backlash in pro-plaintiff jurisdictions because the plaintiff was not like the jury."

Empirical studies indicate that venue has less effect than is often assumed and, in any event, is a highly nuanced factor. Analyzing what is popularly known as the "Bronx jury effect" or, simply, the "Bronx effect," American Bar Foundation Research Fellow Mary Rose and Duke University law professor Neil Vidmar compared jury verdicts rendered in the Bronx between 1981 and 1997 with verdicts rendered in seven other New York counties. They concluded that "statistical tests of differences found no evidence that the Bronx awards exceeded others in any reliable way."[23] Their results supported the conclusion reached earlier by Cornell University professors Theodore Eisenberg and Martin Wells that "there is little support for strong stereotypical views of demographic influences on observed trial outcomes."[24]

The most recent research regarding the effect of venue on win rates and damages awards, based on the 2001 Civil Justice Survey of State Courts, was conducted by Issa Kohler-Hausmann, a Ph.D. Candidate at New York University. She concludes that the variation in win rates "does not seem to be associated with any of the county characteristics typically cited in trial folklore as being 'pro-plaintiff' such as poverty rate, minority population rates, or alternatively, income inequality." When she analyzed the *amount* of damages awards, however, she found that "both county poverty rate and the level of low-end income inequality in a county were positively correlated with damages in plaintiff win cases." Although poverty rates and income inequality were significant predictors of higher damages awards, "neither black nor Hispanic population rates emerge as statistically significant predictors of the level of damages awarded to a plaintiff."[25] Thus, trial attorneys may develop a fuller understanding of damages awards in counties like the Bronx – where the majority of citizens are black or Hispanic – when they consider the county's income characteristics rather than its racial composition.

11.13 Attorney Skill and Trial Experience

Many plaintiffs' attorneys thought that defense counsel and insurance companies did not give adequate consideration and weight to their skill and trial experience. Although that may be an accurate observation for defense counsel and insurers in general, it does not accurately describe defense counsel's conduct in this study. In fact, study attorneys representing defendants mentioned their adversaries' skill and trial experience as an evaluative factor more often than their colleagues on the plaintiff side. These comments by defense counsel reflect the attention given to the quality of plaintiffs' counsel:

---

[23]Rose, Mary R., & Vidmar, Neil. (2002). The Bronx "Bronx jury": A profile of civil jury awards in New York counties. *Texas Law Review, 80*, 1889, 1897.

[24]*Id.*

[25]See Kohler-Hausmann, Issa. (July 14, 2009). Community characteristics and tort law: The importance of county demographics and inequality to tort trial outcomes. CELS 2009 4th Annual Conference on Empirical Legal Studies Paper. Available at SSRN: http://ssrn.com/abstract=1434231. This paragraph refers to Kohler-Hausmann's revised version of that article, dated April 23, 2010, forthcoming in the *Journal of Empirical Legal Studies*.

- The adjusters take a look at the plaintiff's attorney. They ask, "Where is this guy in the food chain?" They want to know who the lawyer is. Another factor is whether the plaintiff's attorney has a reputation for going to trial. They know who will fold the day of trial.
- Some of your adversaries are really great. I consider them to be my most dangerous adversaries. It's not so much the amount of the damages; it's the attorney representing the plaintiff. I value cases to some degree based on who the attorney is. It's based on their record – how they prepare and present cases. Some lawyers are sloppy. That goes into your valuation.
- The quality of the attorney does matter. If it's one of the stellar plaintiffs' attorneys, then the case could be worth more, and we definitely let the carrier know. ... The better the plaintiff's attorney, the more likely they are to be balanced and objective in their evaluation. Lesser-experienced attorneys don't cede any ground. For that reason, I prefer to work with more talented plaintiffs' attorneys. There's less hiding the ball and more open exchange and a candid recognition of what's weak with the case.
- The second most important principle – assuming it can be won or lost – is the talent level of your opponent. A talented lawyer can make it a much tighter horse race. There are huge disparities in the talent level of attorneys. It reminds me of the expression, "Good lawyers are expensive – and bad lawyers are really expensive."

One study attorney specifically considered the law school from which the plaintiff's attorney graduated: "One of the first things I look at with a new case is where the attorney went to law school. I've always felt uncomfortable about where I went to law school, so if the attorney on the other side is from one of those [highly-ranked] schools I prepare a little more and work a lot harder."

11.14   Evolution of Case Evaluators

When asked whether their case evaluation methods had changed over the course of their career, some study attorneys indicated they had learned to place greater emphasis on the parties' appearance and their likely impression on jurors:

- I focus more on how the client will come across at trial because I hear this from mediators and some of the best attorneys. I've learned that you can have good facts but bad presentation, like when the client is arrogant.
- In large part, it's the same as I was taught 30 years ago. You look at the medical bills, the economic loss, income loss, hard dollar figures. You look at what kind of injury and then you come up with a value. What has changed is taking into account my client's appearance. I'm much more hesitant to take a case with an unappealing or argumentative client – or just a client that does not give a good appearance – to trial. Juries tend not to take into account anything they say; they stop listening. Juries mentally block the testimony and not just the parts they

don't believe or disagree with. It kind of works that way with successes, too. When they like the witness, they tend to take it all in. In one case where we got a defense verdict, the plaintiff was unreasonably weepy and emotional. So from experience, good and bad, this is the one thing that has changed the most because of those experiences.

- I'm better at evaluating people, better at thinking like a juror, looking at the emotional aspects and being more objective. I try to see when I'm being too analytical, too objective.

For one plaintiffs' attorney, his evaluation method may have changed, but the ultimate decision to settle or try a case remains dependent on the defendant's offer. "In some cases you still don't really have a choice and you're forced to go to trial," he states. "When you've got a zero offer situation, even a weak case has to be tried because it's worth something."

After they had discussed their case evaluation methods, some study attorneys were asked, "If I had spoken to you 20 years ago, would your view of case evaluation and settlement have been different?" Responding to that question, a defense attorney explained how an attorney's case evaluation and negotiation skills are interwoven with personal development:

> Yes, my answers would have been different 20 years ago. I would have been wrong. I evaluate a case more emotionally now. Back then I didn't have a family; I didn't have a house and a mortgage. I understand what people go through in their lives now. I'm wiser as to human nature now. One thing I said earlier is attorneys don't look at how cases will affect people. As you get more experienced, that changes. I was more black and white back then. A case was either defensible or indefensible. But I've lost cases I should have won and won cases I should have lost. As confident as you feel, there's always a risk. . . .
>
> Whether you're raising a child when you're 25 years old or 35, you raise them very differently. The way you evaluate a case when you're younger is very different than you evaluate when you've done this for 20 years, just as you would raise children differently at different stages of your life. It's an evolutionary experience. You have to look at it from your human experience. That's how you grow as an attorney.

Chapter 12
Client Interviewing and Counseling

In interviewing and counseling clients, the study attorneys are authoritative, prob-ing, independent, directive, forceful and, at times, brutally candid. Although many other attorneys function as professional conduits for client decisions, deferring to client prerogatives and preferences provided they are ethically permissible, the study attorneys generally adopt a strong and affirmative role in advising and guiding clients. They define and assume control of the attorney-client relationship at an early stage, and they have refined their ability to detect, avoid and, if necessary, rehabilitate clients with unrealistic expectations or difficult personalities. To understand the study attorneys' methods of client interviewing and counseling, this chapter examines both the initial client interview and post-retention counseling.

12.1 Initial Client Interview

Perhaps the most critical test of an attorney's counseling skills occurs in the initial client interview, often called the "intake" interview. That interview presages the quality of attorney-client communications and the client's satisfaction with the ultimate case resolution. For the study attorneys, this first contact with the client serves two major purposes. First, it presents an opportunity to determine the client's objectives, risk tolerance, fears and expectations. Second, it affords a preview of the client's demeanor at deposition and trial. Because it is an introductory meeting, it is the most opportune time to decline to represent a client; and the study attorneys devote considerable time to this interview to consider whether the case is meritori-ous, the client's expectations are realistic and the presentation is credible. "We spend a lot of time counseling clients," a plaintiffs' attorney states. "Counseling skills are really important – and really being perceptive."

R. Kiser, *How Leading Lawyers Think,*
DOI 10.1007/978-3-642-20484-5_12, © Springer-Verlag Berlin Heidelberg 2011

12.1.1 Available Remedies

The threshold assessment in interviewing clients is whether the client has a "legal problem" – a problem for which the law affords a remedy. Despite grievous loss, disfiguring injury or lasting insult, the prospective client may have no recourse through the legal system:

> The key factors for me are, first, what the law is. What law will apply? What are the legal remedies for that wrong? Second, what are the client's objectives? The law may not have a solution for that problem. Maybe the law cannot satisfy that objective. What you have to assess early on is what are the legal remedies, what are the jury instructions? I have to ask what elements of proof can I prove. Just because you're sympathetic does not mean there's a remedy. Law is a business – I can get you money, but I cannot get God to smote someone down. Third, probably, is personality. Assess what kind of person they are – who your client is and who the other side is.

Sometimes the most valuable advice an ethical attorney provides is informing a prospective plaintiff that a case should not be brought in the first place or advising a defendant that the courts will not vindicate their position or restore their status. Candidly explaining the limitations of the civil justice system is every bit as important as highlighting its powers. "The system can be unfair," states a plaintiffs' attorney. "You can end up with a $1,500 to $2,000 check for the death of a child with $15,000 [insurance] policy limits after paying the attorney and the funeral expenses and the other bills."

12.1.2 Client Expectations

For those clients who present a legally cognizable problem and recoverable damages, the next inquiry is whether the client has unrealistic expectations that will inevitably cause conflicts in the attorney-client relationship, deep disappointment in the case outcome, unpaid attorneys' fees and, in extreme cases, legal malpractice claims. The study attorneys recognize that client satisfaction is ultimately subjective, and although they are capable of achieving objectively sound results, those results may be meaningless or unacceptable to clients with overly optimistic expectations. For that reason, one plaintiffs' attorney asks each client, "'What do you want out of this?' The client says, 'That's why I came to you' – but I need to know what the client wants before I decide to take the case."

Surfacing and addressing client expectations is a primary function of the initial interview, and the study attorneys distinguish their counseling objectives from other attorneys whose goal is to get the retainer agreement signed:

- I talk with the client about settlement from the very beginning. That's why I find out what they're after and whether they're going to be realistic about what I can do. Almost all of my cases come from referrals and so I want happy clients. If a client is unrealistic, they're going to be unhappy, so I don't take the case. At that stage I want to give them a straight opinion. I would rather give them a lower assessment.

- The biggest mistake a plaintiff's attorney will make is giving the client false expectations in the first or second meeting. Ninety-five percent of clients will ask in the intake interview, "What is my case worth?" I tell them, "Any attorney who answers that either is lying to you or does not know what he's doing, and you should run like hell. When the time comes, I will tell you what your case is worth."
- A lot of attorneys will give a client an unrealistic expectation and will gouge them. I call them one-shot Charleys because that client will not go back to them. If I have to give an evaluation, I say, "It may be in this nebulous range but don't hold me to it because it is impossible to tell."
- If you don't know the policy limits, you can't possibly tell the client what a case is worth. But that's what happens when you're selling your soul to the devil just to get the case – it will just be a miserable case for the duration.
- Never give your client unrealistic expectations. That's the difference between a professional and a non-professional. I turn away more cases than I take because I'm this way.

Although attorneys are commonly blamed for endorsing or raising client expectations, this support may stem more from inexperience than avarice. As one attorney comments, "Ninety-eight percent of the attorneys who tell their clients they have a great case are sincere; they are not greedy or malevolent. They just are making a premature assessment."

12.1.3   Client Preconceptions

How often do clients develop preconceptions of case value before they have met with an attorney? The study attorneys reported wide variances in client preconceptions; about 70% of the attorneys responding to this question noted that most clients have formed some opinion "early on." For individual clients (as opposed to corporate clients and insurers), these opinions range from ideas about liability to beliefs about specific monetary outcomes:

- There are two main types of clients. Some have a very specific idea of case value and what should happen, usually based on some relative who got a big recovery and was hardly hurt. The other type is the client who believes something should be done but is not sure what.
- They usually have a feeling about whether someone was injured and should be compensated. On the plaintiffs' side you get more variance between rational actors and irrational actors and people who don't even think it through.
- Some clients develop their own sense of what should happen. Part of it is they want you to know who the boss is.

- Clients have an idea – I don't know if it's accurate. They sometimes assume things will go into evidence that won't come in – like "I paid property taxes for 30 years." But this has no effect on fair market value [of real property]. They personalize things and this affects their opinion.
- Often one of the first questions to me is, "What is this worth?" They don't know and that's why they ask me. They don't know what to expect, but someone with a blind quadriplegic kid is not expecting $2,000. I don't find clients have a preconceived idea of what to expect. They might be angry, but it's more emotional venting than anything else.

"The clients that are highly opinionated you learn to avoid," remarks a plaintiffs' personal injury attorney. Looking back on his cases, he adds: "I've gotten better at selecting clients. Unhappy experiences with clients teach you to be a better judge of clients."

Corporate executives and insurance company adjusters also develop preconceptions about liability and recoverable damages:

- Corporate clients will talk about the value – they need to establish a reserve. They tend to be pretty much on line once they get past liability. They may start by disputing liability, but if you ask them to assume there's liability their numbers are pretty good once you get past the liability threshold they have. Otherwise, they scream, "No liability."
- It does happen. Clients can have impressions about lawsuits and claims. The degree of challenge varies quite a bit. The longer you have known them, the easier it is to get them to reevaluate.
- In business cases, clients have opinions. Sometimes it's way off the mark.
- For the most part, I work with the adjuster who has handled the case pre-lit. They may have already taken a statement over the phone. Seventy-five percent of the time when they come to me, they have some idea of what the case is worth. Most of the time they're willing to listen to me.

Client preconceptions appear to be largely shaped by the media, family members, friends and co-workers. Noting that clients "get their ideas from the media," a plaintiffs' attorney states, "They hear about these cases and people with high verdicts and they think they will get that as well." Sometimes the clients' expectations "come from hearing attorneys on radio and TV," according to one defense attorney. "Advertising has changed everything," he asserts. Other attorneys report that clients rely on "word of mouth from people who don't know what they're talking about," an aunt or a brother who received "a large recovery for an injury that seems minor," "an opinion from another attorney," "cases and people with high verdicts," and "a lot of outrageous publicity about trial results." And now, another attorney notes, "The Internet is your client." Although the source of client preconceptions may vary with the client's sophistication level, the tendency to form expectations may be universal. A former judge, for example, noted that highly educated people can be recalcitrant and difficult to counsel: "In Berkeley, everyone is a genius; they all have Ph.D.'s. They all know more than you."

12.1.4 Underestimation

Although stereotypes depict plaintiffs as having unrealistically high expectations and their attorneys as reinforcing those expectations, it is important to realize that expectations also can be unreasonably low. As one plaintiffs' attorney states, "Some clients have unrealistically low views of what their case is worth. It works both ways." Another plaintiffs' attorney elaborates:

> On big cases, clients usually expect low. They don't know what a case is worth. On larger cases, clients' expectations are always low.
>
> Most clients with catastrophic injuries are not getting optimal care. So they cannot value their damages. Most of my quadriplegic clients are getting two shifts a day, but in other states clients are getting two hours a day instead of 16, or even two hours per week. They need two shifts to clean their butts and turn them over and they don't know a lot of the people doing this are not qualified to take care of them. They are getting paid $8 per hour to care for these patients, but the patients need someone paid at least twice that amount, $16 per hour. When an expert figures out what it will actually cost to get the right care for these people for the rest of their lives, the amount is way beyond anything the client would imagine on their own.
>
> These people are lucky to be alive, so they've adapted and lowered their expectations. Some are suicidal for their entire life. They have gotten used to it, but juries are hearing it for the first time.

The fact that some clients have low or no expectations and rely almost exclusively on their attorney to engage experts, ascertain their damages and guide them through settlement negotiations is emphasized by another attorney: "In plaintiff cases I would have trouble saying there is something typical. In the two cases we've talked about, neither client had any preconceived notion – they would have taken anything we recommended." The clients with unrealistic expectations, he adds, are "upper class" clients. "You are put in the position of bringing them back to earth."

12.1.5 Client Risk Tolerance

In addition to determining client expectations, the study attorneys attempt to understand the client's risk tolerance. Clients with substantially identical claims may have entirely different risk tolerances, resulting in disparate concepts of a successful outcome. For risk-averse clients, the uncertainty of protracted litigation can eclipse the economic benefits of a settlement obtained through prolonged negotiations or a favorable judgment entered after years of extensive, disruptive discovery. Litigation success thus is often defined more by the client's risk preferences than the case's legal merits.

"Sometimes the clients are super risk-averse or 100% risk takers," observes a commercial litigator who also has served as an arbitrator on many attorney fee dispute panels. "The problem is that some attorneys don't know what type of client they have; they don't take the time to understand what the client is trying to achieve." In his experience, the most common problem in fee disputes is "poor communication." What starts as a communication deficiency in failing to ascertain the client's risk tolerance then becomes a fee dispute about failing to align the case strategy with the client's risk profile.

The study attorneys seem to be effective in avoiding those types of communication problems. They are proactive in discerning and adhering to the client's risk preferences and note that both individuals and insurers have varying risk tolerances:

- I'm very clear on this and always ask the client, "How much do you want to risk?" Different clients have different attitudes about risk. For a client making $500,000 per year, a $250,000 settlement won't change his life, but a $250,000 offer for someone making $50,000 will.
- Most clients are risk-averse. They do not want to go to trial. They go to trial when the insurance company's offer is abusively low. But other clients are not risk-averse. Certain people cannot comprehend that they could lose.
- Carriers go through cycles. Sometimes they want to make an example of everyone and other times they just want to avoid risks and close the files. Each cycle lasts a couple of years.
- Yes, there's a broad range in the risk tolerances of carriers. A lot depends on their recent experience. If they got hit with a big verdict recently, they may be more inclined to settle. One will pay $100,000 [to settle] and one will take a verdict. Medical malpractice carriers take a little less business approach. General liability carriers are more business oriented. The med mal carriers know the physicians have to consent and there are other issues for the physicians other than the payment.

Because clients have different risk tolerances and expectations, notes a plaintiffs' attorney, "some clients are pleased with settlements that I don't think are great settlements."

The conventional assumption is that risk-averse clients prefer settlements to trials and, if possible, early settlements over later settlements. But for some clients, risk aversion dictates that a case be tried instead of settled:

> Some clients are stubborn and just want the jury to decide. In some ways, jury trials are less risky than settlement. If the jury comes out with a bad result, you just say, "The jury did it." Otherwise, if you're the one who authorized a settlement, you get second-guessed and someone else is in there saying, "Why did you pay that much?"

Risk aversion in large organizations often means ducking the call so that the responsibility for recommending or authorizing a settlement cannot be squarely affixed on the attorneys or the executives. When a jury awards an amount significantly higher than a plaintiff's settlement demand, one study attorney notes, it is not a defendant's case evaluation error but rather reflects group dynamics. "Mistakes sometimes occur because all the people on the defendant's side cannot agree ultimately on an offer," she explains. "Separately, they may know what a realistic number is."

12.1.6   Testing the Client

In the initial interview, clients may think they are interviewing and selecting their attorneys, but for the study attorneys, the process is reversed. The study attorneys, in fact, are interviewing and screening the clients. In many respects, the initial interview serves as the client's audition for trial. To direct and obtain maximum benefit from that audition, the attorneys probe for characteristics that foreshadow a favorable settlement or verdict: Is the client credible? Is the client likeable? Can the client handle the stress of protracted litigation? How will the client perform under cross-examination? In answering these questions, the study attorneys change lenses, adopting the viewpoint of a juror and trying to counter their own personal biases. "The bottom line," states a plaintiffs' attorney who previously managed claims for a national insurer, "is how they will go over to a judge or jury."

12.1.7   Credibility

The study attorneys expressed some skepticism about client claims and indicated the initial interview is critical in assessing credibility:

- No case will ever get better after the first meeting with the client – it will only get worse. Clients try to impress you so that you'll be excited about taking the case. Don't make the assumption that something bad won't come along. Like a client lies about prior experience and little by little you hear a different story and find out they've been in other accidents and claimed the same injuries.
- I don't believe clients when they come in. I scrutinize them like the defense would.
- I tell clients I want to know all the bad crap first – "tell me the bad stuff."
- Until informed otherwise, believe just half of what the client tells you, especially in more complicated cases like employment cases. Be prepared for the fact not everything your client tells you is true.
- I look at facts more analytically and objectively and have learned not to believe anything the client tells you, unless it's independently verified. I tell clients, "I need to know all the dirt because if I don't know it ahead of time I can't protect you from it."

Some of the attorneys were especially skeptical about clients intent on vindicating a principle. "If someone comes in with an agenda and says it's the principle," states an attorney who represents both plaintiffs and defendants, "it will be the exact opposite. They will be all over you on the fees." Another attorney expresses a similar sentiment: "I want to find out whether it's the 'principle of the thing' because the client is less likely to resolve the case if it's just the principle of the thing. When it's their principle it could be my fee, too."

12.1.8   Demeanor

Apart from assessing credibility, the attorneys test prospective clients to determine whether they can appear trustworthy and pleasant, convey their story and convince a jury:

- The most important factors are the client himself or herself – sincere, honest, down-to-earth people, not flighty. Can they answer a question without getting fidgety and going all over the place in answering a question? What's the history? Do they have all the paperwork? By asking them to bring the paperwork for the first meeting, I try to find out if they've got some sense of organization and are sincere.
- Females make better witnesses and can express the depth of their distress. Males cannot express their emotions well.
- A client's ability to express themselves is one of the most important factors. The difficulty with some clients is that they cannot articulate their pain. When the client cannot describe for the jury how they feel and the effect on their life, the lawyer has to think about settling for the best number they can.
- The most important factor is the client. If I believe the client, I can sell the client to the judge, the jury, the insurer, and opposing counsel. The client's appearance is important. I tell them, "You're not going to be wearing those rings" or "You should wear a shirt to cover those tattoos."
- You assess people differently each time – they're individuals. But you have to have that skill when you're dealing with defendants who will come after you with 15 to 16 freight trains.

One of the most common errors attorneys make, according to a defense attorney, is "misjudging your own client and the client's ability to communicate or relate to a jury."

Even when the client is credible and likeable, the study attorneys probe deeper to see how they will perform under cross-examination:

- I spend two to three hours on an intake. When I just listened to the client highlights, you get screwed. I get adversarial with clients because I want to know what happened. When a person gets stressed, what are they looking for – the lucre gene, the righteous indignation gene? Can they keep a clearness of purpose? It's like a military battle. You know you won't win every skirmish, but can they win the battle? Is there an inner calm?
- I look for that contact back – how antagonistic is the client, is there a hint of antagonism toward me?
- If I take a case, it's because I like the client and the case. Whenever I've had a bad feeling about a client in the past, 100% of the time I was right and regretted it.
- So I found another category of clients that I don't like – ones that cannot multi-task and see where they're going. I don't know if you'd call it diarrhea of the mouth, but she did not perform in deposition. We lost the case on summary

judgment. I'm mentioning this so you understand, it's more complicated than whether the client is confident and can handle testifying. She was very confident. She just didn't know when to stop talking.

In testing the client's ability to handle questioning at deposition and trial, many of the study attorneys benefit from their experience as temporary judges and mediators as well as their own trial experience. Explaining why he tests clients at an early stage, one attorney states: "As a neutral [mediator], I was always asking, 'How much is this the attorney's case?' A weak client can hide behind a strong attorney – he's a hell of a client with the attorney holding his arms and legs."

12.1.9   Public Safety Officials

Some law enforcement officers and other individuals responsible for public safety have a special vulnerability in cross-examination. Their careers are dedicated to protecting the public, and many simply cannot endure the accusation that they have violated the public trust and their own creed:

- Officers spend a lot of time testifying in court, and you could get the wrong impression that they're great witnesses. Many are experienced witnesses, but they have not had the experience of being a defendant, of an attorney saying in front of 12 jurors, "This guy murdered my client's son." There's a different psychology of being a defendant in a civil rights case, being accused of being a murderer. You have to prepare them psychologically for being accused.
- It's important to see how they react to being in a court as a defendant. Some are unable to cope with being accused of being a murderer. A few years ago I had a clean case but the officer could not handle being a defendant. In the mock cross-exam the officer was so angry he nearly walked off the stand. We settled.
- The attorney has to know how the client is inside. Otherwise they may fall apart on the stand. Some clients – even ones who were not directly involved in the incident – cannot handle the idea that someone thinks they're responsible for a death. In one case I'm thinking of, an officer retired and is working in a different career. It [plaintiff's claim] hit him like a ton of bricks.

Whether the defendant is a police officer accused of murdering a young father or a park equipment maintenance supervisor alleged to be responsible for a child's full body paralysis, he may be psychologically incapable of defending his actions at trial. Thus, a key function of the initial interview is to look beyond the superficial confidence of authoritative people and discern whether the legal merits of the client's behavior will be subsumed by anger, defensiveness, self-doubt or distress on the witness stand. The great benefit and annoyance of the witness stand is that it levels its occupants, stripping them of the prerogatives that attend roles and titles and placing society's most elevated and most disgraced members in the same seat. This can disadvantage and aggravate clients – corporate officers, physicians, professors, and public safety officers – who are unaccustomed to having their views challenged and their integrity questioned.

12.2   Counseling After Retention

After the study attorneys have accepted a case, the counseling methods and objectives are different from those employed and achieved in the initial attorney-client interactions. The attention shifts from the clients' expectations, risk tolerances and credibility to the long-term prospects for case resolution. The attorney has established the ground rules, developed the client's trust and conveyed at least a partial assessment of the case. As the case progresses through the discovery process – "maybe we'll learn some good stuff, maybe some bad stuff" – the attorney becomes more evaluative, weighs the advantages and disadvantages of settlement and emphasizes the risks of jury trials:

- I give them the best legal advice I can and tell them what the law is and tell them even if they think they know exactly what will happen at trial, they don't. I stress – I compare it to gambling – that it's devastating when you lose. I try to explain the downside of costs, expert's fees. I always tell them 90% of cases settle, and clients are relieved to hear that.
- My role is to give them advice regarding the risks and opportunities and be as candid as possible. Tell them what the jury could do. We need to tell them a number. They ask and we'll tell them what a jury could do.
- We spend a lot of time talking with injured clients about liability – how it happened. Some clients find this annoying because for them the most important thing is they're injured. But the injury can be a secondary factor if liability cannot be established. For a lot of lawyers there's a tendency to focus on bad injuries, but where plaintiff attorneys seem to make mistakes is on liability issues. I have done a fair amount of med mal – medical malpractice – and I've seen the same mistake – looking at the injury instead of liability.
- How do you get it across to a client who does not have the life experience to make this decision? I try to sit down with the client and explain, "What you may have seen or read is not an accurate picture of the court system. The average case will not be the subject of a newspaper article or a TV program." Sometimes it has been difficult – not a pleasant experience – explaining what has happened in other cases. A win may not be a win. It can be less than your analysis. You have to evaluate very carefully the strength of the witnesses.
- I'll show them what we can get at trial, and this is what we can get at settlement. I give broad ranges and make recommendations. I explain that we'll go to the carrier, and the amount we demand will be 30–45% higher than what you'll get. So they know from the start that my negotiation position is different from what they should be prepared to accept. I tell them, "You need to know this ahead of time." I don't think attorneys get down to the nitty gritty and discuss the real potentials.

Bluntly describing a jury trial, a plaintiffs' attorney tells clients, "Keep in mind jurors don't want to be there anyway. They have their own problems." The client's case, he advises, "will be decided by a jury of 12 people who have not figured out how to get out of jury duty."

12.2.1   Differences Between Plaintiffs' and Defense Counsel

In discussing the difficulties of counseling clients about settlement and trial, some of the defense attorneys made sharp distinctions between plaintiffs' attorneys and defense counsel. These distinctions reflect fundamental differences between the business models and structures of the two practices and indicate that the type of practice could affect case evaluation and client counseling:

- When a client is paying hourly, you have to have an accurate evaluation. I can't afford to be wrong, but the plaintiff can. Most of my clients I've known for 20 years. If I make a mistake, I lose the client. If something goes wrong, it's my fault. As I say to the other attorneys in my office, "there are no bad results, only bad reporting." For plaintiffs everything is different. Their clients are one-shot deals, so they don't have the same incentive to get it right every time. There's not necessarily anything wrong with the way plaintiffs do things because they are not paying for your fees.
- My relationship with clients is very different from plaintiffs' counsel. I don't have to do a lot of pushing and shoving to get my client where I think he needs to be. Plaintiffs' attorneys have it rough. On every case they have a different client with a different perspective, different goals, and each time they have to prove themselves. There's a lot more posturing and bluster with plaintiffs' counsel because they have to convince the client they're on his side. I don't have to go through that routine because I already have the credibility with my clients.
- On the plaintiff side, lawyers are the most influential. On the defense side, you're dealing with management. They want your recommendation. They will very seriously take it into account, but they will act independently. They want to know how many times you would win this case – like "if it was tried ten times how often would we prevail?" I ask, "Why do you want to take it to trial?" Sometimes they tell me, "We want to see what a jury does with it." They are looking at a much bigger picture than my case.
- On the defense side, attorneys are pretty good about recognizing the reality of the case. There's definitely a high degree of accuracy. They know a likeable plaintiff can overcome any chinks in the armor. Defense attorneys want to do the right thing for the client because they're getting paid on an hourly basis and have repeat business with the client. For the plaintiffs' attorneys, it's usually a one-shot deal with the client so there's not the same level of accountability. Defense attorneys know that if their valuation is wrong, the client pays twice – once for

the bad advice and again for the verdict. It also helps to have two sets of eyes on the case when you're working with an insurance company. Plaintiffs' attorneys don't have to report to anyone except the client.

Whether one agrees or disagrees with these opinions, it seems evident that defense firms are more likely to bill on an hourly basis, represent repeat clients, report periodically to insurers and obtain input from claims executives. These factors present different economic incentives in processing and evaluating cases and provide an additional layer of communication and accountability. Limited data suggests that these factors – combined with extensive databases, adjuster training and adequate financial resources to pay investigators and expert witnesses – reduce evaluation errors.[1] Insured defendants, for example, appear to experience fewer adverse outcomes at trial than uninsured defendants.[2]

12.2.2   Bad Witnesses

Perhaps the most critical and difficult aspect of counseling is informing clients that they will be unbelievable or unlikeable witnesses. Once an attorney has observed the client testify during deposition, however, the attorney is ethically obligated to integrate any unfavorable impressions into the overall assessment of the case and candidly communicate that assessment to the client:[3]

- It's really, really, really tough to tell your own client he will not be a good witness. Tell them it looks like it's difficult to decide who to put on the stand because people will disbelieve you. It's the most difficult message to give to a client and is part of what you have to see when you first decide to take the case. Both the attorney and the other side are looking at how the client comes across.

---

[1]See Kritzer, Herbert M., & Silbey, Susan (Eds.). (2003). *In litigation do the "haves" still come out ahead?* Stanford, California: Stanford University Press. Guthrie, Chris & Rachlinski , Jeffrey J. (2006). Insurers, illusions of judgment & litigation. *Vanderbilt Law Review 59*, 2017. Vanderbilt Law and Economics Research Paper No. 06–28. Available at SSRN: http://ssrn.com/abstract=952493.

[2]Kiser, Randall. (2010). *Beyond right and wrong: The power of effective decision making for attorneys and clients* (pp. 73–76). New York: Springer Science + Business Media.

[3]Model Rule 2.1 states: "In representing a client, a lawyer shall exercise independent professional judgment and render candid advice." Comment 1 states: "A client is entitled to straightforward advice expressing the lawyer's honest assessment. Legal advice often involves unpleasant facts and alternatives that a client may be disinclined to confront. In presenting advice, a lawyer endeavors to sustain the client's morale and may put advice in as acceptable a form as honesty permits. However, a lawyer should not be deterred from giving candid advice by the prospect that the advice will be unpalatable to the client."

- You also have to tell them that maybe they do not have the rapport with the jury. A lot of attorneys have this problem, too. You cannot be arrogant or too aggressive in front of a jury.
- If your client makes a terrible witness you need to tell them right after the depo, not on the eve of trial. How can you explain it then?
- I have a very good ability to understand how an average juror will look at this. Sometimes it seems so obvious. Like I represented a physician at a deposition. His head was darting, his eyes were shifting all the time. I told the carrier right after, "We have to settle."

A defense attorney tells clients, "At a deposition you are auditioning for trial. Are you a good or bad witness? Are you going to hold up or fold?" For the deposition to serve its purpose, then, some clients invariably have to be informed that the audition went poorly and, if they are fortunate enough to settle the case, they will not be getting a callback for trial.

12.2.3 Physicians

Like public safety officials, physicians bring a special sensitivity to civil litigation. Their self-perceptions often cannot be reconciled with the base allegations of negligence, ineptitude or inattention asserted in a medical malpractice action. They have invested years of education and training to become a physician and practice in a rarefied environment characterized by deference, autonomy, latitude and respect. Since they believe their lives are dedicated to treating disease and saving lives, the concept that they have caused injury or death is anathema. "As a group," explains psychiatry professor Sara Charles, "physicians are acutely sensitive to any suggestion that they have failed to meet the standard of care or are not 'good' doctors. Their honor – that sense of personal integrity that most people cherish – is at issue, and the threat of its loss is devastating."[4]

Counseling physicians in medical malpractice actions, the study attorneys relate, requires a high degree of emotional intelligence as well as legal acumen:

- Physicians live in a world where they have control. Being sued changes that completely.
- All of them are benevolent in their motivations. When they're sued, their reputation is attacked, their ego hurts, their feelings are hurt – they tried their best. Because of this, my work involves a lot of psychology.
- They're scared. They realize this ain't the hospital, that it's not "whatever you say doctor" anymore. Earlier in my career I was near the end of an initial

---

[4]Charles, Sara C. (2001). Coping with a medical malpractice suit. *Western Journal of Medicine*, *174*(1), 55–58. See Charles, Sara C., & Frisch, Paul R. (2005). *Adverse events, stress, and litigation: A physician's guide*. New York: Oxford University Press.

meeting with a doctor. I said, "You can relax now. I'll be taking care of this. I'll do the worrying now." I knew it was a dumb thing to say. I had said it before to other doctors, but I was trying to make him feel better. He was really upset. He stood up in front of my desk and said, "How can I relax when I'm being sued? This is my career." I never said that again. Now I say, "I can only educate you about the process. There's nothing I can do about your anxiety."

- Some of the young doctors are terrified. Many, many times I've seen physicians who settle one case, then settle another and settle another. Then they get a letter from the medical board and the licensing problems start. It has other consequences, too, from Blue Cross dropping them to their insurance carriers. When they are thinking about settling a case that should not be settled, I will tell them, "You are making a mistake. You will quit practicing medicine."
- I tell them, "We have two systems that don't blend. Your system is empirical and ours is adversarial. For every position I take another attorney will say 90% of what I think is wrong." After a while they begin to understand this is a very different system than what they trained for. The key is gaining trust and being open about facts.

Unless an attorney takes the time to understand the physician's ethos, even good legal results can exacerbate the physician's sense of insult and offense. Upon obtaining a dismissal of a physician from a malpractice action, for instance, an attorney telephoned what he imagined would be his grateful client. Elated to convey the good news, he told the physician, "We got you off the hook." After a long silence, the physician responded, "I was never on the hook."

Chapter 13
Adversaries and Judges

In this chapter, the study attorneys describe how they relate to opposing counsel and judges. They consider how professional relationships have changed during the last 50 years and discuss their own style in communicating with adversaries. They also talk about the tension between being an officer of the court and an advocate and the attorney's role in protecting clients from undue judicial pressure to settle a case. Reflecting on the judiciary, they note that statutes and programs designed to expedite litigation have changed some judges' roles from being a trial judge to a case manager, and they express concerns about the relatively new phenomenon of judges retiring to join private mediation services.

13.1 Adversaries

Attorneys and judges in general perceive an increase in incivility. Urging attorneys to "rekindle" their heritage, honor, and self-respect, former California State Bar President James Heiting writes, "At times I get so tired of dealing with needlessly antagonistic lawyers in litigation. It is widely recognized, as you are certainly aware, that civility among lawyers, promotion of justice and respect for each other and the law as an institution has been eroding."[1] Surveys indicate that 40% of lawyers and judges identify "lack of civility and professionalism as a significant problem;" and, depending on the region in which they practice, up to 62% of attorneys and judges think "civility is lacking."[2] In a survey conducted by the

---

[1]Heiting, James O. (2006, May). A new approach to civility. *California Bar Journal*, p. 1.

[2]Mashburn, Amy R. (1994). Professionalism as class ideology: Civility codes and bar hierarchy. *Valparaiso University Law Review 28*, 692. Daicoff, Susan. (1997). Lawyer, know thyself: A review of empirical research on attorney attributes bearing on professionalism. *American University Law Review, 46*, 1344–1345. Hansen, Mark. (1991, July). Incivility a problem, survey says. *ABA Journal*, p. 22. See Daicoff, Susan. (2006). *Lawyer, know thyself* (pp. 102–112). Washington, D.C.: American Psychological Association.

American Bar Association's Commission on Professionalism, 68% of judges and corporate executives thought professionalism among lawyers "had decreased over time."[3]

In his article, "Rambo Litigation: Why Hardball Tactics Don't Work," Robert Sayler, a litigation partner at Covington & Burling, asserts that excessively aggressive tactics "are pernicious and on the rise."[4] He identifies six characteristics of uncivil litigation conduct that block objectivity and place attorneys in "untenable" negotiation positions: (1) a mindset that litigation is war and that describes trial practice in military terms; (2) a conviction that it is invariably in your interest to make life miserable for your opponent; (3) a disdain for common courtesy and civility, assuming that they are ill-suited for the true warrior; (4) a wondrous facility for manipulating facts and engaging in revisionist history; (5) a hair-trigger willingness to fire off unnecessary motions and to use discovery for intimidation rather than fact finding; and (6) an urge to put the trial lawyer on center stage rather than the client or his cause. The most frequent context for incivility, according to one survey, is discovery proceedings, followed by "routine matters" and "in-court proceedings."[5] A judge responding to the survey wrote, "Too many litigators think winning every point is the name of the game. They often seem to have a compulsive and childish need to fight over everything."[6]

13.1.1   Changes in Attorneys' Communications

The study attorneys shared some of the concerns voiced by judges and other lawyers about increased incivility. The study attorneys view incivility, though, as part of the larger problem of decreased communication between opposing counsel. Reflecting on changes in practice styles resulting from technology, discovery, mediation and the sheer increase in the number of attorneys during the last 50 years, the study attorneys observe:

• When I started practicing you didn't write this letter confirming everything; you picked up the phone. Everyone knew each other; there was this mutuality of trust. [Interviewer: What has changed? Why are attorneys confrontational?] It's the number of lawyers, the experience of counsel, the attitudes of attorneys. With

---

[3]Mashburn, Amy R. (1994). Professionalism as class ideology: Civility codes and bar hierarchy. *Valparaiso University Law Review 28*, 692.

[4]Sayler, Robert. (1988, March 1). Rambo litigation: Why hardball tactics don't work. *ABA Journal*, pp. 79–81.

[5]Hansen *supra* note 2 at 22. Friedman, Paul L. (1998, March 13). Fostering civility: A professional obligation. Remarks by Judge Paul L. Friedman, United States District Court for the District of Columbia, American Bar Association Section of Pubic Contract Law. Available at http://www.abanet.org/contract/operations/proceedings/sigdocs/friedman13mar98.html.

[6]Hansen *supra* note 2 at 22.

the number of attorneys, the attorneys are so scared and lacking in confidence. The surfers have an expression, "No 'tude [attitude] here." I think we need the same. So many attorneys think you have to pound on the table and argue instead of speaking softly with substance.

- I'm pretty old school and started when we were a small community and everyone knew each other. This discovery stuff did not start until the 1980s. It's defense driven, billable hour driven. Back in the 1970s we would go to trial with just a manila folder in our hands. Now the practice is less civil, especially among younger attorneys.

- So much of lawyering has changed. I worked with an attorney who always called a day before trial to see if they could settle. Now there is little informal exchange. People are more cautious. They send faxes instead of talking and are more formal all around.

- [Interviewer: Are you in the school of attorneys who think attorneys have become less civil to each other?] No, I'm not. But I think it has gotten more sterile in the relationships attorneys have with each other. ABOTA [American Board of Trial Advocates] has been presenting a program in the law schools on civility. It's important to start when they're in law school, so they don't think you have to be an a-hole to be a successful attorney. Another offshoot is it brings respect back to the profession and the courts.

- There's so much more in writing now, not just a few things but a lot of things – emails, faxes – that has reduced the frequency of personal interaction and elevates the intensity of advocacy. If you say something in writing it's much harsher than if it's said in the course of a conversation. An aspect of practice has not been lost, but has been diminished. Mediation is a forced meeting between attorneys who may not be communicating very well. [Interviewer: Is this a generational difference between attorneys in communication styles?] It's not so much generational as experience, learning how to relate, how to talk with another attorney. To have a good level of interaction with another attorney requires a high level of confidence – that takes time. The emphasis is on the paper.

- The attorneys I have the most success with there's often a collegial thing – two people see the same things, and we don't do the stuff we're always accused of doing. With the other attorneys, there's two basic problems. The first step is posturing, and the second is taking advantage of trust or familiarity. With some attorneys you think you're having a candid discussion and then you get a confirming letter saying you said something you never said or misstating what you said.

Another study attorney commented, "Incivility is a major problem. We had to let go of one of our own attorneys because of aggressiveness."

Despite the frequently voiced concern about incivility, a few study attorneys strongly believe that opposing counsel have become less aggressive over time and that younger attorneys in their own firms have changed the law office environment.

They recall early careers being subjected to inconsiderate people not only in depositions and courtrooms but also in the office next door:

> The business has changed dramatically within the last six to seven years. People are a lot nicer than they used to be. Everyone is really nice, where before they were not nice. The people I worked with early on were tougher and meaner. They were tough guys, complete jerks, constantly drank, chased secretaries, never said a kind word to anyone, always chasing secretaries. They were a different breed of people. People are raised differently. The Me Generation, they don't work that much anymore. It's hard to find someone here after 5:15 [p.m.].

This perception of increased congeniality within the profession appears consistent with what professor Julie Macfarlane calls "the new lawyer" – the attorney who eschews traditional adversarial behavior, places a greater emphasis on being an effective negotiator and communicator and "offers a participatory model of compassionate, client-centred, professional service instead of the traditional 'trust me' detachment of the old lawyer."[7]

13.1.2 Study Attorneys' Communications with Adversaries

When asked to describe their own relationships with opposing counsel, the study attorneys emphasized cooperation and collegiality, justifying that approach as both more professional and practical:

- There's a significant shift into mediation. It's a replacement for a simple phone call. But it doesn't mean I'm less civil to the other attorney because we're not discussing settlement directly. I always try to have a good relationship with opposing counsel because if I'm mad at the other attorney, I'm focusing on the wrong thing. I need to focus on the plaintiff, not the attorney.
- I take a pretty relaxed attitude about discovery and am pretty accommodating about the minor things. It takes too much effort to be a jerk. If you have had a contentious relationship before trial, that will build up walls and you won't be able to listen to them when they have a rational figure to present. We have an adversarial system, but the adversariness is supposed to come up at trial.
- You don't have to be hostile or confrontational with the other side. You just slowly, politely, efficiently, methodically cut their balls off.
- My goal is to be straightforward and honest. I've done my share of posturing, and it doesn't do me any good. The idea is to take the negotiation process out of the war zone – have respect for the other side and recognize he is as smart as I am. You have to have openness without fear that it will come back to haunt you. With one attorney – I won't mention his name – everything he does is posturing. Any attempt to take down the barriers is used against you.

---

[7]Macfarlane, Julie. (2007). *The new lawyer: How settlement is transforming the practice of law* (pp. 22–23). Vancouver, British Columbia: UBC Press.

The study attorneys' attitudes track those of noted trial attorney and law professor Michael Tigar. In dealing with an abusive adversary, he urges attorneys to "keep calm, keep on track, and keep on your plan." He admits, "I have so often faced this temptation to strike back or change course abruptly. When I have yielded to this temptation, I have almost always regretted it."[8]

13.1.3 Reputation and Specialization

When they are interacting with a small group of specialists or other attorneys who have distinguished themselves by their stellar reputations or trial results, the study attorneys encounter incivility less frequently. In some practice areas, the attorneys are familiar "repeat players" and have established patterns of discovery, reciprocity and negotiation. The importance and advantages of reputation and specialization are illustrated by these remarks:

• Eighty-five percent of my practice is medical malpractice; the rest is serious personal injury. In the medical malpractice area, they are old school – we voluntarily send documents instead of requiring a formal request. We're at the same experience level and have the added factor of being in the same field. We will roll around on the courtroom floor at trial but have a glass of wine afterwards and discuss who the next day's witnesses will be.
• When you're working with really experienced plaintiff's counsel, the situation is different. That case settled in 2–3 months but would have taken 2–3 years with other plaintiffs' attorneys. Old pros are different because they know what a case is worth. He served a 998 offer right at the beginning, and I knew his number was very close. We had a cordial relationship and settled that case early on.
• Because it's a small group of lawyers in this field, reputation is the most important thing. As I tell law students, you only have one reputation, and it only takes one screw-up to ruin it. Judges all eat lunch together and they discuss which attorneys miscite cases and misrepresent facts. Your reputation gets around. It takes decades of integrity to build up a reputation.
• The attorneys I work with are different, generally more sophisticated. There's a tendency to evaluate cases early on. You work with the same attorneys. This overcomes the hurdles with most attorneys. We have discussions regarding the problems. We abbreviate the discovery statutes. We exchange experts more than

---

[8]Tigar, Michael. (2009). *Nine principles of litigation and life* (p. 232). Chicago: American Bar Association. See Tucker, John C. (2003). *Trial and error: The education of a courtroom lawyer* (p. 71). New York: Carroll & Graf Publishers. ("I had learned from Jim Sprowl that litigation could be conducted calmly with polite respect for your opponent and his client, without losing anything in the way of effectiveness. And I had learned from another partner of the firm and a couple of opponents that litigation could also be conducted like a street fight, without really gaining anything.")

120 days before trial. Six out of ten attorneys will go along with this. With one attorney, I said, "Let's not take depos – let's sit down and talk." I have no qualms about opening the door to him.

When asked why he thought some plaintiffs' attorneys overvalued their cases, a defense attorney expressed a preference for working with senior attorneys: "A lot of it is stupidity and inexperience. Most older plaintiff attorneys have a good sense of what a case is worth. They have stopped taking minor cases."

13.1.4   Advice to New Attorneys

Recognizing the importance of maintaining a professional relationship with opposing counsel, the study attorneys offered this advice to newly admitted attorneys:

- Never ever get contentious with opposing counsel and don't personalize it. Explain the reasons for your client's position, explain why you have constraints, respect the other person's position, tell them what you think their position is, never demean it, be comfortable with your position, and practice, practice, practice.
- Try not to think you have to be hyperbolic with the other attorney. Try to develop some rapport. There's no reason to take advantage of someone because sooner or later it's going to haunt you.
- I also recommend they act civilly to other counsel. If they're a bulldozer, that reputation will stay. I tell attorneys, "You can be adversarial but you don't have to be enemies."
- Do not try to approach the opposition the same way with every case. There's a time to be a tough guy when the conditions require it, and now I start off pretty even. I give the other side the benefit of the doubt until they do something that says I need to be different. Sometimes I've taken cases all the way through trial and still been friendly with the other attorney.
- It's very hard to go back to opposing counsel to discuss settlement if the case goes south and you've taken a tough, "I'm going to bury you" attitude. I'd rather have a cordial relationship with opposing counsel so I can talk to them if things change.

This advice is consistent with research demonstrating that attorneys who assume a "problem-solving" attitude toward negotiations are more effective than attorneys adopting an "adversarial" attitude.[9] In one study, only 9% of the attorneys perceived to be effective negotiators by their peers exhibited combative, inflexible, self-centered and arrogant behavior, while 91% of the attorneys perceived to be effective negotiators displayed trustworthy, personable, communicative, perceptive

---

[9]Schneider, Andrea K. (2002). Shattering negotiation myths: Empirical evidence on the effectiveness of negotiation style. *Harvard Negotiation Law Review, 7*, 143–233. Craver, Charles. (2002). *The intelligent negotiator*. Roseville, California: Prima Publishing.

and adaptable behavior. In that study, an attorney described a "problem-solving attorney" in terms that would apply to many of the study attorneys: "He advocated for the client – kept coming back to the table – and proposing alternatives – was effective in making emotional appeal – got a good deal – was friendly and courteous – never took it personally."[10]

13.2   Judges

While discussing case evaluation and resolution, the study attorneys agreed that judges play a critical role throughout the case. They pointed out that judges exert tremendous power in attempting to settle cases and that attorneys often underestimate the wide discretion judges exercise at trial in admitting evidence and interpreting the law. They also observed that legislative efforts to expedite trials have resulted in increased pressure to settle cases and decreased time for voir dire. As they talked about judges, they looked beyond their own cases and expressed some general concerns about the loss of experienced civil settlement and trial judges who retire and join private dispute resolution firms. Their observations and concerns are elaborated below.

13.2.1   Trial Delay Reduction Programs

Programs designed to reduce the time between the filing of a lawsuit and its disposition through settlement or trial – as exemplified by California's Trial Delay Reduction Act and New York's Comprehensive Civil Justice Program – have been heralded as an "unqualified success." In New York, for instance, the average time for case resolution has been reduced from 606 days to 380 days.[11] Although these programs have shortened the time for case resolution, the study attorneys indicate that they also may have changed judges and trials:

- Judges are evaluated more rigorously now on how fast they administer cases. The courts keep track of how many cases they're assigned, how many are resolved within a certain period. This started to change with the Trial Delay Reduction Act. Judges will never admit it, but they do pay attention to this.

---

[10]Schneider *supra* note 9 at 163–165, 167.

[11](Spring/Summer 2005). Report proposes changes in civil case management. *Benchmarks*, *1*(1), 4. New York State Unified Court System.

- Judges now view it as a personal failure if they don't settle the case. This places a lot of pressure on attorneys. Back in the 1970s and 1980s, judges put less pressure on settlement. Now fewer and fewer judges come up through the civil arena. Experienced judges are leaving in droves and no civil practitioners are being appointed.
- Also, the rocket docket has created a lot of problems. Judges became abusive and became aware of the power they could abuse. Even when attorneys stipulate to a continuance or an attorney needs a continuance because his client has just been brought in as a Doe [a defendant whose identify is unknown at the time the complaint is filed], the judges deny the motions. They follow this in the trial. One judge gave each side 32 hours to put on its case and made each party stick to it. Except for one or two judges, they are all that way. Justice has definitely taken a back door since the rocket docket. Judges have to process cases more expeditiously. Looking back on trials, I think some judges signal earlier in the trial where they're going, what the result probably will be so you see their direction and settle the case.

Another study attorney thought that some judges now see themselves more as case managers than trial judges and are reluctant to commit court resources to trials that frequently last two to four weeks: "Some judges do not want trials in their courtroom; they just want to be case managers. They have statistics and goals they have to meet."[12]

13.2.2   Settlement Conferences

Prior to trial, judges can exert a strong effect on case outcomes through their rulings, scheduling orders, comments and evaluations and, in some cases, direct pressure to settle a case. Law professor Judith Resnik notes that judges have adopted a "more active, 'managerial' stance" and have moved away from the dispassionate, disengaged adjudicator role: "In growing numbers, judges are not only adjudicating the merits of issues presented to them by litigants, but also are meeting with parties in chambers to encourage settlement of disputes and to supervise case preparation. Both before and after the trial, judges are playing a critical role in shaping litigation and influencing results."[13]

---

[12]In a data-driven courthouse, metrics may not fully capture the precedential and democratic values of civil jury trials. In this respect, it is notable that the United States now ranks 11th among 35 countries and 11th among 11 countries with similar income levels in "access to justice." Agrast, M., Botero, J., & Ponce, A. (2010). *WJP rule of law index*. Washington, D.C.: The World Justice Project.

[13]Resnik, Judith. (1982). Managerial judges. *Harvard Law Review, 96*, 376–377.

Some study attorneys expressed gratitude for judges' attempts to settle cases, while other attorneys reacted unfavorably to these efforts. Attorneys with a positive view of judicial intervention remarked:

- One factor we haven't talked about is trial – the effectiveness of the trial judge. The trial judge's role is critical. You have some who sit back and are not active participants and others who work very hard to resolve the case and just act in a neutral way to see if the parties can settle it. Particularly in med mal, if you can get a good judge they are in a unique position of identifying value. A trial judge sitting in Queens County or the Bronx knows what the value is. They tell you what the settlements and verdicts have been. [Interviewer: Do you trust that information?] It's trust as to whether they could get more money. Typically I do trust the trial judge. They always remember; they never forget. And remember, they trust you, too, if you've been around for a while.
- I remember a judge telling me that in auto cases the plaintiff did not win a single case in his court. I asked, "For how long?" He said, "For the whole year." You can believe that case settled.
- When insurance companies value cases, it doesn't take into consideration an individual trial attorney's skills. A judge who is familiar with the plaintiff's attorney can explain this to them.
- In the old days we got a lot of mediations from the judges who would try the cases. That can have a hell of an effect. We certainly had several cases we settled where the judge basically tried the case right there and told you what would happen. Those early mediations got a lot of cases settled.

Other attorneys related difficulties they had encountered with judges' evaluations and their conduct in settlement conferences:

- When you go to settlement conferences, some judges play a significant role. One judge for example says in front of everyone what a jury in that county will do. He says, "Don't ask for pain and suffering and cut off chiropractic after three months." He'll also tell defendants that they're offering too much. It's horrible because what do I tell my client – the judge doesn't know what he's talking about?
- Never take a judge's evaluation of your case if you believe in your case. I've come across the craziest judges. Do not lose the faith. Don't lose your confidence. Don't let the judge or the mediator give you a value. Don't take a third party's value. You have lived with the case, lived with the client. You know the strengths and weaknesses.
- You can't be intimidated by the judge if you are sure he's not doing the right thing. In one case the judge conducted a settlement conference shortly before trial. When it looked like the case would not settle, the judge said he would consider a motion to dismiss if filed by the defendant. I told the judge, "This is not right. You asked us to participate in a settlement conference to see if the case could be settled. Now that we've openly discussed our cases, you're using that information to encourage the other side to file a motion to dismiss the

case." The judge said, "What do you want me to do?" I said, "Assign us to a trial department with a judge who is not you." The judge agreed.

- I start getting to a point where I worry I might be sued for malpractice or get a complaint with the bar association because I thought my client would do better than the defendant offered and then I go to trial and don't do any better. I know costs [physicians' expert witness fees] will be at least $1,000 if I go to trial and there's just a tremendous amount of pressure on the defense side to pay less and hope on the plaintiff's side you'll get more. So you hope the other side has made a mistake and the jury will award more than what the settlement conference judge says.

13.2.3   Admission of Evidence and Interpretation of the Law

One of the largest variables in predicting case outcomes is the trial judge. Although judges are determined to act impartially and follow the law, empirical studies indicate they are subject to the same decision-making biases that afflict the general population. In their study of judges' decision-making processes, based on questionnaires answered by 252 circuit court judges, law professor (and current dean) Chris Guthrie and his colleagues conclude:

> We believe that most judges attempt to reach their decisions utilizing facts, evidence, and highly constrained legal criteria, while putting aside personal biases, attitudes, emotions, and other individuating factors. Despite their best efforts, however, judges, like everyone else, have two cognitive systems for making judgments – the intuitive and the deliberative – and the intuitive system appears to have a powerful effect on judges' decision making. The intuitive approach might work well in some cases, but it can lead to erroneous and unjust outcomes in others.[14]

Defining "intuitive" processes as spontaneous, emotional, effortless and fast and "deliberative" processes as rule-governed, controlled, effortful and slow, Guthrie finds that "judges tended to favor intuitive rather than deliberative faculties."[15]

The study attorneys note that the wide discretion judges exercise in ruling on evidentiary issues and interpreting the law is a major factor in evaluating cases:

- Most of us can predict whether the jury will like the facts or not like the facts, like the witnesses or not like the witnesses, get angry or not get angry. The intangible factor is how the judge will interact with the attorney and the evidence, what they'll let in or exclude. That kind of interaction can have an impact.

---

[14]Guthrie, Chris, Rachlinski , Jeffrey J. & Wistrich, Andrew J. (2007). Blinking on the bench: How judges decide cases. *Cornell Law Review, 93*(1), 43. See Guthrie, Chris, Rachlinski, Jeffrey J., & Wistrich, Andrew J. (2001, May). Inside the judicial mind. *Cornell Law Review, 86*(4), 777–830.

[15]Guthrie, Rachlinski & Wistrich (2007) *supra* note 14 at 17.

- There are so many wild cards. A lot depends on the judge. Some judges are dumber than me, and that is hard to believe. Judges are not the end-all and be-all of legal issues.
- If a case goes sideways, it's usually because of testimony. Another reason is an interpretation of law. A jurist deciding the case may not like the result – you cannot always predict how a judge will interpret.
- One judge said, "Oh, this is just a soft tissue case." I said, "Judge, almost every case is a soft tissue case. That's what we're made of." I never lost a threshold issue. All of these words – "serious injury," "significant limitation" – are really subjective. You have to know how to persuade the judge.
- Ninety-nine percent of law is clear and easy. The judge's discretion in the admission of evidence is huge. It's a large part of that 1%. Attorneys need to appreciate the important role of discretionary rulings on evidence.

When asked to recall cases that turned out differently than he had expected and the reason for those unexpected trial results, a defense attorney commented, "In most of them I had some problem with the judge in a jury trial – hard to get evidence in, but I still got it in. In cases I had trouble with, I also had trouble with the judge."

13.2.4   Judges' Settlement and Civil Trial Experience

The increasing popularity of mediation, in tandem with reductions in court budgets, may have the unintended effect of accelerating judges' retirements and reducing the number of judges with civil settlement and trial experience. Study attorneys thought that judges with a reputation for resolving civil cases had few incentives to remain on the bench and that many had already retired to serve as neutrals for private alternative dispute resolution companies:

- In Southern California, the Tier 1 judges are retiring. The older judges are saying, "I don't need this anymore." They have heavier caseloads and the courts are closed one day every month. There's a lot of burnout on the bench. A lot of very good judges have left the bench.
- The state of judges is appalling. ADR has sucked all the good judges out. This problem with bad judges started during the last seven years when ADR really took off. The good judges on the bench are thinking, "I could be making $400 per hour, working less and not have to listen to all this shit." So they leave and join an ADR company. The ones that are really good at working with attorneys leave the bench; they know they'll have to be selected and can't rely on getting cases like they do in the courtroom.
- About one-half of the judges are qualified, in my opinion. My two biggest disappointments with the system are, one, the quality of the judiciary, and, two, how easy it is to get an expert to say anything you want. It will get worse.
- Judges are jumping ship and going to private mediation firms.

- My expectation of judges has been significantly undermined. I no longer anticipate what a judge will do – even if it's black and white. Many judges have
no experience in civil trials. Many of the good judges are off the bench. I don't
know if that's due to retirement or resigning to become a mediator.

"There are fewer experienced judges now," comments a plaintiffs' medical malpractice attorney. "Mediation has stolen away many of the better judges."

If effective settlement judges continue to resign or retire from public service,
private mediation will be the proverbial self-licking ice cream cone. As dispute
resolution skills become increasingly portable and monetized, judges will continue
to leave the bench once their reputation as an effective case resolver has reached the
threshold necessary for commercial success. Parties and their attorneys, in turn, will
feel compelled to retain private mediators because the remaining judges will not
possess subject matter expertise or settlement skills comparable to private mediators.
The public courts, like many public schools, may become second-choice alternatives
for ordinary citizens, selected because of their lower cost rather than their perceived
advantages.

Chapter 14
Insurance

Insurance may be seen as the lubricant of the litigation engine, but in many cases it is the engine itself. The conventional issues upon which legal analysis is grounded – liability and damages – quickly become irrelevant when the defendant is uninsured, illiquid or otherwise judgment proof. Insurance not only facilitates payment of meritorious claims but also in many cases is the only practical source of recovery. Although the law nobly declares that "there is no right without a remedy," it has little to offer a claimant with the more prosaic problem of a good case without an insured defendant.[1]

In his insightful article, "Liability Insurance as Tort Regulation: Six Ways That Liability Insurance Shapes Tort Law in Action," University of Pennsylvania law professor Tom Baker argues that liability insurers play a major role in developing beliefs and norms about litigation and that "those beliefs and norms constitute the *real* tort law for far more people than does the tort law on the books."[2] Liability insurance impacts "tort law in action" in at least six ways, he explains:

> First, for claims against all but the wealthiest individuals and organizations, liability insurance is a de facto element of tort liability. Second, liability insurance limits are a de facto cap on tort damages. Third, tort claims are shaped to match the available liability insurance, with the result that liability insurance policy exclusions become de facto limits on tort liability. Fourth, liability insurance makes lawsuits against ordinary individuals and small organizations into "repeat player" lawsuits on the defense side, making tort law in action less focused on the fault of individual defendants and more focused on managing aggregate costs. Fifth, liability insurance personnel transform complex tort rules into simple "rules of thumb," also with the result that tort law in action is less concerned with the fault of individual defendants than tort law on the books. Sixth, negotiations over the

---

[1] *Ubi jus ibi remedium* ("there is no right without a remedy" or "there is no wrong without a remedy"). See California Civil Code Section 3523 ("For every wrong there is a remedy").

[2] Baker, Tom. (2005). Liability insurance as tort regulation: Six ways that liability insurance shapes tort law in action. *Connecticut Insurance Law Journal, 12*(1), 10. Available at SSRN: http://ssrn.com/abstract=911565.

R. Kiser, *How Leading Lawyers Think*,
DOI 10.1007/978-3-642-20484-5_14, © Springer-Verlag Berlin Heidelberg 2011

boundaries of liability insurance coverage (which appears nowhere in tort law on the books) drive tort law in action.[3]

Liability insurance thus acts as a gatekeeper in determining which tort claims will be paid. In many instances, the existence and extent of insurance and the insurer's claim management practices will be more determinative of a case outcome than a legislative enactment.

Because insurance has an enormous effect on which claims are paid and how much is paid, this chapter focuses on the study attorneys' perceptions and opinions of insurers and their claims management practices. These perceptions and opinions relate to five topics: (1) insurers' case monitoring and management; (2) consideration of defense counsel's analysis and recommendations; (3) insurers' trust and confidence in defense counsel; (4) insurers' case evaluations and settlement authority; and (5) software programs used to evaluate cases.

14.1   Case Monitoring and Management

Many study attorneys believe that insurers have become more active in case monitoring and management and attempt to assert a greater degree of control over defense counsel:

- Things have changed a lot with insurance companies and their attorneys. [Defense] attorneys are more and more put out of the loop. The climate has changed as far as who is driving the bus. The carriers tell their attorneys what a case is worth.
- Ninety-five percent of the insurance companies have taken the cases over. The attorneys are puppets. They're manhandled by the insurance companies. The attorney's role on the defense side is to do the usual stuff, take depositions, get records, send interrogatories. They used to make recommendations and the insurance companies generally paid attention to them. Now their role is limited. They're very frustrated, extremely frustrated. It's almost like being castrated. These guys have some serious egos – you don't stay in this business unless you have a strong ego – and it's hard on them. [Interviewer: When did you start noticing this change?] I'd say it's been 10 years and becoming more so all the time.
- I'm finding that insurance companies seem to be involving themselves in cases more than they used to. They are insinuating themselves more than they did in the past. Now the real tough sell is to the insurance company. Before, insurance companies kind of understood it was just their job to pay the bills. Now the insurer gets into strategy issues and who the mediator should be. The most heated discussions and debates I have now are with the adjuster. The insurance

---

[3]*Id.* at 3–4.

companies insinuate themselves into the substance of cases, and the client's general counsel also is more involved than they used to be. This may be a reflection of the economy. There's just less money now than there used to be.

- The biggest thing I see is in the economic factors. They are on us constantly on how much time we're spending, requiring us to justify what we're going to do. The expenses, especially experts, have gotten more expensive over time, and the carriers are trying very hard to control and keep the costs down. Yes, it is different – a lot more pressure on attorneys to save money and fees and expenses.
- The insurance companies want to tell you exactly what you can and cannot do on a case and how much the case should cost. They go by rote. Have you see any Coen Brothers movies? Well, in those movies nobody knows what the shit they're doing. If you get a good claims person, the case goes very well, but if someone with an attitude, a moral outrage, is handling the case, it's almost impossible.

A defense attorney made an important distinction between case management and strategy issues when asked whether the carriers had become more involved in cases: "No, I don't think they're more involved in strategy issues. I think it's more case management and monitoring. Once you're in trial they so much want you to succeed, they don't get in the way."

14.2   Consideration of Defense Counsel's Analysis and Recommendations

Apart from case management issues, some study attorneys thought that the role of insurance defense counsel has fundamentally changed and that insurers do not elicit – and sometimes ignore – counsel's evaluation and recommendations:

- There's a complete switch. The defense counsel used to be someone they took advice from. It would settle if the attorney told you that's what the carrier should do. Now most carriers don't even want to know what their attorneys think. They may ask but they really don't care. Defense attorneys apologize to me and just say, "Sorry, I'm out of the loop."
- For defendant lawyers, I don't know if it's the defense attorney or the insurer. When I started, the insurers listened to us and almost always gave us the authority to settle at our recommendation. But this has all changed. My friends on the defense side say, "They don't listen to us at all."
- When there's insurance, attorneys don't call the shots, it's the adjusters. For years they have compiled data to calculate the value for jury purposes. Attorneys who handle these types of cases have no authority to settle and only make recommendations. They just say there is this probability of this kind of verdict and the adjuster makes the opinion. The adjuster says this is what we pay for this

type of injury. My impression is that they want to settle for as little as possible so there's a lot of hyperbole, a lot of exaggeration that occurs that shouldn't.

- My evaluation may not matter that much. I may think that a case would be dismissed on summary judgment, but we would have to take the plaintiff's depo first. Sometimes the client and its carrier don't want to go through all that. They just want out, so the case may settle for more than I think it's worth.

When asked about an attorney's role in the client's decision to settle or try a case, a defense attorney noted that some insurers act independently: "Some companies don't want your opinion. They tell you, 'Don't give me your independent judgment.'"

Other study attorneys believe that insurers remain attentive and deferential to their case assessments and recommendations, despite the fact that they often authorize amounts lower than the attorney's recommendation:

- I tell the insurance company what I think it should do. I think the client respects my opinion, but it's not unusual for me to say, "I think this case is worth $250,000," and they say, "I'll give you authority to settle for $200,000."
- They're giving a file to you, and as long as you're presenting your opinion and it's not completely unjustified, they listen and respect what you think. I would say they are very deferential to us. For the most part, what we say is what we'll do.
- We gather all the information. We take the depos; we see how the parties and witnesses testify. Most [claims representatives] listen with a degree of respect to our opinions about the subjective appearance of the plaintiff. They always ask us how our client did.

Whether the insurer relies on defense counsel's evaluation or its own internal assessment, they "have a philosophy about how they will litigate cases," observes a study attorney. "They have the idea that the attorney will win the case or fall on his sword if they fail." The lawyers who maintain an ongoing relationship with insurers, he says, know "they expect lawyers to take the fall. The claims representative knows what happened, but they remember and know the attorney protected my back."

14.3 Insurers' Trust and Confidence in Defense Counsel

To the extent insurers are exercising more control over case management and strategy and relying on their own evaluations, this change may reflect a degree of distrust between insurers and defense counsel, according to one defense attorney:

> You have to understand what's changed in this business. For most of my career the insurance companies saw the plaintiffs' attorneys as the bad guys. The insurers and the defense bar were united against the same enemy; we were all going after the same dirt bags. Then everything changed with the insurance companies. They went from thinking all

plaintiffs' attorneys were the bad guys to thinking *all* attorneys were the bad guys. Some are
very difficult to work with. My work is almost all defense, but I refuse to work for [lists
three major insurance companies].

An insurer's distrust may be evident in its disregard of an attorney's recommendation or its constant scrutiny of attorneys' time and statements. This sense of distrust
can lead to adverse outcomes and demotivated counsel. One of the most common
causes of case misevaluation, states an attorney with extensive experience as a
mediator, is "a claims adjuster who fails to listen to a seasoned defense lawyer. The
lawyers have seen the witnesses; the adjuster has not." Another attorney notes that
technology enables insurers to monitor attorneys' billing daily: "One of my friends
got a call the day after he billed 10.2 hours. That was questioned because it doesn't
fit into a 9-to-5 day mentality. That's frustrating, it's angering."

The reason insurers rely on their own evaluations, opines a former defense
attorney, is that they have "gotten wise" to the defense bar:

> When defense attorneys say they can't get the carrier to go with their recommendation, for
> the most part that's a cop-out for the defense attorneys. Here's where the system works
> against the defense bar. They say, "I'm being usurped by the insurance company." But
> what's going on is the insurance companies are responding to the way attorneys evaluate
> cases. They've gotten wise to it. The attorney has to write an extensive pre-trial report. In
> this you have to make a valuation. From time immemorial, that's the CYA. Invariably they
> will evaluate the case higher than they expect. In a way you have to do that because in every
> case that goes bad, the shit goes downstream. Everyone is pointing fingers. Your estimate
> gives you the leeway to say it's within a range.

When asked whether there is an upward or downward bias in providing evaluations
to insurers, another attorney responded, "There is a tendency by all of us to tell the
client a higher number if there is exposure, so that the client is prepared. If the case
comes in under the number, the client is satisfied but you've also prepared them for
the downside." A different defense attorney noted that his approach depends on his
relationship with the insurer: "If it's a long-term relationship, I underestimate
because it's easy to move up. You already have credibility with the carrier." But
when he's representing a new client, "You take a higher number because it's going
to be easier to come down from a high number than going up." With respect to
preparing a litigation budget for insurers, a fourth attorney said, "I've learned to use
big numbers, to think of more of a worst-case approach because it's almost
impossible to estimate, and clients and insurance companies place too much
emphasis on it. But maybe it's for their own budgeting, so it's better for them to
be prepared."

14.4   Case Evaluations and Settlement Authority

The study attorneys expressed mixed opinions about the validity of insurers' case
evaluations. Not surprisingly, plaintiffs' attorneys tended to be more critical of both
the ultimate offers and the processes that generated those offers:

- Their approach is the same on every case – for example, if the property damage is less than $1,000, they say they won't pay for anything else. They say you have to have a tangible loss to recover other expenses – "no crash, no cash" and "no ding, no ring." They have lots of these silly expressions.
- What's happening now is going way back. The posture now is institutionalized. Defense attorneys tell me, "We're just being told to try every case." Only the large cases get a thorough review. The other cases are take-it-or-leave-it, usually lowball offers.
- The problem is each case is different, but they treat all of them the same. Insurance companies have done a tremendously good job of intimidating clients. This leaves [plaintiffs'] attorneys with very little leverage. The chance of getting a big verdict has changed a lot during the last 20 years. Insurance companies did not tighten up until they started collecting the data. There used to be rules of thumb like three times specials [medical expenses], but not any more. Now you're lucky to get two times. I've seen a dramatic change in the tightness of insurance companies to pay settlements.
- What comes to mind is cases that have a lot of upside, and the problem is that they were not handled correctly before and the insurance company has not evaluated it correctly. The cases have not ripened up to their potential. The insurance company is way behind. The client has had surgery, and they're thinking that surgery was just future meds. My pleasure in a case like that is opening up the policy.
- Defense attorneys are deprived of discretion to handle the negotiations in the way they think they should go. It happens more now than it did before. The attorneys and the mediator all agree on the case but the defense attorneys still have to go through the steps the [insurance] company wants followed. Sometimes what they do makes no sense.

A defense attorney noted that, even when claims representatives have a good relationship with a mediator, they occasionally take intractable settlement positions: "But even with mediators they respect, the claims people stick to their positions sometimes. It's like trying to lever a big rock into the ocean with a toothpick."

Study attorneys felt that some adjusters' inexperience, intransigence and hostility impeded settlement negotiations and delayed case resolution:

- [I]nsurance companies come in [to mediation] and say, "This is the number and we don't have authority for any other figure." A major problem now is adjusters who have no knowledge, no experience. They have short-term experience and are only interested in saving money in the short term.
- In another case, I never met the adjuster until she showed up at trial. The first thing she does is give my client the finger [gesturing]. After the trial they paid $100,000 more than what they could have settled for.
- These cases can be very agenda oriented, and the probability of misevaluation goes way up. ... The ones with agendas are young, inexperienced. Many are lawyers who found the practice of law to be stressful, not remunerative enough.

They tend to be better educated, are well informed. They have a large caseload. They are interested in the cases in the middle of the bell curve. [Interviewer: What is the agenda you're referring to?] Anger at the plaintiff or the plaintiff's lawyer. A plaintiffs' lawyer may have won a big case against them or been abusive. ... Adjusters with an agenda think plaintiff lawyers are greedy, opportunistic, and they want a free lunch.

An insurer's misevaluation and arrogance "creates an opportunity," claims a plaintiffs' attorney. "When the cases are not evaluated correctly or are not reviewed by the right people, the offers can be so low that the client has to go to trial." Another plaintiffs' attorney comments, "You can make good money taking advantage of how insurance companies are run these days. Sometimes you can hit it big."

In looking at how insurers now evaluate cases, defense counsel point to major changes in the insurance industry, large increases in adjusters' caseloads and potential biases in reporting and evaluation:

- People used to stay with the same insurance company for a long time and had a lifetime career. There's tremendous turnover now – they overwork them. An adjuster has 180 cases instead of 60. Their jobs are on the line, and they don't have a clue about what's going on. We send them regular reports, but they don't have time to read or don't remember. I just got an email from one asking whether a trial is still set for April. There's no trial in April.
- They're under tremendous pressure. It's a dramatic change. Groups of MBAs come in and change the company. They reduce payments and bring cases in-house.
- There's a whole syndrome with insurers because of the structure. There's the adjuster, the supervisor, and the branch manager. The defense firm gets all the cases from the same insurer, and the defense lawyer has to be providing them with objective advice. But reporting [sometimes] takes on a personality consistent with what the adjuster expects. You can't be sure the supervisor is getting the complete picture. With some insurance companies there's a complete disconnect.
- On the defense side, the issue is whether they have the time to make an accurate evaluation. Their view is more jaundiced by costs.
- I've seen different adjusters in the same company do different things – it's whimsy, night and day.

The attorneys also explain that claims management is affected by cyclical trends in "balancing between payouts and costs of defense." A defense attorney describes this process: "For the last three years payouts have gone up, so the cycle will turn to spending more money on defense. After a few years, they'll look at how much they're spending on defense costs and start pushing early evaluation and settling cases before they're in litigation or settling them earlier if they're in litigation."

14.5   Software Programs Used to Evaluate Cases

One of the most prevalent criticisms of insurers is their reliance on software programs to evaluate cases:

- A common thread with defense lawyers is they don't, they're not evaluating
  cases like we used to. Their hands are tied. This is attributable to software
  programs like Colossus. The offers we get make no sense. The defense lawyer
  is saddled with that.
- Before we had Atlas and Colossus we evaluated cases very closely. We did not
  take the risks they do today. When you thought a case should be settled, you
  would just beat the claims manager to a pulp until they wrote a check [to avoid a
  bad faith claim]. Anybody who will mess with a case with a $100,000 policy and
  a million in medicals, you don't belong in the business.
- The mistakes they make are driven by computer programs. I had another
  case where there was a $750,000 offer, but the jury verdict was [in excess of
  $4,000,000].
- The insurance companies use software programs that have even changed the
  plaintiff's treatment. Client used to go to chiropractors. But those bills aren't
  worth much in the software programs. You need an orthopedist to refer a
  client to physical therapy. They have neutralized the chiropractor cases down
  to nothing.
- The insurance companies use computers to tell them what the case is worth and
  how much they'll pay. This makes a delicate balance between your obligations
  to the [insured] client and the demands of the insurance company.

Noting that statistical assessments overlook factors important to jurors, a plaintiffs'
attorney remarks, "I don't think the statistical analysis can take into consideration
the hooks that persuade jurors. It's a mistake overweighting this kind of analysis."

Chapter 15
Negotiation

Settlement is the predominant method of resolving civil cases, and the percentage of cases tried to verdict has steadily declined from nearly 20% in 1938 to about 2% today.[1] Although attorneys and mediators often assert that 95% of cases are settled, that conclusion is derived from the estimated 5% of cases that are resolved by bench or jury trials and overlooks the substantial percentage of cases that are disposed of by summary judgment, remand, motions to dismiss, default judgment, voluntary dismissal and orders following a failure to serve, prosecute or comply with procedural rules. A finer grain analysis shows actual settlement rates ranging from 58% to 72%.[2] These settlement rates are significantly affected by case type. One study indicates that the aggregate settlement rate is 82% in tort cases, 68% in contract cases and 67% in employment discrimination cases. That study also shows that, in every circuit, "the settlement rate was lower in employment cases than in the other two case categories [contract and personal injury tort cases]."[3] Regardless of case type, the data demonstrates that "settlement rather than trial has emerged as the dominant endgame of civil litigation."[4]

Reflecting the importance of settlement negotiations and the reality that most cases are resolved without trials, this chapter looks at the study attorneys' settlement strategies, tactics, results and attitudes. This chapter first discusses the close relationship between negotiation and case evaluation skills and shows how the study attorneys determine settlement values and negotiate settlements of their cases. The attorneys then describe the most significant obstacle to resolving cases – excessive plaintiff demands and lowball defendant offers. Lastly, the study attorneys reflect on

---

[1]Nagareda, Richard A. (2010, March 10). 1938 all over again? Pre-trial as trial in complex litigation. Vanderbilt Public Law Research Paper No. 10–12; *DePaul Law Review*, *60*, (forthcoming 2011). Available at http://papers.ssrn.com/sol3/papers.cfm?abstract_id=1568127.

[2]Eisenberg, Theodore, & Lanvers, Charlotte. (2009, March). What is the settlement rate and why should we care? *Journal of Empirical Legal Studies*, *6*(1), 115, 132.

[3]*Id*. at 140.

[4]Nagareda *supra* note 1 at 1.

R. Kiser, *How Leading Lawyers Think*,
DOI 10.1007/978-3-642-20484-5_15, © Springer-Verlag Berlin Heidelberg 2011

the frequency with which defendants pay plaintiffs more than they would have accepted and plaintiffs accept less than defendants were willing to pay.

15.1 Settlement Negotiations and Case Evaluation

This chapter follows the chapters regarding case evaluation, client interviewing and counseling, adversaries, judges and insurers because these factors are interdependent. Unfortunately, negotiation is often taught as a distinct subject, leading some law students and attorneys to conceive of negotiation skills as a set of goals, strategies, tactics and maneuvers that can be superimposed over any civil case. In fact, teaching negotiation skills independent of case evaluation skills and the intricate legal context often leads to impasse when valuations, arguments, positions, bluffs, bottom lines and assessments of best and worst alternatives to a negotiated agreement (BATNAs and WATNAs) bear no relation to litigation reality. Even the most adept negotiator flounders when he cannot distinguish between a marginal case with a 20% probability of recovering $200,000 and a strong case with a 75% chance of netting $2,000,000 after costs. At the core of many impasses in litigation negotiations is a smart, well-trained advocate who bypassed case evaluation and sincerely believes he is selling BMWs instead of VWs.

Jeffrey Krivis, a well-respected mediator and author, explains how case evaluation errors impair case resolution at the outset and prolong, disrupt and sometimes sabotage settlement negotiations:

> The negotiation of a products case begins the moment you put a price tag on its value. ... The price tag will be your compass for how you invest in the case, and often becomes an unrealistic goal of what you should achieve on the case. This is where trial lawyers create their first obstacle to settlement. The value you place on the case and the ultimate settlement number are often very different, and the reason for that difference will usually unfold as the evidence in the case develops. This "ideal" value is tantamount to having a best-case scenario driving your every move. ... It is impossible to reach, generally exists only in your mind and becomes a mental construct for the ultimate negotiation in the case. When you as a trial lawyer send a signal to the other side that you are looking out at the horizon on this case, the settlement result is often failure, frustration, disappointment, predictability, depression and impasse. Before you have even come to the negotiating table you might have developed a huge "gap" between what is a fair and actual result and the ideal outcome that has been delivered in your messages to the other side.
>
> When the defendants see the plaintiffs as trying to achieve their ideal result, they have no choice but to commit substantial resources toward defending the case in order to prove you cannot achieve your ideal. A negative cycle begins to occur as you continue to invest resources to justify your decision to seek your ideal outcome and the costs of failure rise. You can't change strategies at that point because it would be a sign of weakness. Both sides are now involved in a cycle of taking irrational risks by investing more financial resources into a case in which risk could have been managed far better.[5]

---

[5]Krivis, Jeffrey. (2010). The mind of the advocate in a product liability mediation. Available at http://www.mediate.com/articles/krivis25.cfm.

"That is not to say that putting a value on the case is not a good idea," Krivis adds. "The key is to do it in a way that sends clear messages to the other side that an ideal value will not trump a realistic or fair outcome."

The study attorneys express similar concerns that unrealistic case evaluations can impair, disrupt and terminate settlement negotiations. When asked about common errors that attorneys make in settlement negotiations, some attorneys point out that the most common mistakes occur because of poor case evaluation skills, not deficient negotiation skills. In some instances, inaccurate case evaluation – unduly optimistic *or* pessimistic assessments – may be compounded by arrogance, rudeness and immaturity in pre-filing communications with the insurer, as a study attorney explains:

> I'd have to look at this from my work as a mediator. It's not a negotiation thing; it's a misevaluation thing. On the plaintiff side, if the attorney had been a better evaluator, maybe 40 to 50 percent of the time they could have gotten a better settlement. I see it a lot on the plaintiff side. If it's on the defense side, there may be an underlying reason that I won't know about. Maybe the plaintiff's attorney pissed off the claims adjuster. [Interviewer: Is this irrational?] It's very rational. They want to teach that attorney a lesson he'll remember. That's why I tell law students, "Do not motivate the other side. If you get disrespect, return it with respect; if you get incivility, respond with civility." If you've messed up and the claims adjuster assigned to your case is told to take it to trial, you cannot settle that case.

Another study attorney who also serves as a mediator notes that attorneys negotiate settlements without a full understanding of their own case. Reflecting on the insights he has gained as a mediator, he says, "You'd be surprised how easily you can learn about negotiations and what people have overlooked in their own cases."

15.2 Settlement Valuation

A threshold issue in understanding settlement negotiations is the difference between settlement value and trial value. By its very nature, a settlement value reflects a compromise and the financial advantage derived from saving attorneys fees and reducing risk at trial and on appeal. When asked whether there is a difference between trial value and settlement value, the attorneys responded:

- Yes, for plaintiffs settlement value is less than trial value. On the defense side, it's more than what you think would happen at trial.
- Trial value is not your absolute best day in trial but a decent award in your favor. Settlement value reflects the certainty of getting the case resolved, avoiding the emotional distress and the cost of trial. Once clients understand the economics they can make decisions quickly. Once you have to bring in medical experts, it's very difficult to net at trial more than you can get through settlement.
- I'm not settling a case based on what the jury is going to do. It's a rough calculation, but settlements do not necessarily reflect what a jury will do. The more the variables in a case, the greater the risk on both sides. That's what the

settlement number is about. So when the number of variables is smaller, like when liability is stipulated and the issue is damages, then the settlement number is closer to what I think a jury will do.

Because settlement value may be less than trial value and strong claims may never realize their full potential without a trial, some plaintiffs' attorneys were ambivalent, even wistful, about settlement:

- This is a problem all attorneys face. You never make the real money unless you go to trial. You never hit the home run at settlement. It's a bittersweet experience.
- The toughest offer is one too close to walk away from. It's not trial value, but it's enough to want to avoid the risk of trial.
- I only make money on the cases they make me try.
- Settlement is about taking less than the home run. A lot of singles and a few doubles will produce more runs than a home run, and for cash flow purposes it makes it a lot easier.

Despite these reservations, the study attorneys generally express a positive attitude toward settlement. "I'm a firm believer if you have two reasonable attorneys, you can resolve it short of litigation," comments a commercial litigation attorney. A medical malpractice defense attorney echoed that sentiment: "It is generally inefficient to litigate. Parties should settle, especially when both sides are on the meter."

15.3   Timing

Timing and the complementary traits of patience, perseverance, prescience and a good poker face are critical factors in settlement negotiations. Plaintiffs' attorneys stressed the importance of avoiding early settlements, and defendants emphasized the importance of adequate discovery:

- It's a very delicate balance between settling too early and having a good enough handle on your case. But this isn't brain surgery.
- Ted Williams [Baseball Hall of Fame member known as "The Thumper"] loved to stand way back in the batter box. The longer you have to evaluate, the better the chance you have of seeing where the ball is going to go. Never make your best bid first. The longer you wait, usually the better the deal you'll get. You don't get any serious discussions unless you're there and a judge or jury is ready to go. Stand in the back of the batter box.
- A lot of people like to settle too early. You'll never get your best offer early in the case. The longer you hang in there, usually the better, but I have hung in there too long sometimes. You have to have a poker face when this is happening.
- I know from being in the defense business you have to be willing to say "No" and let time pass. The insurance companies know that they can settle some cases

for very low amounts, and they always have to start low for that reason. If a case is worth $400,000, just using that as an example, and the offer is $100,000, it's distasteful to you, but if the client is risk averse, they may not want to take it to trial. They may not want to take it any further.

- The last 90 days are when the serious things happen – especially within the last 30 days. In many cases insurance companies want to wait until the expert opinions are in. Those reports don't come in until the case is fairly close to trial.
- It has become a process, and process is what is important to the carriers. So you have to go through the dance and just tell them, "No." It could be the second, third, fourth or fifth time before you settle the case in mediation.

The key to successful negotiation is "keeping them at the table," asserts a plaintiffs' attorney. "What they say is less important than what they're doing. If they are still there and not disrespecting you, you are still in negotiations, whether you know it or not."

15.4 Willingness to Try the Case

In his book, *Nine Principles of Litigation and Life*, Michael Tigar, the renowned trial attorney and law professor, urges attorneys to have the courage to say, "let's go to trial." The best settlements, he believes, occur when "parties are ready to try their cases effectively, and show that they are not afraid to do so."[6] The decision to decline a settlement offer, however, "is not based on bravado, or ego. It is a practical decision about evidence, juror sentiment, and the power of a story."[7] Tigar's conviction that defendants make their best offers to attorneys who have a reputation for trying cases is reiterated by a few study attorneys:

- The system is set up to settle the case for the lowest amount they can. Many plaintiff lawyers are more concerned about getting a payday than a good settlement for the client. The insurance companies feed on that. If a defendant is confronted with a plaintiff who is willing to take it to the mat, the whole system is turned around. This causes grave concerns on the defense side. Despite the bravado, everyone is concerned about their job; they don't want to get clobbered. The fear of the plaintiff taking the case to trial is that you will not have a chance to settle this case once it starts. If you have managed the perception, they double their number.
- [T]hey knew I'd take anything to trial. I fight not just when cornered but when aroused – and sometimes just for the hell of it. You drive the other side crazy.

---

[6]Tigar, Michael. (2009). *Nine principles of litigation and life* (p. 54). Chicago: American Bar Association.

[7]*Id.* at 49.

- I start with a very conservative figure and move up from there. I'd like to think it gives me more credibility. I've handled over 500 cases against [health care provider]. The awards have never been lower than my demands. I tell them in advance, "This is what I'm going to do. It's worth $3 million. I'll 998 [refers to a statutory offer of compromise under California Code of Civil Procedure Section 998] you at $2.5 million. If you don't want to make the savings, it's totally up to you." I know it's more typical to come down, but that's not the way I do it. I'm a conservative lawyer. The advantage I get from this is I carry some weight. I try not to drink the Kool-Aid.
- In one case, the adjuster tried to play games with me – [mimicking adjuster] "your expert was terrible." The case went to trial, and we got what I expected. If you burn someone once or twice, they do not want it to happen again.

The belief that "you cannot settle a case that you are not prepared to try" applies with equal weight to plaintiffs and defendants. In asserting that lawyers need the "let's go to trial" courage, Tigar notes that the pharmaceutical company Merck & Co. negotiated a favorable settlement of the Vioxx claims because its general counsel (now chief executive officer), Ken Frazier, was willing to take the cases to trial. After a few cases were litigated to verdict, Merck had "a meaningful market for the value of Vioxx-related claims."[8] The trials – which resulted in mixed verdicts – "illuminated the key issues better than any settlement negotiations ever could."[9]

15.5 Reputation and Repeat Player Effects

Negotiation behavior is altered by "repeat player" effects. Negotiators' communications, positions and moves are affected not only by the frequency of transactions and the resultant bargaining patterns observed by repeat negotiators but also by the reputations that are established during serial negotiations.[10] Multiple negotiations with the same parties tend to be characterized by more cooperative than competitive styles. Single-shot negotiations, in contrast, are associated with low levels of trust, short-term objectives and instrumental rather than affiliative values. Although the aphorism holds that "familiarity breeds contempt," at least among serial negotiators

---

[8]*Id.* at 54.

[9]*Id.* at 54.

[10]See Emmelman, Debra S. (1996). Trial by plea bargain: Case settlement as a product of recursive decisionmaking. *Law & Society Review, 30*(2), 335–360. Peppet, Scott R. (2005). Lawyers' bargaining ethics, contract, and collaboration: The end of the legal profession and the beginning of professional pluralism. *Iowa Law Review, 90,* 475–538. Tinsley, Catherine H., *et al.* (2008). Reputations in negotiation. In Schneider, Andrea K., & Honeyman, Christopher (Eds.). *The negotiator's fieldbook: The desk reference for the experienced negotiator.* Available at SSRN: http://ssrn.com/abstract=1169286.

it is more accurate to find that familiarity fosters respect, cooperation and relatively predictable offers and counter-offers.

Attorneys who have developed a reputation for cooperative problem solving "achieve better substantive results and increased peer respect" writes Jamison Davies in his award-winning article, "Formalizing Legal Reputation Markets."[11] A positive reputation "does not produce superior outcomes in and of itself," he notes. "Rather, a good reputation encourages parties to exchange information by limiting the fear of exploitation. Information transfer, in turn, enables problem-solving negotiation behaviors by each party: sharing interests, presenting alternatives, and discussing priorities honestly."

The study attorneys' insights into their own settlement negotiations indicate that a strong reputation bias and an "in-group/out-group" bias, based on repeated interactions and professional reputations established over decades, affect both the credibility of an adversary's case evaluation and the mode of negotiation. These biases are particularly strong in the medical malpractice field, sometimes affecting the extent of informal discovery and determining whether a claim will be accorded a tentative presumption of validity or invalidity.[12] Professional reputation also denotes whether plaintiff's counsel is adequately capitalized to represent the client through trial, an especially important qualification in medical malpractice cases due to the high costs of expert witnesses and other pre-trial expenses.

A sense of respect, familiarity, collegiality and acceptance characterize "in-group" attorneys:

- There's a small number of plaintiff attorneys I respect in this field. We belong to the same organizations, see each other at the same events. I know they know what they're doing. They will have been very selective in the cases they bring. When one of those attorneys is on the other side, I know it's going to be a dogfight. [Interviewer: What percent of plaintiff attorneys are in that category?] Probably twenty to twenty-five percent. They're high-class plaintiff attorneys who know what they're doing and select good cases. About fifty percent of the other plaintiff attorneys are fringe, bottom feeders, and the rest are young attorneys who don't know what they're doing, or they may be regular plaintiff attorneys who don't normally handle med mal cases.

---

[11]Davies, Jamison. Formalizing legal reputation markets. *Harvard Negotiation Law Review, 16* (forthcoming Spring 2011). Law professor Robert Condlin notes that "explicit" legal argumentation is "less prominent in negotiations between experienced lawyers who bargain with one another regularly (e.g., personal injury plaintiffs' lawyers and insurance company counsel, prosecutors and criminal defense lawyers.). Perhaps this is because personal familiarity and common experiences give lawyers shared views about what law is settled and what evidence counts as persuasive, and enable them to play out arguments privately in their heads so that they need discuss only novel or controversial points openly." Krieger, Stefan H., & Neumann, Richard K. (2007). *Essential lawyering skills* (p. 300). New York: Aspen Publishers.

[12]See Harris, Catherine T., *et al.* (2008). Does being a "repeat player" make a difference? The impact of attorney experience and "case picking" on the outcome of medical malpractice lawsuits. *Yale Journal of Health Policy, Law and Ethics, 8,* 253–282.

- The plaintiffs' bar has always been behind in investigating and ultimately disposing of cases. But the good ones will kill you. They get the information early on and build the case. They know you settle your dogs and try your good ones. They never over-evaluate. I used to watch one firm's pre-trial demand offers and the other side's offers. This one firm was always right. If they made a $250,000 demand, the verdict was $250,000. There was a big lesson to learn from that firm.
- The economic analysis is different for those who are familiar with the [medical malpractice] practice. They have a special screening process. The non-specialists end up back-loading expense. You can see this when you take the expert's deposition and find out he was recently retained. When I hear this I think, "Oh, one of those again." The specialized attorneys have built up a war chest over the years and can finance experts early in the case. This requires a little more layout up-front but saves you a lot of grief down the road.
- The really well-known attorneys get great settlements and verdicts, and those guys are very good at what they do. But you have to remember they get the great cases to begin with. They can pick the best ones. Part of their success is that the clients sell themselves.

The mutual respect displayed by "in-group" attorneys fosters more open communication between them and expedites case resolution. Information that escapes formal discovery processes but could be dispositive at trial – often missed because the deposition or interrogatory questions are not sufficiently precise or critical information is obtained later – may be exchanged informally to show why an adversary's evaluation is inaccurate or incomplete. These informal exchanges between well-regarded specialists also supply information otherwise missing or overlooked in expert reports and medical records. As a medical malpractice defense attorney notes, "I don't need a mediator if I'm working with the other eight people in this field who I respect."

15.6   Offers of Compromise

Statutory offers of judgment under Rule 68, Federal Rules of Civil Procedure, and offers of compromise under California Code of Civil Procedure Section 998 are cost-shifting mechanisms. They impose specified costs on parties that fail to achieve a better financial result at trial than the amount stated in the offer of judgment or compromise. For plaintiffs, the failure to obtain a verdict *higher* than the amount of a defendant's offer of compromise may render them liable for the defendant's court costs and expert witness fees from the date of the offer. Defendants who fail to obtain a verdict *lower* than the amount of plaintiff's offer of compromise under Section 998 may be liable for interest from the date of the offer of compromise, in addition to costs and expert witness fees. The ostensible purpose of these statutory cost-shifting mechanisms is to encourage settlement and penalize parties that take unreasonable positions in settlement negotiations.[13]

Despite the seemingly strong penalties imposed by Rule 68 and Section 998, the offers are used sparingly and produce mixed results, according to the study attorneys. A few attorneys who regularly use statutory offers comment on their efficacy:

- Everyone basically ignores 998s. There's not enough cost or value to alter my perception of the dynamics. In most cases I come in with a higher number after [I serve] a 998 demand. I always come in conservative with the lowest conservative number than I can beat. I'll raise the demand after the 998 expires. An attorney will call six months after a 998 demand expires and says he'll accept it. I tell him, "That's not on the table anymore. The number is higher now." That's why I call them before serving the first 998, so they won't be surprised.
- I use 998s a lot and keep it very low. It's not a number I especially like, but it's low enough that I think I can do better at trial. I notice that triggers the insurance company's radar and they have to assess the possible cost transfers that will happen. That's when they start looking at what the case is and stop listening to attorneys.
- That's one reason I serve a 998. If there's a 998, the plaintiff has to know they are not looking at "zero to infinity" but they could actually owe us money if they don't do better than the 998 offer.
- I keep them [insurance companies] in check in regards to evaluation by giving them a policy limit/time limits demand. I don't do it just once but sometimes twice before filing. Then I give them a third chance after filing with a 998 offer at policy limits.

A common problem with defendants' statutory offers, states a plaintiffs' attorney, is that the offers are not close enough to the anticipated trial result "to make us worried – they don't push us to the edge." The defense attorneys, he believes, suggest realistic figures that could force a settlement, but their clients prefer figures that are symbolic, conveying a message of confidence rather than increasing the likelihood of closure.

A more fundamental problem with the federal offer of judgment statute – "among the most enigmatic of the Federal Rules of Civil Procedure" – is that it apparently was never intended to encourage settlements.[14] Acknowledging the universal view that "Rule 68 was meant to encourage settlements by forcing

---

[13]See *Taing v. Johnson Scaffolding Co.*, 9 Cal. App. 4th 579, 583, 11 Cal. Rptr. 2d 820 (1992). *Taing* was distinguished in *Bihun v. AT&T Information Systems*, 13 Cal. App. 4th 976, 6 Cal. Rptr. 2d 787 (1993).

[14]Bone, Robert G., (2008). To encourage settlement: Rule 68, offers of judgment, and the history of the federal rules of civil procedure. *Northwestern University Law Review*, *102*, 1561. Boston University School of Law Working Paper No. 08–02. Available at SSRN: http://ssrn.com/abstract=1081423.

plaintiffs to think hard before rejecting an offer," Boston University School of Law professor Robert Bone asserts that this view is unsupported by the rule's history:

> What is puzzling is how a Rule with that purpose could possibly have been drafted the way Rule 68 was. The Rule operates only one-way (in favor of defendants); the penalty is too small to be meaningful; the requirement of a judgment (rather than just a settlement) discourages its use, and the Rule's timing requirements are puzzling. ... The solution is simple but surprising: the conventional view of Rule 68 is wrong. The original FRCP drafters did not adopt Rule 68 for the purpose of promoting settlement in the way we understand settlement promotion today. In fact, they did not give much thought at all to Rule 68's purpose, but simply adopted the offer of judgment rule that existed in the state codes. Those state rules were not designed to promote settlement as such. Their purpose was narrower: to prevent plaintiffs from imposing costs unfairly when the defendant offered what the plaintiff was entitled to receive from trial, and to enable defendants to avoid paying those costs when the plaintiff persisted with the suit. The text of Rule 68 makes much more sense when it is viewed in these fairness terms.

"The prevailing settlement promotion view became entrenched in the 1970s and 1980s," Bone sums up, "when concerns about litigation cost, case backlog, and litigation delay grew acute and interest in settling cases intensified."[15] Thus, the apparent ineffectiveness of Rule 68 and the state statutes from which it was derived stems from the fact they were not drafted to promote settlement; they do not achieve an objective beyond their original purpose.

Previous research also suggests that statutory offers of judgment or compromise – like sanctions and other cost-shifting rules – are counter-productive and may heighten risk-taking behavior.[16] Plaintiffs served with a 998 offer by defendants are more likely to experience adverse outcomes at trial, obtaining a trial award below the 998 offer, than plaintiffs who received non-statutory settlement offers. For defendants who receive and decline offers of compromise from plaintiffs, the incidence of settlement decision-making errors more than doubles. One hypothesis is that offers of compromise trigger "reactive devaluation" – the tendency to assume that any proposal from an adversary must be inferior and unacceptable because adversaries never make proposals beneficial to opponents. Esteemed mediator Don Philbin calls this the "It's a trick because they offered it" phenomenon.[17] Unfortunately, plaintiffs served with an offer to compromise may regard the

---

[15]*Id.* See Katz, Avery W. & Sanchirico, Chris William. (2010, November 2). Fee shifting in litigation: Survey and assessment. University of Pennsylvania Institute for Law and Economics Research Paper No. 10–30. Available at SSRN: http://ssrn.com/abstract=1714089. Lynch, William P. (2009). Rule 68 offers of judgment: Lessons from the New Mexico experience. *New Mexico Law Review, 39*, 349–374.

[16]Kiser, Randall. (2010). *Beyond right and wrong: The power of effective decision making for attorneys and clients* (pp. 58–62). New York: Springer Science + Business Media. Kiser, Randall, *et al.* (2008). Let's not make a deal: An empirical study of decision making in unsuccessful settlement negotiations. *Journal of Empirical Legal Studies, 5*(3), 572.

[17]Philbin, Donald R., Jr. (2008, Winter). The one minute manager prepares for mediation: A multidisciplinary approach to negotiation preparation. *Harvard Negotiation Law Review, 13*, 290.

offer as a floor on their recovery when, in fact, it is the ceiling; for defendants, plaintiffs' offers to compromise may be regarded as mere aspirations when in reality many are conservative compromise proposals.

15.7 Negotiation Styles

Negotiation styles are generally classified as cooperative or competitive, problem-solving or adversarial, and value-creating or value-claiming.[18] The study attorneys generally display many of the attributes of effective problem-solving negotiators – realistic, astute, careful, wise, perceptive and adaptable.[19] But their negotiation style does not fit squarely into the existing nomenclature and would be more accurately characterized as "reputational." Many of the study attorneys adopt a low-key approach to negotiations and rely on their reputations – especially major victories in publicized cases and verdicts obtained against defendants with the same insurer – to legitimize their positions and motivate their adversaries. Neither committed nor resistant to settlement, they convey an attitude of practiced indifference about settling or trying a case. As one defense attorney who has tried cases for more than 40 years commented, a plaintiff's attorney who threatens to take a case to trial "will have to do a lot more than that" to settle it. "After 40 years of trying cases, the fear of having a loss is not one of the motivating factors for me," he says. "I've lost my share of cases and I can accept it." Buttressed by extensive trial experience, the study attorneys' negotiation style could be perceived by adversaries as convincingly confident or borderline arrogant. In some cases, their settlement demands and offers are unemotional ultimatums, flatly declaring what they believe is the natural, ordinary and direct consequence of the case facts and personalities.

The study attorneys discussed their general approach to settlement negotiations and then described some tactics. Their comments convey a broad range of negotiation styles and attitudes:

- I know most of the attorneys in this field. I will already have spoken with them to see if we can get rid of it. I try to speak casually with them; usually they're not receptive. But I do have credibility when I talk with them because I've tried 120 cases to verdict with [fewer than 15] losses.
- I'm not saying this as a criticism of other attorneys, but my cases are worked up better than 95% of other attorneys. I usually go into mediation with admissions. Most of the time the attorneys did not understand the significance of my questions during depositions and don't realize the case for them was over back then.

---

[18]Schneider, Andrea K. (2002). Shattering negotiation myths: Empirical evidence on the effectiveness of negotiation style. *Harvard Negotiation Law Review*, 7, 149–152.
[19]*Id.* at 168.

- I'm a hard-ass negotiator, but I'm a realist. I look it up, look at the jury sheets. What's a broken leg worth? This goes back to PAD [paying attention to detail]. I'm cautious, I'm pretty conservative. I have a pretty good idea of the range of values.
- When I'm discussing settlement with the attorney, I'm thinking, "Do you not get it?" My numbers are pretty constant. I tell them up-front – this is what the number is, and this is what the number will be at trial.
- I'm a very good negotiator. I like to negotiate. I learned about bargaining from my dad at the Paris flea market. There should be no pride in negotiations. Negotiation is all lies. Everyone says what their bottom line is, but it's not true. Negotiation is a free-for-all – whatever happens, happens. If they don't know my strong points, I never give the strong points away.
- At the beginning of a case I'll call the defense attorney and say, "Today I'm representing a person injured in a crosswalk by a drunk driver driving a beer truck. You can do whatever you want over the next two or three years – throw 10 to 15 attorneys on the case between now and trial. But on the first day of trial, I'll still be presenting a person run over in a crosswalk by a drunk driver who ran a red light."

Reflecting a modest and understated approach to negotiation, a defense attorney states, "I don't even tell another attorney what will happen at trial." He recalled how his reluctance to predict outcomes was shaped by a case earlier in his career: "I did that once after a mistrial, 8–4 in favor of the defense, and was surprised by what happened in the second trial. That's the only time I can remember telling another attorney what will happen at trial, and I haven't done it since."

Some study attorneys emphasized the value of experience and noted that their overall strategies had changed over time:

- With experience your ability to assess outcomes becomes better. Early in one's career, you learn you always have a chance to settle your good cases, and after a while you realize you've tried the bad cases and settled the good cases. And when you finally figure this out, you change your strategy. Now I do the opposite. So you realize, let's settle the lousy cases and try the good cases, instead of the other way around. You learn things as you go. You also learn with experience that sometimes you're the last one to know what's wrong with your clients.
- Sometimes you cannot figure out why the other side is doing what they're doing. In one case I thought they had done everything right and told them so, but I never saw their file. There must have been something in there because they kept raising the amount they were willing to settle for. I realized it doesn't matter that I don't think they did anything wrong as long as they think they did something wrong.
- And what really matters is trying cases. You see what is bluster and what is not bluster. When you start off, you really are terrified by what the other side says is going to happen. After a few years of trials, that stuff doesn't mean anything to you anymore. The distinction is experience.

The attorneys also discussed specific negotiation tactics and their view of settlements:

- If you argue too hard, it comes back to haunt you. In one case, a party's interest in a house was being valued. The party who wanted to stay in the house tried to show the house had so many problems that she should almost be paid to stay in it. I then flipped their argument and said we would buy her out at that price – we would be glad to pay her value and take the house off her hands. That's what we told the mediator. That case settled because you can push your argument too far. One thing you have to be prepared for is the other side may buy your bullshit.
- When you're looking at the upside, you still have to ask, "Do we have more to lose than to gain?" After you consider the trial costs, especially expert witnesses and sometimes the possibility of paying the defendant's costs, most of the time you settle.
- When I started representing plaintiffs, my first case settled for $900,000. That's a case I would have paid $75,000 for if we represented the defendant. Everybody is afraid – plaintiffs and defendants laying out all of this money. You have to manipulate the other side's fear and have none yourself. Fear equals the perception of risk – not even risk, but the perception of risk.
- It's sometimes easier to settle a $500,000 case than a $50,000 case. The exposure is greater and the range of possible settlement is larger.
- I took a negotiation class from Professor Craver [currently a law professor at George Washington University Law School]. Every day in class we had to negotiate. You had to see it to believe it. I learned you can't just go in with a number, even if it's a totally fair number, because there is always some expectation that there will be some give and take. You have to give yourself some reasonable room to negotiate.
- Hiding the smoking gun means the positions will have hardened – that the other side will just ignore the document or testimony.

The attorney who learned how to negotiate at the Paris flea market says, "I never ask for a bottom line – I ask for a range. When they give me a range I ask, 'Where are you in that range – Maine or Florida?' When an attorney told me 'around Georgia' I knew we could settle it."

15.8 Playing a Strong Hand

A study attorney described a complex case that, if litigated to verdict, would have had far-reaching consequences for an entire industry and might have encouraged similar claims. When asked, "What was your negotiation strategy when you had that type of leverage, a case that had implications beyond the specific case you're negotiating?", he replied:

> Never do I say that. The minute you start rattling that cup, you're perceived as trying to do them in. You do that, and they act like a rat that's cornered. The lawyers know what's at stake. They know what you've got, what will happen if you don't settle. I kept it low key. As a consequence, it settled for more than it may have been worth. I knew at least not to rattle their cage.

"Braying, bragging, threatening, expressly or implicitly, will draw a conclusion that you are not as good as you want them to think you are," he elaborates. "Understatement creates more anxiety in your opponent than braggadocio and will produce a better settlement."

15.9 Effect of Excessive Demands and Lowball Offers

The study attorneys identified excessive demands and unreasonably low offers as being the major impediment to settlement negotiations. Plaintiffs' attorneys thought that low offers sometimes provoked their clients to abandon negotiations altogether, and defense attorneys noted that unrealistic demands often led directly to trial:

- Part of the process is called the "no-brainer offer." When the other side makes a ridiculous offer, there's really nothing to talk about.
- We had nothing to lose. That makes such a difference. That type of case makes heroes out of attorneys. They may have been just regular attorneys before, but the other side makes them heroes.
- I feel that you can eliminate the settlement negotiation process where you start very low and move up a series of steps that are absurd. Game playing at low levels and at high-end cases serves no purpose other than insulting the client.
- Thirty-five years ago all the cases went to trial, and you used to bill based on how you did. If you made a high demand and did worse at trial, it reflected on you. It affected your reputation and your negotiations in the future. It worked against you to have high demands. You lost your credibility. I'm not sure why plaintiffs' attorneys make such high demands nowadays. I think they think the case then goes higher up the food chain in the insurance company. This has been a slow evolution. When I started attorneys did not bullshit around – when an attorney said something he meant it.
- The thing I would like to see is if both sides came in with realistic positions. If both sides could come in with economically viable plaintiff and defendant positions you could avoid the alienation and anger that is the reaction to the first offers and demands, before the negotiation dance is over, which sometimes make plaintiffs unable to see an offer as reasonable when it finally comes in at the end of the negotiation process. Some plaintiffs get angry early on and decide to go to trial.
- In the case you found me in, the carrier just missed the ball. It offered a ridiculous amount of money – put me into a position where we have nothing to lose. That's stupid because when you have nothing to lose you go for the fences.

Lowball offers had the ironic effect of freeing institutional plaintiffs from the responsibility of seriously considering an offer that could be better than the net trial result and, if rejected, could expose the decision makers to criticism and potential liability. Recalling an offer of less than $50,000 in a case later resulting in a verdict close to $1,000,000, the plaintiff's attorney comments, "In that case, I told the client, 'They did you a favor. You won't have to be looking over your shoulder and wondering whether you did the right thing or have other people second-guessing you.'"

15.10 Settlement Results

Study attorneys were asked to think about cases they had settled and answer two questions. The first question was, "Looking back on cases that settled, do you think the other side could have negotiated a better deal for itself if it had been a better negotiator or case evaluator?" The second question was, "When cases settle, how often do you think the other side would have achieved a better result by going to trial instead of settling?" These questions generated very different responses. Most of the study attorneys thought an adversary could have negotiated a better settlement, but very few thought that trial would have resulted in a better result for the adversary.

When asked whether adversaries could have negotiated better deals, the study attorneys were contemplative and aware that their responses might seem self-serving or counter-productive:

- I shouldn't say this, but I would take a lot less on some cases. I walk away from a lot of cases thinking I would have taken less. Some attorneys get more than I do; most do not.
- In a lot of cases a little more is paid than it should be. That's because there is a large variation in risk-taking by carriers. Some are very protective of the insureds; some are not.
- I'd like to say "yeah," because that would mean I'm a great negotiator. But really some clients probably pay a few bucks more or a few bucks less by the time the case settles. I can't really think of cases where the other side paid too much if they had competent counsel.
- I know some cases where they could have gotten a better result if they knew what they were doing. In some cases, the attorney did not know the law.
- You have to separate the hacks from the quasi-hacks. The better the attorney, the less likely they will leave money on the table. But it does happen. I had a case where we did a two-butt shuffle [two virtual trials], and one jury came in at $1.5 [million] and the other came in at $1.8. The case settled for [less than $1,000,000]. Did they [plaintiffs] leave money on the table? Yes, but all they wanted was a house, and they got enough money for that.

- Ordinarily, the mediators have squeezed everything out of the case they can. The defense has gone way beyond what they thought they'd pay, and the plaintiff has come far down from their number.

Reflecting on the question of whether settlement results could have been better, another attorney was philosophical: "Everyone leaves money on the table."

When asked how frequently an adversary could have negotiated a better settlement, the attorneys expressed a wide range of opinions:

- This happens all the time. It's a pretty high percentage. It's not 3 to 4%; it's closer to 25 to 30% of the time. I have to look at this from the defense side. You often get a situation where the plaintiff's attorney is lazy. They haven't done the work and they don't want to do the work. Competence of the other side is the most important thing. Reputations are made. You know from the get-go whether you might reduce the value of the case by a certain percentage because of that.
- Not often, but often enough to make me feel that I'm a good liar. ... When this happens, it's usually with either the high-end or low-end cases.
- It happens all the time. I hear that all the time from attorneys – "I had $100,000 but the plaintiff asked for $35,000." All day long I talk with attorneys about injuries, so I see it.
- If you consider all cases, including the small cases, maybe 25%, maybe a third.
- Fifty percent of the time, maybe 70%, they leave money on the table. But not a lot more. I rarely get pushed to the drop-dead number. It's an intangible because you never know exactly where your client would have gone if the negotiations continued. But as I think about it, the other side could say the same thing about me – it probably balances out because in 50% of the cases maybe I could have paid less.
- About 90% of the time. Only once was I out-prepped [prepared] and I told myself that it would never happen again. I was too close – forgot to look at the big picture. After that I created a master timeline for every fact, every event and document in the case. I knew more about the plaintiff than she [the plaintiff] did.

When asked whether an adversary would have obtained a better result at trial than through settlement, the attorneys generally thought this was an uncommon event:

- Once you consider the risks, the unknowns, the costs and the stress you're avoiding through settlement, I don't think anyone would have been better off trying a case. The costs of trial are incredible, even apart from the attorneys' fees. Jury fees and court reporter fees are really high – there's no small cases anymore.
- In my cases, 5% would have gotten better results at trial.
- Most of the time plaintiffs get better results by settlement after considering the costs of trial. They end up with more in their pockets.
- Pretty often, but not if you consider the attorneys' fees. Attorneys' fees play a major role.

- Not often. In the grand scheme of things, you're happy if 50% of the settlements are under what would happen at trial and 50% are over.
- We keep track of this. Plaintiffs get more in settlement than they would get at trial. In 65% of the cases that go to trial in this office, plaintiffs get less than our settlement number. You can't be sure that would happen in all the cases that settle because maybe there's a reason they settle and the other ones go to trial.

If these comments are representative of attorneys in general, clients may be assured that their settlement is superior to the likely trial result. But they may wonder whether the settlement amount could have been measurably different.

Chapter 16
Mediation

Law professor Marc Galanter describes the American civil justice system as "litigotiation." As he explains, "only a minority of eligible claims are made and only a minority of these proceed to disposition by trial; the vast majority are resolved by settlement, abandonment, or ruling at an earlier stage. It is important to recall that America does not have two systems, one of litigation and one of negotiation, but a single system of 'litigotiation' – that is, of contesting claims in the vicinity of courts, where recourse to the full process of adjudication is an infrequent occurrence but at every stage an important option and threat."[1] Beginning in the mid-1980s, with the widespread adoption of alternative dispute resolution programs in federal and state courts, mediation became an integral component of this system of litigotiation.

For attorneys practicing before the advent of court-ordered or court-annexed mediation, settlement negotiations with opposing counsel were voluntary – initiated and conducted by attorneys without court intervention or the presence of a mediator. As Guy Kornblum, a distinguished trial attorney, mediator and co-author of *Negotiating and Settling Tort Cases*, recalls, "the words 'alternate dispute resolution' or 'ADR' were not in our vocabularies."[2] When he started practicing law in the mid-1960s, he writes, the word "mediation" was hardly spoken:

> I am not sure I heard the word more than a couple of times while in law school. As a young trial lawyer, the common practice was that settlement was not really discussed until a mandatory settlement conference right before trial. Before that, if a case settled, it was because the attorneys did so, or the insurance adjuster jumped in and negotiated "the file" directly with the plaintiff's lawyer. Often the first real opportunity to negotiate a case was the "Mandatory Settlement Conference," which later became part of the court rules, and

[1] Galanter, Marc. (1993). The regulatory function of the civil jury. In Litan, Robert E. (Ed.). *Verdict: Assessing the civil jury system* (pp. 61–102). Washington, D.C.: Brookings Institution.

[2] Kornblum, Guy. (2010, August 23). More on the case for mediation: Understanding the process better. Available at http://resolutionadvocate.blogspot.com/2010/08/more-on-case-for-mediation.html.

R. Kiser, *How Leading Lawyers Think*,
DOI 10.1007/978-3-642-20484-5_16, © Springer-Verlag Berlin Heidelberg 2011

which ordinarily was held quite close to trial. Other than direct negotiations, there was little involvement by the court in settlement talks before then. At that time there were no Case Management Conferences.

The number of federal court cases tried to verdict peaked in 1985, and between that year and 2002 "the number of trials in federal court has dropped by more than 60 percent and the portion of cases disposed of by trial has fallen from 4.7 percent to 1.8 percent."[3]

Because many of the study attorneys practiced in both pre-ADR and post-ADR eras, they were able to compare attorneys' settlement negotiation behavior during the last 50 years and reflect on the advantages and disadvantages of institutionalized mediation. In this chapter, they describe how mediation has changed the timing, tenor and content of settlement negotiations. After providing that historical perspective, they discuss mediator selection, mediation procedures, mediation negotiation tactics, qualities of effective mediators and evaluative mediation. The chapter concludes with their overall assessment of mediation.

16.1 Effect of Mediation on Timing and Nature of Pre-trial Negotiations

The attorneys were asked whether mediation had affected informal settlement negotiations between counsel or the timing of those negotiations. Many if not most of the attorneys had not considered the issue previously and gave considerable thought to the question before responding. They indicated that mediation had affected the negotiation behavior of younger attorneys in particular, who had started practicing when referrals to mediation were common. Others noted that mediation had the practical effect of curtailing negotiations between counsel before a scheduled mediation, but those negotiations were not very successful anyway. These comments illustrate the range of opinions regarding the effect of mediation on direct negotiations between attorneys:

- It probably has decreased communications because attorneys defer to a mediator. The problem with the mediators we use is that, by and large, they are successful in bringing us together. But that comes at a cost. It tends to decrease the likelihood that the attorneys will talk openly between themselves.
- Maybe my experience is not typical, but mediation has not affected my interactions with other attorneys. There was not much going on anyway. I was with a gung ho trial firm when I started, and they did not spend much time talking with the other side about settlement, so I haven't seen that mediation

---

[3]Galanter, Marc. (2004, November). The vanishing trial: An examination of trials and related matters in federal and state courts. *Journal of Empirical Legal Studies, 1*(3), 461.

made a change that way. I'm more capable today of having a discussion with my adversaries than I used to be when I was younger.

- Definitely, yes, it has affected both the timing and the way we communicate. Years ago the two lawyers would talk with each other and get the case settled. Today you don't really discuss settlement until it's time to discuss who to select as the mediator. ... Mediation is a product of fast track [trial delay reduction programs] and for the courts to manage their cases.
- When I started, mediation was the exception to the rule. Now it seems we can't enter into meaningful settlement negotiations without a mediator. Before mediation, I'd say 90% of the cases settled between the attorneys, and now it's reversed. Ninety percent of the cases settle in mediation and only 10% of the cases settle between the attorneys. People are unwilling to talk settlement without a mediator.
- Absolutely. Attorneys just say, "We'll get into it at the mediation." There's a mindset now that we must go to mediation. We used to go with the other attorney and have a nice lunch and drinks. Sometimes you took the claims person with you. The case got settled over lunch.
- It's a sign of weakness to call the other side's attorney to discuss settlement because settlement now takes place in mediation. I used to call the other attorney to talk about the case and now I only do it in extreme cases, like when I want to send a message that we're not paying anything. ... So I only discuss settlement on my own when I'm taking an extreme position, not on a regular case.

"One of the latent effects is that attorneys have turned into terrible settlement attorneys," states a defense attorney. "Most attorneys, if they're honest, will tell you they have not settled a case on their own – except maybe a $15,000 case – in years."

The attorneys also were queried about the effect of mediation on the timing of informal settlement negotiations between counsel. Some attorneys indicate that, in addition to affecting how counsel interact, mediation has changed the timing of attorney interactions:

- It has delayed informal negotiations but is more effective. It's better for someone else to talk with them because they're not listening to me and don't want to make any concessions.
- Everyone says, "Let's wait for the mediation because I don't want to bid against myself." This is kind of a generational gap when I think about my practice over [about 20] years. They don't know what it's like to negotiate and settle cases without mediators. For the more experienced attorneys, who discuss settlement before mediation, most of those who have done it forever are not worried about looking weak.
- If I know mediation is scheduled, I don't start negotiations because I'll just give up ground. I'll give them my demand, but I won't start negotiations before then.
- No, a good attorney still will want to contact the other attorney to get a reasonable settlement. The mediation itself does not delay settlement; it's the case itself, how the carrier wants to handle it.

- Absolutely – many clients and attorneys find it difficult to settle their cases until a mediator tells them what's going to happen at trial. Attorneys don't talk about settling before mediation. Being proactive used to mean trying to settle a case early in the game; now it means just trying to get the other side to mediation, not talking about settling.
- Mediation seems to be for those people who are floundering, who are more concerned about a sign of weakness if they try to discuss settlement before mediation. If an attorney calls me who has tried 30 to 40 cases, they don't need to play games. It is only perceived as a weakness if the attorney is not willing to try the case.

Mediator Scott Markus has observed the "non-starter" policy that prevents some attorneys from discussing settlement before mediation. In a recent case he describes, plaintiff's counsel spoke with the mediator separately before mediation and told him, "We have a policy of not making a demand before mediation." In a later, separate call with the mediator, the defendant's attorney told him, "We have a policy of not making an offer unless we get a demand and plaintiff's counsel will not give us a demand before mediation."[4] In his mediation practice, Markus finds that "counsel never discussed any amounts with each other before mediation. Each just assumed the other would see the case their way, and if not, the mediator would convince opposing counsel of her 'misevaluation.'"[5]

16.2 Effect on Client Counseling

Apart from its effect on the nature and timing of settlement negotiations between attorneys, mediation may affect how attorneys counsel clients. Some attorneys and mediators note that mediators are asked to convey negative aspects of the client's case and "work their magic" because case weaknesses have not been fully discussed with the client, the client is not listening to the attorney or an attorney has client control problems:

- Some do, generally if they're having trouble. Some attorneys use the mediator to lean on the client to give the bad news.
- Sometimes attorneys rely on mediators to tell the clients the weaknesses of their cases.
- Yes, attorneys are constantly looking for assistance in that counseling function.
- I have gotten some cases where the attorney says a mediator needs to be involved because we have client control problems.

---

[4]Markus, Scott. (2010, August 27). "If I had known that ..." Avoiding the "non-starter" in mediation. *Daily Journal Verdicts and Settlements*, p. 2.
[5]*Id.*

"It's a mistake for counsel to abdicate responsibility for client education," states a plaintiffs' attorney who practiced law for decades before mediation became prevalent. "The client is looking to the attorney, and the attorney makes a mistake when they shove the responsibility of advice to the mediator. It's a mistake for the attorney to think the mediator knows their case better than they do."

Some attorneys thought that plaintiffs' attorneys rely on mediators' intervention more than defense attorneys:

- From my experience as a mediator, 20 to 25% of plaintiffs' attorneys are using mediators to inform clients of the negative aspects of the case. I talk with the attorneys first and see if there is a client control problem. Most of the time it's the attorney who has caused the unrealistic impression.
- Frequently what happens is the plaintiff's attorney is persuaded, but his client is not. The mediator needs to be there because it is the plaintiff client who has the unrealistic idea this is a $5 million case when in reality it's a $200,000 check.
- On the defense side, we don't wait for mediators to tell us the downside. Attorneys who do that have a problem. This happens more often on the plaintiffs' side. I don't know if it's a fear of losing the client but, yes, some attorneys rely on the mediator to talk about the negative side of the client's case.
- I don't believe that really happens on the defense side. We do not need mediators to tell us the strengths and weaknesses. On the plaintiffs' side, what happens in mediation often remains a mystery to us. I have seen cases where the plaintiff's attorney is relying on the mediator to explain what has not been explained before or has not sunk in. Plaintiffs have clients who want $5 million because of the McDonald's case. They rely on the mediator to bring the client down. Plaintiffs will be hearing this for the first time and feel they are being attacked. And they are often very angry.

A defense attorney sees an advantage in the mediator conveying negative information to a client: "Even the best, most experienced attorneys can benefit from mediation because the attorney-client relationship can be harmed by being brutally honest." As an example, he mentions the difficulty of informing a client that the client is a bad witness. "They may need to listen to the mediator for that," he explains. "Some clients can handle personal information, but most clients have a hard time making a difference between what you're telling them the jury might think of them and what you think of them."

16.3 Mediator Selection

Because mediation is often the most critical event in civil litigation, study attorneys devote substantial time and thought to selecting the mediator:

- Deciding who should be the mediator is very case specific. I spend a lot of time thinking about who is the right mediator for the case. Sometimes you want someone who's more academic, like a patent case. Other times, like death of a child, you need highly developed emotional skills. Another time you may need a bankruptcy specialist. You have to see what the sensitivities are. You know how it works. I get to designate three mediators, so I pick two I know they'll strike and end up with the one I wanted to begin with.

- Mediation is the final resort if you're trying to avoid trial and you think there's a good chance of settling. Sometimes you want a plaintiffs' attorney as a mediator; sometimes you have to disabuse your client of what they think the case is worth, and you don't want to do this yourself. So it helps to get another plaintiffs' attorney opinion so the client knows it's not just your opinion or so the client hears what another plaintiffs' attorney thinks it's worth.
- I use retired [defense] counsel because I will get more traction out of someone who used to work for the type of people who will be paying the money – very capable defense lawyers. I almost exclusively use retired defense attorneys.
- The best mediator is the one the other side is comfortable with because my clients are sophisticated and have a good idea of what a case is worth. I need a mediator who has a good relationship with the other attorney and has the credibility to tell the other attorney that he has gotten everything out of me that he can. My clients are not that affected by what the mediator thinks the case is worth, so the most important connection is between the mediator and the other attorney.
- On the defense side we are looking for knowledge of how insurance companies and claims departments work. On the plaintiffs' side, for me, as a defense lawyer, the mediators that are successful with plaintiffs have sufficient rapport or caché with plaintiffs and plaintiffs' attorneys to convince them they are not getting screwed. That is why I like to use plaintiffs' attorneys as mediators, so they can say to the plaintiff, "I've represented people like you and have handled cases similar to yours."
- Picking the right mediator will be the key. Some mediators are really retired. I'm not paying $400 per hour for a judge who is really retired. I don't want a mediator to massage me and tell war stories. The ones at [major ADR provider] do a great job of massaging. But my clients can't afford a day of massaging.

Some plaintiffs' attorneys indicated that they have few options in selecting mediators and usually defer to the preferences of the defendant or its insurer:

- You have to understand that large companies who pick the mediators have their in-house mediators, the ones they've used before. I don't mean the mediators are employed by the companies; it's just the ones they've worked with at [major ADR provider] and think they see things the way the companies do. I go along with those mediators because that's who they feel comfortable with.
- Carriers will insist on X, Y, or Z mediator. I will always go with who the carrier wants. The carrier wants another set of eyes on the case. It's an insurance policy for the claims adjuster.
- Usually, you get the mediator the insurance companies like. The insurance companies play a large role in selecting the mediator. There's no sense in picking a plaintiff mediator because the insurance company won't take them.

- Certain mediators I and my firm are more comfortable with. Other ones you know they are not the impartial mediators they're supposed to be. But you go in with your eyes open. Sometimes we do this just to get someone to focus on the case. It brings in the decision makers. It's the insurance companies that may not have focused on all the persons who will need to be involved. When we use those types of mediators [selected by insurance companies for settlement days] a difficult case will get resolved as long as the plaintiff is reasonable. You walk in not trusting, but you walk out with the case resolved.

16.4   Mediation Procedure and Conduct

The study attorneys expressed mixed views about mediation procedures, some regarding joint sessions as highly beneficial and others contending they are inflammatory. They also voiced concerns about mediations scheduled prematurely, attorneys' lack of preparation, the absence of good faith negotiations, the futility of confidential mediation briefs and parties who do not understand mediation and apparently are not adequately counseled regarding the nature and purpose of mediation:

- A lot of mediators like to get the parties together at the beginning. But a good mediator, he or she will separate the lawyers so they don't have to posture in front of their clients. Joint sessions are a goddamn waste of time. The lawyers are trying to convince clients they're determined and completely committed. It's like two male dogs – who's going to back down? There's no way to back down without losing face. That's when all you hear is in your face stuff like, "I'm going to kick your ass."
- What's frustrating in mediation is that we have no control over the plaintiff. I don't get the feeling the plaintiff is aware of the ramifications of settlement and the effect of a 998 offer. That is one reason I prefer it when we start mediation with everyone instead of breaking up the parties and their attorneys from the start. That removes people from other people. When everyone is separated you can't tell whether the plaintiff's attorney is insulating his client, the plaintiff's attorney does not appreciate what the problems are, or maybe the client is not paying attention to the attorney. It could be all of the above.
- I have never understood why someone would submit a confidential mediation brief. What purpose does that serve? Persuading the mediator is not the issue; you have to persuade the other party. Confidential briefs gives me the impression your argument won't stand up if the other side sees it, but you're trying to get one over on the mediator. It's the starchy firms that seem to do this more often.
- On the defense side, some defense attorneys do not take mediation or the settlement process seriously. They do not give it a good faith effort.
- Lots of mediations depend on where the case is. If a deposition needs to be taken, it is not going to settle. More thought should be given to when the mediation is

scheduled. In one case I did not have an IME [independent medical examination]. ... Mediation comes down to "Is the case ripe?"

- If it's a sophisticated lawyer, he or she will decide how to use the mediator to control the client. But a lot of attorneys who don't mediate a lot of cases don't understand what to expect at mediation. They don't know what you do at mediation and their clients have not been prepared. The client is completely confused about what's going on because they're expecting something closer to a trial. I don't use a mediator to argue my case; I want him to settle it.

The attorneys' perception that other attorneys and their clients may not be prepared for mediation is consistent with practices observed by Michael Leathes, Honorary Chair of the International Mediation Institute: "It's startling how many attorneys come to mediation expecting the mediator to do all the work, having little idea how to engage the mediator's help, having not worked out their BATNA, and with a poorly prepared client."[6]

16.5 Negotiation Techniques in Mediation

The attorneys' general negotiation strategies and tactics are discussed in the previous chapter, but some of their ideas and advice specific to mediation include:

- One thing plaintiffs don't realize sometimes is that they need to be realistic at the beginning. If a case does not settle at a mediation scheduled early in the case, we may not be scheduling another mediation just so they can take a hard stand at the beginning, like they're sending a message, and then settle it down the road. Old-school attorneys think they should start high at the beginning. That's not the way it works anymore because mediation is expensive. Mediation has gotten really expensive, and it's not true anymore that mediation is always cheaper. If the case does not settle at the first mediation, we might just take it to trial because it could be cheaper. [Major ADR provider] can cost as much as a trial.
- The worst thing you can do is to produce a piece of evidence at a mediation that you think will change the whole case. The lawyer thinks he has a good piece of evidence, but this mediation strategy is counter-productive and ineffective. It does not work because if this is legit you would have shown me it before. Why didn't you produce it in discovery? What you think is a winning move is fraught with peril. In mediation you are trying to assess the case with what you know. But when someone produces something totally new, you can't make progress toward settlement because you have to go back and do more investigation and research about that new piece of evidence. I tell the other attorney, "It's too bad

[6]Leathes, Michael. (2010, April 27). Review of Abramson, Harold, *Mediation representation: Advocating as a problem-solver in any country*. Available at http://www.amazon.com/Mediation-Representation-Advocating-Problem-Solver-Country/product-reviews/1601561083/.

you produced this now because I came here to settle the case and I can't do that now since you've brought in something completely new." I've seen this done time and time again. How do you think attorneys feel about an attorney who does this?

- If I have some secrets, I pull them out at mediation. Depending on how many cards I have, I give them to the mediator and pick which ones to deal.
- I don't want the mediator asking my client questions directly. Clients may give up something early – they'll extract negotiating information from the client like, "What's the bottom line?" That's OK if you know they're not going to share that with the other side, but you have to be careful. I know that negotiation is a process, a dance, and you almost always need to go through a few stages. Clients don't always understand this, and it will affect the result if the client just gives a bottom line to the mediator. That's why it affects value whether the mediator brings in the whole group.
- People do not get serious about numbers until the end of the mediation. If you talk about the numbers at the beginning, it doesn't work. Each party just says the other's number is unreasonable.

A plaintiffs' attorney thought that negotiation strategies in mediation could be reduced to a simple concept. "In mediation," he says, "you try to put more lipstick on your pig than theirs."

16.6   Qualities of Effective Mediators

Previous surveys of mediator effectiveness indicate that key traits include trustworthiness, empathy, compassion, self-awareness, communication skills, imagination, preparation, persistence and mindfulness.[7] A recent study by JAMS mediator Margaret Shaw and Northwestern University professors Stephen Goldberg and Jeanne Brett analyzed differences between mediators who are former judges and mediators who are attorneys without judicial experience. They found that "process skills" like patience, listening, firmness, candidness and diplomacy "were significantly more important for nonjudges," while the "ability to provide useful case evaluations, on the other hand, was significantly more important for former judges than for nonjudges."[8] Mediators with a judicial background had two advantages, the

---

[7]See Bowling, Daniel, & Hoffman, David (Eds.). (2003). *Bringing peace into the room: How the personal qualities of the mediator impact the process of conflict resolution*. San Francisco: Jossey-Bass. ABA Section of Dispute Resolution, Task Force on Improving Mediation Quality. (2008). *Final Report, April 2006 – February 2008*.

[8]Successful mediators wanted: No robe required. *Kellogg Insight*, September 10, 2010. Available at http://insight.kellogg.northwestern.edu/index.php/Kellogg/article/successful_mediators_wanted_no_robe_required. Goldberg, Stephen B., Shaw, Margaret L., & Brett, Jeanne M. (2009). What difference does a robe make? Comparing mediators with and without prior judicial experience. *Negotiation Journal*, 25(3), 277–305.

study found: "clients automatically respect former judges, and lawyers assume they are intelligent." But some judges were criticized for being "unfriendly, self-absorbed or self-important, and/or lacked empathy."

The study attorneys have their own terminology for describing effective mediators. The most frequently mentioned adjectives are serious, helpful, comfortable and quality, followed by confidential and astute. Other highly ranked traits include congeniality, approachable, friendly, non-threatening, committed, determined, unbiased, motivated, objective, even-handed, receptive, delicate, sophisticated, sincere, likeable, analytical, engaging, honest and dynamic. In responding to the question, "What characteristics make a mediator effective?", the attorneys comment:

- Effective mediators have eye contact with the client and they're engaging. They have empathy and tell clients . . . that a jury cannot understand exactly how they feel, and even a serious injury can never be taken away but can be compensated. They know that some clients are looking for validation and vindication, and they have a good way of telling clients that if they go to trial they may never have a sense of validation and vindication.
- Effective mediators have a sense of humor. They have a demeanor that makes people comfortable as soon as possible. They know which clients he has to hold hands for and which clients have to hold their mouth.
- Some mediators have a real knack for persuasion. They are very good listeners and they cater to those needs. Not a lot of mediators understand that for the client "it's all about me." The mediator needs to understand the client and ask, "What is it I need to overcome?"
- The quality of being approachable, non-threatening, friendly. Because so many mediators are retired judges, they tend to carry this silly weight with them and expect you to kiss their ring. They bring the bench with them.
- The attorneys always talk about how someone did at a deposition. But the mediator does not have the benefit of that; they can't see it. So an astute mediator tries to draw the client out on a neutral subject. A retired judge, for instance, says, "Can you tell me a little more about yourself?" The mediator is assessing the client.
- First, you've got to separate the cases where I sincerely want to settle and the cases where I'm there for something else and am not going to settle. If it's a sincere attempt – and you exclude the claims reps who have a hard-on for the plaintiff's attorney – almost anyone, including a 10-year-old, can settle a case. I do not like it when a mediator tells me how I'm going to get my ass kicked, your case sucks and your experts are whores. I don't like it when the mediators separate the attorneys from the clients, and I don't like heavy-handed. What works is listening and asking someone to look at their case in a different way – like what would happen in this case on the best day, what would happen on the worst day? I think empathy is important, too, and trying to get the attorney to separate himself from the representation.

- One thing mediators need to remember is that they should not be trying harder than the parties to settle the case. If the mediator is working harder than one of the parties, something else is going on. If the parties don't want to settle, that's not the mediator's fault. That why I sometimes think it's better to have a mediator who is not a full-time mediator. When they're full-time, it's their whole job and they think their reputation depends on settling every case they get. For the part-time mediator, you have other things to do and you don't feel that every case has to settle.
- One thing that helps an attorney is having a former federal judge saying, "I have overseen 3,000 cases." They tell plaintiffs about how they've seen plaintiffs with good cases get nothing and how defendants with good defenses got hit with huge verdicts. At least I hope that's what they're telling the defendants.

With some mediators, a defense attorney complains, "Too many times we spend hours listening to war stories." An attorney who represents both plaintiffs and defendants emphasizes the importance of subject matter expertise and cautions, "If you're a retired judge, you may have lost a lot because you try so many different cases; you can't control the type of cases in your courtroom. Having a judge as a mediator can be just like you're in trial in front of a judge who does not know the law – this happens."

16.7   Evaluative Mediation

"Evaluative" mediation, the American Bar Association's Task Force on Improving Mediation Quality notes, "is something of a land mine in the field of mediation."[9] Although different mediators and attorneys ascribe different meanings to the term, evaluative mediation is generally understood to occur when a mediator "asserts an opinion or judgment as to the likely court outcome or a 'fair' or correct resolution of an issue in dispute."[10] The study attorneys were asked to step directly on this land mine and respond to three questions: When does evaluative mediation occur? Is evaluative mediation helpful? When mediators become evaluative, are they accurate predictors of case outcomes? On each of these subjects, the attorneys expressed disparate views that were not dependent on whether they represented plaintiffs or defendants.

---

[9]ABA Section of Dispute Resolution, Task Force on Improving Mediation Quality *supra* note 7 at 15.

[10]Kovach, Kimberlee K., and Love, Lela P. (1998). Mapping mediation: The risks of Riskin's grid. *Harvard Negotiation Law Review, 3*, 80. See Riskin, Leonard L. (2003). Who decides what? Rethinking the grid of mediator orientations. *Dispute Resolution Magazine 9*(2), 22. Riskin, Leonard. (1996). Understanding mediator orientations, strategies and techniques: A grid for the perplexed. *Harvard Negotiation Law Review, 1*, 7. Available at SSRN: http://ssrn.com/abstract=1506684.

Asked to describe when mediators become evaluative and whether one or more attorneys had asked the mediator for an evaluation, the study attorneys responded:

- Most mediators are reluctant to provide evaluations unless someone wants it. When the mediator does it on their own initiative, I'd say half the time it's because the parties are at an impasse, and about half of the time it's right at the start of the mediation. The mediator says, "I've looked at this case and this is what my opinion is." It's not very helpful – it can actually cause some problems – to get this upfront.
- Some mediators provide opinions without the parties asking for them. This usually occurs when the parties have already come up with a figure. It usually reflects the parties' numbers. It's not their [the mediator's] own opinion anyway since it's somewhere between the numbers the parties have already discussed.
- More experienced mediators do not easily give up. They will tell you what they think of the case only in very difficult cases when the other side needs to get their head out of the clouds. On my own cases, when I'm the mediator, I stay away from taking sides and having opinions about the case.
- With good mediators it's only when requested and usually not in the presence of the other party. With bad mediators, it is on their own initiative and often in front of the other party and its attorney. Sometimes it's in front of my client, which also creates a problem. I don't want a client hearing different opinions or advice before I've heard it from the mediator. I firmly believe the mediators who are most respected don't even get into that.
- Most of the time it occurs when the other side wants it. I would say it's a minority of cases where the mediator expresses an opinion.
- Some mediators just give their opinion of value anyway, not necessarily because a party requested it. Sometimes I ask myself, "Why did I go to law school if I really needed somebody else to evaluate my case?" Most of the time, though, I'm open to hearing anything.

An attorney with a general civil practice representing plaintiffs and defendants says, "It usually happens when you have impasse. The job of a mediator is to poke holes in everybody's case and tell them what a piece of crap it is. When they can't get people in their mindset, they say, 'You will get your head handed to you if you take this to trial.'"

The second question regarding evaluative mediation sought the attorneys' opinions about whether it was helpful. Some welcome the intervention, while others emphatically assert it is improper:

- You want an independent third-party's opinion of the case. I like to hear a true evaluation of my case – and if he or she is giving a true evaluation, I assume he is giving the other side the same.
- It's not a mediator's principal role to give an opinion about trial outcomes. It's commonly not done. There's a mild social stigma about doing that, sort of a special consent that would be required. In that narrow subset of cases – less than 50% – it depends on the mediator's experience. Most mediators won't have as

much experience in this field as I do. If they wanted an expert opinion they would need to contact someone like me. The dominant view is that evaluation is not appropriate without consent.

- In my opinion, unless both sides want them to do it, you can't do that, in my opinion, because that's rendering an opinion, like an arbitrator. This is not appropriate. I've walked out of mediations when that happens.
- I generally find it helpful, but it depends on the mediator. If you're dealing with a retired judge or a lawyer who has great familiarity with the area of law, that can be invaluable. You learn something about your case. It's insightful when a judge tells each side the strengths and weaknesses of the case. But it's not effective when they just talk about weaknesses. The problem is that it just comes across as wanting to make a deal. They first have to show they understand the case.
- I don't want a mediator to give me a number or tell me what will happen at trial. I've already given that a lot of thought before going into mediation, and my opinion on those issues probably isn't going to change. But that's different from a mediator who says, "I think this case can settle at this amount." That's effective.

"I'm disappointed if they're not evaluative, especially about the result at trial," comments a managing partner of a general civil practice. "The only way to get past an impasse is with a mediator's proposal or laying it out about what's going to happen at trial."

The third question about evaluative mediation addresses a central issue: When mediators become evaluative, are they accurate predictors of case outcomes? In a sense, this is the most important question because inaccurate evaluations are misleading and may be harmful regardless of whether they are initiated by the mediator or requested by the parties, or appropriate or inappropriate. A slight majority (55%) of the attorneys who had opinions on this subject thought that mediators were accurate predictors of case outcomes. In responding to this third question, the attorneys relied on their experiences and their perceptions of mediators' motivations. Attorneys who hold a positive view about mediators' predictive capacities state:

- Good mediators are accurate predictors of case outcomes. Sometimes a mediator is wrong in their original valuation because there's something they just don't quite get until we talk privately. It depends on how open-minded the mediator is. Good mediators solicit information and ask, "Is there something I'm missing here?" A lot of mediators won't do this.
- Mediators are good and proper sources of evaluation. I don't know anything about California, but in New York we have many retired judges who have a very good sense of value. Appellate court judges are particularly good because they understand a broad range of issues. They're invaluable.
- I'd say in my experience the mediators I've used were generally relatively accurate about the range of trial outcomes. When I think about the cases that did not settle and went to trial, I'd say their ranges were pretty close. And the mediators did a good job of identifying the important issues.

- Mediators are good predictors for the ones we pick. But you have to keep in mind we only pick the ones we know have expertise in this specific field. Good ones have become familiar with what would happen.
- When mediators become evaluative, it is a good source. Typically, you have selected someone who is astute, so their opinion of value is a reliable source – keeping in mind they have an agenda.

Attorneys who had some reservations about the accuracy of mediators' predictions said:

- Mediators can be like arbitrators and try to split the baby. The mediator does not want to piss anyone off. It's almost an inherent conflict of interest. Instead of calling it black and white, they look for a middle ground. So whether it's a mediator or arbitrator, it depends on their experience and how concerned they are about taking the middle ground and avoiding ticking off either party.
- I'm concerned about the motive. The mediator's motive is to clear the docket – resolution of the case, a feather in their cap, a successful resolution. But, yes, I go to mediation with an open mind, but I know their agenda is not my agenda.
- I don't rely on them. Some of them are excellent – maybe three to four percent of them. Others will tell you, "My only client is settlement." They don't give a damn if it's settled for a few bucks on the dollar; they just want to get it settled. It really varies with the mediator, especially if the mediator is a former judge. It's such an individual thing.
- Their evaluation is not from real life or a juror's perspective, but from an attorney's perspective. Once they become evaluative, you need to have an experiential basis to have an opinion; you need a broader base than just being a mediator.
- But there's a whole other group of judges who have just come off the bench and may not have experience in the field, or very little. Some think, "I'm a judge. Listen to me."
- Some are, some aren't, and I wouldn't say most are. It depends on their background. Some have not been on the bench since I was wearing diapers, so I don't know where they'd get their opinions from.

A plaintiffs' attorney expressed a practical, bottom line perspective that may be representative of many attorneys trying to do their best for clients while managing a significant caseload: "Some mediators are strong-arm mediators, but it may not matter. At the end of the day, I'll go with the mediator who has a strong personality and gets the job done. Is he an accurate predictor, who knows?"

16.8   Overall Assessment

The study attorneys were generally enthusiastic about mediation, although some expressed concerns it was being misused for discovery purposes. Other attorneys thought it had become so popular that attorneys were unable to evaluate and settle cases without mediators or unable to try cases when an adversary's offer or demand was inappropriate. Attorneys supportive of mediation expressed views like these:

- Sometimes lawyers, if they're not on the "A" list, cannot admit they lack confidence or are suspicious the insurance company is selling them a bill of goods. If there's a disagreement between me and plaintiff's attorney regarding valuation, and I'm not making progress, mediators can be helpful. Monetary offers of settlement from the defense side are often viewed with great suspicion, so I prize very highly mediators who have considerable background in plaintiffs' work.
- There is an inherent lack of trust among attorneys because no one wants to show his hand. I may offer $35,000, and the plaintiff's attorney may be at $410,000. You would think that case cannot be settled, but we're actually closer than you think. Where a mediator is of great value is I can go into a room and tell the mediator what the case is worth. You get to be honest with an intermediary.
- One of the most valuable aspects of mediation is that first of all they cannot dictate anything. But emotional barriers can be overcome by working with mediators. It also helps in evaluation.
- Overall, though, I want to be clear: mediation is invaluable. It's worth its weight in gold. Anytime a third party can give an independent view, there's a value in that, looking with an objective ear and eye. It removes the subjectivity. Most cases are crying out for a third party to sit in between the two. It's an art; it's a craft. The ones that do a better job have the desire to render a fair resolution.

Attorneys who thought that the value of mediation was overestimated or that it had some negative effects voiced these types of concerns:

- I am a proponent of mediation, but it is often misused. It's often used by the defense for the opportunity for discovery – trying to get more information through mediation and often used to force lower settlements from plaintiffs.
- A lot of lawyers love mediation because they don't want to try a case, don't know how to try a case, or are scared to death of trying a case.
- Mediation started off as a good idea but has become a waste. It's just a business now. Half the guys at ABOTA [American Board of Trial Advocates] talk about being mediators. Everybody's a mediator now. You're retired or else your practice went to hell in a hand basket.
- Some [attorneys] don't even know where the bathroom is unless the mediator tells them. It's a good institution, but not as good as the quality and ethics of the people in it.
- The mediation process has become totally abused by insurance companies. It's used to intimidate plaintiffs and plaintiff lawyers. They use it to make the process more expensive and drag things out, but they [mediations] can be beneficial for plaintiffs because you never walk out stupider than you were when you walked in. Oftentimes you find very critical information that can help you with trial strategies.

A plaintiffs' attorney felt that, regardless of the outcome, mediation invariably benefits both parties: "Overall, mediation has improved the quality of decision making. You go there to settle, but even if you don't settle, you get a new evaluation. Both sides get an objective look at their case."

Chapter 17
Jury Selection

Few aspects of civil litigation have generated as many war stories, tips and stereotypes as jury selection. Largely based on anecdotal evidence and presumed characteristics of nationalities and races, old advice on jury selection may have reflected society's preconceptions more than jurors' predispositions. In *The Art of Selecting a Jury*, first published in 1979, the author sets forth these "generally accepted rules and principles to be used in selecting a jury:"

- Mexican-Americans tend to be passive.
- A homemaker's attitudes, in particular, are influenced by her husband's occupation.
- Athletic persons often lack compassion.
- Women are often prejudiced against other women they envy, for example, those who are more attractive.[1]

Another source advised attorneys: "you are not looking for any member of a minority group;" "old women wearing too much makeup are usually unstable;" and "'women's intuition' can help you if you can't win your case with the facts."[2]

Beginning in the early 1970s, jury selection became a popular subject of social science research, eventually producing an entire trial consulting industry.[3] This research advanced attorneys' understanding of jurors' decision making but did not necessarily change their reliance on stereotypes and the tendency to associate a person's opinions and beliefs with "some easily observed characteristics (e.g., sex,

---

[1]Wenke, Robert. (1989). *The art of selecting a jury* (2nd ed.) (pp. v, 75, 78, 80, 88). Springfield, Illinois: Charles C. Thomas. The author of that book cautions readers, "Generalizations based solely on such factors as race, age, and occupation can be inaccurate when applied to a particular person."

[2](1973, June 4). The law: Women, gimps, blacks, hippies need not apply. *Time*.

[3]See Wiener, Richard L., & Bornstein, Brian H. (Eds.). (2011). *Handbook of trial consulting*. New York: Springer Science + Business Media.

R. Kiser, *How Leading Lawyers Think*,
DOI 10.1007/978-3-642-20484-5_17, © Springer-Verlag Berlin Heidelberg 2011

age, race, income, education, etc.)"[4] Despite this tendency to divine behavior from
a few features, research regarding juror judgments "shows that individual juror
demographic characteristics (such as race, gender, and socioeconomic status) are
generally weak predictors of juror judgments, although the links between certain
attitudes and judgments are somewhat stronger."[5] Emphasizing the risks of relying
on demographic features, DecisionQuest, a leading trial consulting and research
firm, advises: "there are general tendencies in terms of age, race and gender, but
they are so general and so weak that relying on them is dangerous to a fault." It
further cautions, "There are no longer easy clues to reading people, no simple slots
to put them into, and no substitute for learning what they think through voir dire."[6]

The study attorneys acknowledge that jury selection is one of the most difficult
aspects of their practice and complain that judges do not allow them sufficient time
to ask jurors about the experiences, values and relationships that may strongly
affect their judgments. In describing the challenges they encounter in jury selection,
the study attorneys address five subjects: (1) the importance of jury selection;
(2) jurors' preconceptions, biases and prejudices; (3) limitations placed on voir
dire; (4) jury selection strategies; and (5) the effects of race and religion.

17.1   Importance of Jury Selection

Study attorneys recognize that jury selection is one of the most important litigation
skills, although it is often neglected as attorneys concentrate on the more dramatic
and controllable elements of a trial:

* There was a time when I thought voir dire was a waste of time – just take the first
  12 jurors. My attitude is completely different now. Jury selection is the hardest
  skill. You have to get jurors to understand. Experienced lawyers do that pretty
  well. Most lawyers spend their effort on cross-exam, not jury selection.
* Picking a jury I have found to be the most critical aspect of putting a case
  together. That comes with experience. I look for older people. Within trying four
  to five cases I learned this is the most important thing. I prefer someone who has
  been in the service, maybe World War II or the Korean War. They are not as
  affected by death and the sight of someone who's been shot.

---

[4]DecisionQuest. Trial tip: Jury research – used and abused (part two). Available at http://www.
decisionquest.com/utility/showArticle/?objectID=500.

[5]Feigenson, Neal. (2000). *Legal blame: How jurors think and talk about accidents* (p. 42).
Washington, D.C.: American Psychological Association.

[6]DecisionQuest. Trial tip: The danger of relying on juror stereotypes from the nationwide
juror perception project. Available at http://www.decisionquest.com/utility/showArticle/?
objectID=586. DecisionQuest. Trial tip: Jury research – used and abused (part two). Available
at http://www.decisionquest.com/utility/showArticle/?objectID=500.

- Picking a jury is integral to what we do and the most important part of what we do. Once you pick a jury, the case is over. It's important to find fair-minded, honest people.
- If there is any intelligence an attorney brings to the case after trial begins, it's in picking the jury.

Anticipating how a prospective juror will respond to a case, states a renowned plaintiffs' attorney, is "extremely hard to do – probably one of the most elusive skills. You don't even know who the jury pool will be."

17.2   Jurors' Preconceptions, Biases and Prejudices

Jurors bring a host of preconceptions, biases and prejudices into the courtroom, and the study attorneys are realistic about their ability to discern and mitigate those attitudes:

- Cognitive dissonance is what it comes down to. My view of juries is that cognitive dissonance is the major determinant of jury conduct. People have outcomes they endeavor to reach based on their own experience. They filter out information that does not fit into their preconceived notions.
- Jurors have prejudices about a lot of things – being overweight, insurance, race. Maybe I have not done a good enough job with understanding the prejudices of jurors and some jurors' distrust of my client. Jurors assume your client has already gotten paid with insurance – like in another rear-ender, the jury gave my client nothing and when I talked with them afterward, they said, "She was asking for too much." But liability was clean.
- Jurors say they don't believe in pain and suffering either sincerely or to get out of the panel, and once they make that pronouncement they feel compelled to stick with it through deliberations. It also taints the entire pool because you'll hear other jurors say they agree after one says it.
- I don't think trials are pro-plaintiffs. [Places palm on lower back and grimaces, imitating trial testimony.] Jurors look at this and think, "My back hurts, too, and welcome to real life."
- There is no such thing as an unbiased jury. In a lung cancer case – just using that as an example – if you exclude jurors who would be prejudiced against a smoker, you're not left with neutral jurors. You've got jurors who probably feel that a defendant is responsible for their [the plaintiff's] condition.

A plaintiffs' attorney felt that the present jury selection system thwarted serious efforts to probe for and understand prejudices: "We need to change the system to educate jurors about how their prejudices affect their neutrality – make them think, 'How does my perception of this individual affect my willingness to award damages?' There should be more latitude in juror questionnaires or voir dire regarding those prejudices."

Plaintiffs' attorneys were particularly concerned about jurors' biases in an economy that had left many of them unemployed or threatened with joblessness:

- We're living in different times now. Jurors don't want to be there. They don't even have jobs.
- Another mistake is believing juries will be more sympathetic than they are these days. Jurors have gotten worse with the economy but they have always been conservative, sometimes skeptical about plaintiffs. What's different now is that jurors are very angry, very hostile.
- They are looking to punish whoever is responsible for wasting their time. The lawyer's job is to disabuse the jurors' tendency to believe it's the plaintiff's fault that they're there. Jurors don't perceive that defendants cause trials because of their offers.
- We're in a time of flux. I don't know how the current economic situation affects trial outcomes. My sense is that more claims are probably more likely to be pushed into mediation in this economy. I'm very concerned about how jurors will consider plaintiffs' claims in this economic climate.

These concerns are consistent with two recent trends in jury selection: (1) a large increase in the number of jurors asking to be excluded for hardship, either because they are unemployed or "fear they may be setting themselves up for unemployment by being absent more than a week, or because an employer is already short-staffed because of layoffs;" and (2) jurors who say they "won't even consider compensating an injured plaintiff for noneconomic damages."[7] Some study attorneys indicate that, in a recessionary economy, they are more willing to opt for a bench trial; and journalists report that attorneys are waiving jury trials after they hear jurors' derogatory comments during voir dire. As Gloria Gomez, Director of Juror Services for the Los Angeles County Superior Court, states, "There's a lot of tension, a lot more stress people are dealing with these days."[8]

Although plaintiffs' attorneys were more apt than defense counsel to vocalize their concerns about the effect of the economy on jurors, it appears that jurors' impatience and antipathy affect both plaintiffs and defendants. "There pretty much is a feeling of cynicism across the board towards plaintiffs and defendants," states California Superior Court Judge Jacqueline Connor. She adds: "I do find that it's equal. Consequently, it's fair."[9]

---

[7]Macpherson, Susan. (2009, September). Talking to jurors about damages in a down economy. *Trial, 45*(9), 29.

[8]Williams, Carol J. (2010, February 15). Weighed down by recession woes, jurors are becoming disgruntled. *Los Angeles Times*. See Schwartz, John. (2009, September 2). Call to jury duty strikes fear of financial ruin. *New York Times*, p. A1.

[9]McEvoy, Claran. (2010, December 27). Facing hard times, jurors are in no mood to bestow large personal injury awards. *San Francisco Daily Journal*, p. 1.

17.3 Limitations on Voir Dire

Study attorneys, some of whom had tried cases for more than 50 years, decried the time limitations on voir dire imposed by trial court judges:

- Some judges will only give you 20 minutes. Some up to 40 minutes.
- When a judge puts a time limit on your voir dire, it's impossible to do your job. Time restriction on trials is a serious problem, especially with the type of cases I handle, which usually take at least two weeks to try.
- You don't get a chance to probe a juror about prejudice. How do you very carefully and tactfully get to the prejudices of a juror without alienating them?

The practical effect of these time limitations is to impair the client's "right to speak to the potential deciders and to play a role in selecting them."[10] Because adequate time for voir dire is essential to client representation, David Ball recommends that attorneys serve "well-written, well-reasoned, well-researched motions for voir dire improvements" like a pre-voir dire written questionnaire or two hours instead of one hour for questions. "Given the importance of voir dire," Ball asserts, "a failure to seek improvements when necessary cheats your client."[11]

17.4 Jury Selection Strategies

Leonard Bucklin, a leading trial attorney, identifies four goals of voir dire in his book, *Building Trial Notebooks*: identify the bad jurors for this case; get the judge to send the bad jurors home and keep the good jurors in court; get the jurors to care about your client; and educate the jurors on a key point or two.[12] These goals may be implemented through trial lawyer David Berg's six stages of voir dire: putting the panelists at ease; humanizing the client; asking open-ended questions of the panel followed up by questions directed to individuals; asking questions of individuals about their personal and work lives; creating challenges for cause; and striking the jury.[13] Each of these steps is critical, Berg argues, even if an attorney has only 30 minutes for voir dire: "One serious mistake about a panelist can cost you the verdict – a lesson that every lawyer who tries a lot of cases learns sooner or later."[14]

---

[10]Tigar, Michael. (1999). *Persuasion: The litigator's art* (p. 70). Chicago, Illinois: The American Bar Association.

[11]Ball, David. (2001). *David Ball on damages* (p. 55). Louisville, Colorado: National Institute for Trial Advocacy.

[12]Bucklin, Leonard. *Building trial notebooks* (§19.6). Costa Mesa, California: James Publishing.

[13]Berg, David. (2006). *The trial lawyer: What it takes to win* (p. 81). Chicago, Illinois: American Bar Association.

[14]*Id.* at 109.

The study attorneys discussed their general strategies in voir dire and specific methods of questioning and evaluating individual jurors. Focusing first on general strategies, they remarked:

- I like a cross-section of people, but the real key is picking the foreman. Many lawyers do not recognize this is an issue. Motivation, background, training, where they come from. With teachers and psychologists you know they want to help people, so they're usually good for plaintiffs. I have kicked people off juries although I liked them if I thought they would not be a good foreman. You win by picking the right foreperson. Take that role seriously.
- Try to have good facial contact. Ask non-challenging questions. I'm trying to ask, "Does this person hate my guts?" Part of it is making sure you don't have any enemies on the jury. But even when you know the other side will dismiss a juror, you try to get the most out of them. Try to listen; try to understand people. Who is an enemy? Who is a helper? I try to get educated people with broad experience.
- I focus on deselecting, not just selecting. Look for persons who disagree, not just agree. More often than not, you get 35 people who are looking to hurt you – it's not skepticism, it's cynicism.
- Are there generalities? Yes. Do I rely on them? I think you have to be careful. At the end of the day, defendants bounce a lot of minorities. That's not always the smart thing to do. For me it comes down to questions like, are they a nice person? Is this a nice, kind, feeling person? Is this person bitter or angry? Maybe that will help if you can direct that anger and bitterness in the trial, but it could turn back on you. The goal is to get rid of the monsters, make sure nobody there is going to hurt you.
- Talk to jurors about these economics times. It's especially important for people to know that you know what they're going through.
- I've learned over the years the jurors that decide cases for me are the ones in the middle. The ones at extremes are not my jurors.

Some of these comments reflect a consensus that, "despite good voir dire, jury selection is usually more 'juror deselection.' We can use the process to eliminate, for cause or by peremptory challenge, the jurors we feel are most negative."[15]

When asked how they relate to individual prospective jurors, probing for prejudice and trying to sense how that juror will respond to their client's case and them personally, study attorneys responded:

---

[15]Tigar, Michael. (2009). *Nine principles of litigation and life* (p. 64). Chicago, Illinois: American Bar Association. On the subject of deselecting leaders, David Ball opines: "An unfavorable leader – even just one – can cost you the case or reduce damages by a factor of ten or more. Thus, once you have spotted a leader, try to remove her unless she is very likely to be favorable. You can gamble on non-leaders, but not on leaders. Take no chances." Ball, David. (2005). *David Ball on damages* (p. 305). Louisville, Colorado: National Institute for Trial Advocacy.

- It's in your nose. You know which jurors like you, but you can make mistakes. Mistakes occur when I rely on knowledge – a juror's background, job, people they know. I've learned it's more important how you feel you relate to that juror – do they like you, are they listening?
- I'm not afraid to offend a juror [during voir dire]. If they are offended it's better to find out now.
- In jury selection you have to go with your gut. If you get a bad feel, you have to know these people are not for you.
- You do that by careful listening to all aspects of voir dire, including the judge's preliminary questions. Listen to all that. Look carefully at the jurors. A lot of that comes with experience – you have to do that, you have to listen.
- You have to know the difference between "I'm being attentive because I'm going to fuck you" and "I'm being attentive and I like what you're saying." It's *sechel* – that's Yiddish for good common sense.

Dismissing the idea that a jury consultant can predict with certainty how a prospective juror will decide a case, a plaintiffs' attorney says, "If someone says, 'I'm a great jury consultant and I know what they're thinking,' I just think they're full of bullshit."

17.5 Effect of Race and Religion

None of the study interview questions directly inquired about race or religion. Nevertheless, in responding to the interview questions, study attorneys indicated that race and religion had been factors earlier in their careers and sometimes still affect case outcomes:

- The first trial I had the judge asked me, "Do you take the option?" I never heard the term before, didn't know what he meant. The other attorney said, "Yes." I looked at the attorney from my office who was with me. He nodded, so I told the judge, "Yes." After the case was over, I asked him, "What the hell was the option?" He said it meant we did not want a Black on the jury. I had no idea that's what I had said.
- Stereotypes – some are accurate, some are not. Everybody uses stereotypes. I'm Jewish, and my first job was in a firm where most of the partners were Jewish. I didn't know this when I joined the firm. When I had a trial and we were representing a defendant, they would remind me, "No Jews or Blacks on the jury. They give too much money."
- I did some work on the jury research project at the University of Chicago [Chicago Jury Project]. Until then I did not know you could change the results

just by changing the plaintiff's race – different race, different results. I knew this could happen in [state] but I was surprised to see it happen other places.[16]

- I'm always trying to put myself in the eyes of the jury. But it's so damn unpredictable. I tried a case in [a city where about 40% of the citizens are Black], representing a client who was Black. I expected the jurors to be mostly Black. Instead of being Black, most of the jurors turned out to be from [a suburb with a predominantly White population]. They weren't just White, they were translucent. One of the jurors was a biker with a "Live To Ride" tattoo on his arm. There was only one Black on the jury, a woman. She voted against awarding my client damages. The biker wanted to award more than the other jurors. You can't rely on generalities or make assumptions.
- A lot of the time I say to the jury, "We need to have a Dr. Phil moment. How do you feel about the fact my client is Asian, Filipino? How do you feel about Asians?" Stereotypes are huge and race is a real factor. The first time someone counseled me about gender and race I didn't pay much attention. That was a mistake, and I've learned now.

When asked whether they had noticed any common factors in cases that did not turn out as they expected, some attorneys thought race – either a party's race or a juror's race – played a role. One attorney, for instance, described a jury trial "where three jurors had the same background as one of the parties, and they all voted the same way, even though I know one of them – because of her job – knew it couldn't be right. You can't challenge a juror for those reasons and it ended up having much more effect than I expected."

Racial stereotypes and prejudices are not confined to jurors' perceptions of the parties and witnesses but may extend to their perceptions of the attorneys as well. In their article, "Are Ideal Litigators White? Measuring the Myth of Colorblindness," Professor Jerry Kang and his colleagues describe an experiment in which adult volunteers evaluated Asian and White male attorneys' performance at simulated depositions.[17] All of the volunteers heard the same audio recording of the depositions, but at the beginning of the deposition they were shown for five seconds the photographs and names of the fictitious attorneys taking the depositions. The photographs depicted similarly attractive Asian and White male attorneys whose fictitious names were selected to make their racial identities clear. The White attorney was named "William Cole," and the Asian attorney was named "Sung Chang." The attorney identities were manipulated so that half of the volunteers

---

[16]For information on the Chicago Jury Project, see Abbott, Walter F. & Batt, John. (1999). *A handbook of jury research* (§23.02). Philadelphia: American Law Institute – American Bar Association. Kalven, Harry, Jr. & Zeisel, Hans. (1966). *The American jury.* For a current assessment of the effect of race on jury selection see Equal Justice Initiative. (2010, June). *Illegal racial discrimination in jury selection: A continuing legacy.* Available at http://www.eji.org/eji/node/397.

[17]Kang, Jerry, *et al.* (2010). Are ideal litigators white? Measuring the myth of colorblindness. *Journal of Empirical Legal Studies,* 7(4), 886–915.

heard the same deposition being taken by "Attorney Cole," while the other half heard "Attorney Chang" taking the same deposition.

After listening to the depositions, the citizens who claimed that "they themselves did not hold racial stereotypes about the ideal litigator," but thought that most Americans held those stereotypes, rated the Asian litigator as less competent and less likeable than the White litigator. They also indicated they were less willing to hire the Asian litigator and recommend him to friends and family. Professor Kang concludes, "Because of racial stereotypes operating in their individual minds, participants evaluated lawyers who were objectively indistinguishable as significantly different."[18]

---

[18]*Id.* at 907.

Chapter 18
Mistakes and Oversights

The previous chapters show how the study attorneys think and what they do. This chapter changes the focus to *other* attorneys. In an attempt to better understand the causes of case misevaluations and poor negotiation outcomes, four questions were posed to the study attorneys:

1. Do you think other attorneys adequately counsel their clients regarding what their case is worth?
2. In your opinion, what are the most common mistakes other attorneys make in case evaluation and settlement negotiations?
3. What is most often overlooked or missing in other attorneys' case evaluations?
4. If you could change some things about how other attorneys evaluate and negotiate their cases, what would they be?

These questions are condensed versions of a larger question that perplexes attorneys, clients, insurers, judges and mediators: What causes poor legal judgment and decision making? Although the study attorneys had ready answers to the four interview questions, the larger question will continue to perplex the profession because it is difficult to ascertain errors when case objectives can be recast retrospectively, and attorneys and their clients may have different objectives in a single case. Attorneys also may disagree on the basic issue of what constitutes an error in judgment and decision making. One attorney's brilliant, bold strategy, for instance, may be regarded by another attorney as preternaturally inept. As Lord Acton noted in 1881, "There is no error so monstrous that it fails to find defenders among the ablest men."[1]

The study attorneys' opinions about deficiencies in other attorneys' case evaluation and negotiation skills can be grouped into six broad categories: inappropriate attitudes, lack of trial experience, inadequate skills, bad habits, conflicting incentives and inadequate communication within law firms. What may be most revealing

---

[1] John Emerich Edward Dalberg-Acton, Letter to Mary Gladstone dated April 24, 1881.

R. Kiser, *How Leading Lawyers Think*,
DOI 10.1007/978-3-642-20484-5_18, © Springer-Verlag Berlin Heidelberg 2011

about the study attorneys' opinions is what was not said. The attorneys did not emphasize immutable or intractable problems. To the extent deficiencies were noted, they tended to be behavioral, not innate. The types of problems identified by the study attorneys, though serious, are regularly overcome with strong measures of humility, receptiveness, industry, candor, and restraint.

This chapter begins with the attorneys' general opinions about other attorneys and then conveys their insights about the six general areas in which other attorneys' conduct could be improved. The purpose of the chapter is not to catalog error but to spark improvement. By asking questions that attorneys otherwise would not pose to highly successful colleagues, this study not only provides some guidelines for developing expertise but also explains how attorneys are unknowingly diverted from meeting their own high standards.

18.1   General Assessment

The study attorneys had encountered wide disparities in attorneys' case evaluation and negotiation skills; those experiences are reflected in disparate assessments. Among the attorneys expressing generally positive assessments, these statements were representative:

- Yes, most attorneys give their clients a balanced opinion of strengths and weaknesses. They have to – if they're wrong, and it's just bravado, they will not get the client on the next case. In fact, it may be the opposite. Some attorneys may exaggerate some of the problems just in case they get caught short.
- In a few cases I'm sure they [clients] did not have an inkling of what the case is worth. But if it's a good plaintiffs' attorney, the client knows what they're up against. There are plaintiff lawyers and plaintiff trial lawyers. If they actually try cases, they're right 90% of the time. Attorneys who take cases to trial know what's going on.
- In personal injury cases, if you're dealing with experienced counsel, rarely do you see people who are off base with their assessment. This applies to both plaintiff and defense attorneys. They have a pretty good feel about monetary value in front of a jury. Differences in assessments are caused more by causation issues than damages, to the extent there are differences of opinion. In the employment litigation arena, injuries are more nebulous and there are greater differences between attorneys.
- Attorneys do a pretty good job of helping clients evaluate their cases. In large cases, plaintiffs' attorneys are really good at evaluating cases. They have more experience and because they're good, they've got the big cases.
- Most often attorneys give their clients a balanced view of the strengths and weaknesses. But insurers have a lot of pull with their attorneys.

An attorney who represents both plaintiffs and defendants points out that it is difficult to discern whether a settlement position reflects the attorney's assessment or the client's stance: "In the case you're interviewing me for, it was the client that was driving the settlement negotiations. The attorney has to take the client's position, so you never know whether it's the client that's unrealistic or the attorney is messing up." A plaintiffs' attorney makes a similar observation: "When you look at what defendants are doing, it's hard to tell whether it's the adjuster or defense counsel."

Many of the negative opinions about attorneys' case evaluation skills were directed by defense attorneys toward plaintiffs' attorneys, offsetting, in a rough sense, their criticisms of insurance companies as described in previous chapters. The negative opinions reflect basic differences between the business models of plaintiffs' practices and defense practices and the inherent tension between those practices:

- Some of the plaintiff attorneys don't explain the pros and cons as much as the defense does. On the defense side we usually have a very sophisticated client and you're doing so much decision making and strategy with someone looking over your shoulder. It helps a lot – it's a collective wisdom approach to decision making. On the plaintiff side, it's more of a "trust me" approach with the client.
- Case evaluation is extremely misunderstood by the plaintiffs' bar. They somehow ignore what juries actually do.
- Plaintiffs' counsel does a very poor job of valuing their case. They're dictated by emotion or economic necessity. They don't actually value their case – they push as far as they can go and take a number at the last minute. The amount they take at the last minute usually is based on the attorney's situation or something the client needs, not the case itself.
- Attorneys are reluctant to bring up bad tidings with their clients. When their livelihood is at stake [referring to contingent fee cases], it makes it even more difficult to be realistic.
- It depends on which side you're talking about. On the plaintiff side, attorneys overvalue their cases based on cold facts instead of people. They're not thinking about whether the client is likeable, how the client will come across to a jury, which is probably the most important factor after the law. They look at facts in isolation and don't see how the case will look to a jury. They don't realize that a likable witness can overcome a lot of problems in a case, and an unlikable client can really hurt a good case. And so much of the time they don't care about the economics of a case when it's on a contingency.

These criticisms of plaintiffs are simultaneously substantiated and challenged by empirical research. As discussed in Chapter 10, independent studies spanning a 43-year period indicate that 50–68% of plaintiffs obtain worse results at trial than they could have obtained through a pre-trial settlement. Defendants' decision error rate during that period ranged from 19–26%. But the average cost of defendants' decision errors, as measured by the difference between the verdict and the plaintiff's last settlement demand, is consistently higher than plaintiffs' average cost of error. For California state court cases reported in *VerdictSearch* during the 2002–2007 period, for instance, plaintiffs' aggregate cost of error was

$120,890,536, compared with defendants' aggregate cost of $981,154,097.[2] The frequency of plaintiffs' decision errors, though, may be more salient than the magnitude of defendants' decision errors, leading defense counsel to regard plaintiffs as unrealistic case evaluators.

In opining on other attorneys' case evaluation skills, some study attorneys did not discriminate based on client orientation and indicated that case evaluation errors by both plaintiffs and defendants are widespread:

- Certain people buy into their client's mantra and lose their objectivity. Seventy-five percent do, and 25% don't. This does not vary with plaintiff attorneys and defense attorneys.
- Seventy to 75% of lawyers really do not know how to evaluate a case.
- For both plaintiff and defense attorneys, overvaluation is the number one problem in my opinion. I have experienced good reactions when I evaluate cases properly and bad results when attorneys make ridiculous, outlandish demands. Seventy to 75% of attorneys exaggerate their cases.

A plaintiffs' attorney described trials as case assessment failures, "a breakdown of case evaluation." Another plaintiffs' attorney noted, "When low offers are made and they're dead wrong, the attorney is not attuned with the client, and the attorney did not feel comfortable making a recommendation to the client or had a false sense of bravado. The attorney and the client are not synched. I have to fight with my clients, too, so I know the problem."

18.2   Inappropriate Attitudes

Attitudinal problems interfere with accurate case evaluation and effective settlement negotiations. These problems include aggressiveness, arrogance, egotism, overconfidence, exaggeration, emotional involvement with clients, lack of objectivity, and intransigence. Not surprisingly, these characteristics rarely appear in isolation but tend to cluster in some attorneys. When bundled, they often produce a strong position and a weak result. The study attorneys' opinions about specific attitudes are described below.

---

[2]Excludes adjudicated cases that did not meet the requirements for inclusion in the dataset, e.g., cases with disputed settlement offer or demand amounts and cases in which equitable relief was sought. For a description of the case selection criteria, see Kiser, Randall. (2010). *Beyond right and wrong: The power of effective decision making for attorneys and clients* (pp. 32–35, 431–435). New York: Springer Science + Business Media.

18.2.1 Aggressiveness

No client wants a weak attorney, but some clients are unable to distinguish between assertiveness and aggressiveness, between advocacy and belligerence and between the arguments that make them feel powerful and those that have the power to persuade. For study attorneys, an adversary's aggressiveness can be bothersome, counterproductive and unprofessional:

• Lawyers with small skill sets have a multiplicity of problems – ego, immaturity, inexperience. Like pounding on his or her chest and saying, "I can't wait to get you into the court," or "this is a slam dunk." ... One other thing – these are the problems after you set aside the personality disorders. That's a whole other problem.

• In many cases that go to trial, there's genuine passive-aggressive behavior behind them. The attorneys are incredibly difficult to deal with and I think there are some serious personal problems. I did not think this for a long time, but sometimes it's the only way to explain things.

• Establishing an overly aggressive attitude. This is a style issue and has nothing to do with the merits of the case. Some attorneys have an aggressive style in every case and this can kill negotiations.

• A lot of attorneys are antagonistic. Some do it because they think the clients want them to be mean and nasty. I've never seen this attitude work. It looks good for the moment but it makes me want to fight even harder. [Interviewer: Is it strategic?] The attorneys who act this way do it all the time. It's a style and a personality. It's more of a comprehensive attitude, but for me, when I do it, it's for a purpose. I may take a strong approach at some point in the case, but I do it rarely and only then to make a point, to send a signal.

When asked what he would change about how other attorneys evaluate and negotiate their cases, a study attorney responded simply, "Stopping the overly aggressive tactics." Another attorney replied, "all or nothing attitudes – 'my way or the highway – we're not going to compromise, we're going to kick your ass.'" Expressing a similar disdain for overly aggressive tactics, a defense attorney states: "I'm still surprised when inexperienced attorneys hang up on me. How can I settle a case? I tell them, 'You can hang up on me as often as you want, but I can't get any money for you until we can talk about the case.'"

Frequently associated with aggressiveness are arrogance and egotism, both of which impede accurate case evaluation and stymie settlement negotiations:

• Arrogance is another factor. Other attorneys underestimate us – underestimate our capability to fight all the way through trial if need be. They underestimate our ability to present a persuasive and winnable case. They don't think we're skilled in putting on a compelling case that thoroughly discounts their defenses.

• They underestimate us in two ways. First, they underestimate our will to take a case all the way through trial. A lot of attorneys won't try the case. I assume that I will have to try a case, and I tell clients you'll get your best offer on the day of trial. The second thing is they assume they will be able to lowball, and the attorney will do what's in the attorney's interests instead of the clients. That means less work for the attorney. I don't take the easy way. If I can work hard for the client, then that works for me.

- My opinion is that attorneys tend to disregard facts that are not favorable to them and place too much emphasis on their own skills. They think jurors are stupid pawns.
- Most of the time, for me, errors are made from ego involvement in the case and arrogance. The biggest pitfall is believing their own press and your own press or your client's. We have this ability to package cases and sometimes the package is much better than the product. You need to do this to sell it to the other side.
- Arrogance is the biggest problem; it's the killer for both defendants and plaintiffs. How do attorneys become arrogant? They get locked into a macho macho man syndrome – "I'm a tough SOB. I can kick your ass." I call it the "Big Ten Mont Blanc Pen" syndrome. I've got a 15-cent pen in my hand, and the jury will pick up a different mindset on my side of the table.

"In one case recently," remarks an attorney with a mixed practice, "the lawyer simply had the law wrong. Part of it is sloppiness, part of it is he was cocky, arrogant and thought he had all the answers." Another attorney with a mixed practice thinks egotism is the biggest impediment to case evaluation: "Ego – not stepping back and just being able to separate your argument from your case and your client's interests."

18.2.2 Overconfidence, Overvaluation and Exaggeration

The study attorneys identified overconfidence, overvaluation and exaggeration as serial deal killers:

- On the plaintiff side, the cases that are most problematic are the ones where the attorneys are overconfident and don't understand the realities of the case. There are two types of problem attorneys – inexperienced attorneys who don't know what a case is worth and experienced attorneys who have tried a lot of cases and think that they can a great result in any case, no matter how bad it is. Some of them truly believe they can get six figures but definitely do not know what their case is worth.
- A lot of cases are classic cases of overconfidence – the attorneys are too emotional and attached to the case and the client.
- In terms of mistakes of evaluating cases, the mistakes we most often see come from the plaintiffs' bar. They see their client as more sympathetic than jurors do. They predict a larger non-economic damage award than will happen. I think plaintiff attorneys sometimes underestimate the willingness of defendants to try cases based on causation and damages. Plaintiffs seem to think that just because their client's damages are high defendants will settle the case and will overlook weak causation.

- Yes, a common mistake is that lawyers become true believers in their case – the plaintiffs' bar in particular. They want a likeable plaintiff or very legitimate injuries. A lot of attorneys think they have one or both. Even when the plaintiffs had legitimate injuries, the clients were not as credible as the attorneys thought they were.
- I would say making demands that are not within a remote range of verdicts in the jurisdiction where the case will be tried has become the most common mistake. You lose credibility with counsel, mediators and claims adjusters. The mistakes made in the crunch times are going with a demand that the client feels is their expected recovery.

When attorneys are overconfident, strident and hyperbolic – locked into a "persuasion" mode instead of an "inquiring" mode – they engage in "over-simplified reasoning, self-serving speech, and a reduced loyalty to truth."[3] To be effective, lawyers need to know how to switch between persuasion modes and inquiring modes, alternating between argument and genuine interest, state law professors Stefan Krieger and Richard Neumann. The problem, they find, "is that many lawyers are so locked into persuasion mode that they do not know when or how to switch into inquiring mode."[4]

The study attorneys elaborate on the reasons for attorney and litigant overconfidence and the attendant exaggeration and overvaluation:

- Overconfidence comes from three main sources: underestimated the opponent, defensed so many cases, and did not do the discovery, the work-up.
- I believe that when other attorneys misevaluate cases it's generally because in the venue where our cases are there's a misunderstanding of the jury pool because historically the juries have been so favorable that the plaintiff's attorney starts to assume they'll get the same results. They're not looking at the merits of the case. They're looking at who the client is and who the jury pool is. I think firmly that is a great part in those cases where I get a defense verdict.
- They [attorneys] rely too much on total damages and overlook causation and client presentation. Client charisma can carry the day, but a lot of attorneys get that wrong. They think the client is way more charismatic than the jury sees them.

18.2.3   Undue Emotional Involvement

As discussed throughout this book, the line between passionate advocacy and undue emotional involvement is difficult to discern but easy to cross. The desire to be a

---

[3]Krieger, Stefan H., & Neumann, Richard K. (2007). *Essential lawyering skills* (p. 13). New York: Aspen Publishers.

[4]*Id.* at 14.

zealous advocate for a client sometimes leads an attorney to adopt the client's beliefs, motivations and certitude. However well-intentioned, this emotional involvement reduces an attorney's credibility and effectiveness and is readily apparent to adversaries:

- Many attorneys have a difficult time in evaluating cases because they become emotionally involved with their cases and clients. You do get wedded to your case over time. I can maintain my objectivity. Maybe this is a function of experience. But attorneys, even experienced attorneys, can have an emotional connection from the first meeting with the client and their evaluation is not terribly trustworthy for that reason.
- As soon as they personalize the case – once you sense it you know they will not be objective. You can hear it in their language – there's no distinction between them and their client.
- Two things happen. You get emotionally invested in the client or the case and you lose your emotional distance. You start to treat it like a pro per case. Second, you connect with the client and are committed to helping them. We deal with very sympathetic people and it can affect your objectivity. You fall into believing the client's side.
- Plaintiff attorneys who are good trial attorneys but poor case evaluators make more emotional decisions than rational decisions. This happens because they meet a client and they like them.
- In mediation you see plaintiffs' attorneys who need a mediator to help them work with a client they took on because they liked them or wanted to help them. Getting too wrapped up in a client is a slippery slope – even with the best of intentions.

Although a tendency exists to see plaintiffs' attorneys as being emotionally involved with their clients, undue emotional involvement is a serious problem for both plaintiffs and defendants. As a defense attorney comments, "The cases that go sideways usually have an adjuster who got really pissed at the plaintiff's attorney and started to take the case personally."

18.2.4   Lack of Objectivity

Even when an attorney is not emotionally involved with a client, the attorney's dual roles as advocate and advisor often converge into a single mode of zealous advocacy. The study attorneys indicate that lack of objectivity is an occupational hazard, stemming from a genuine but misdirected professional commitment:

- There's always a danger of losing your objectivity. You can have litigation goggles on. You identify too closely with your client's case and lose your objectivity. You need to evaluate your case objectively before you get to trial. Some attorneys get so involved they cannot see the merits of the other side's case. It's not easy to do [maintaining objectivity] because you get caught up in your own view.

- There's a time when you do lose your objectivity. As you're waiting until you get to that point, everyone gets entrenched and your clients become entrenched. On the defense side, they've been thinking, "it's a defensible case," and on the plaintiff's side, they're convinced it's a win.
- The biggest mistakes are where the clients did not understand the downside or the client did not care what the downside was. With some clients and attorneys they just take a leap of faith. Your brain stops processing information. They keep marching on and end up like a bug on a windshield.
- Trial lawyers approach what they do with a complete lack of adversarial objectivity. They think they're supposed to vigorously represent their client regardless of the facts and they take their happy horseshit all the way to trial. Right up to the trial they cannot get the stick out of their ass and recognize they could lose the case. The longer they have worked on a case the more worked up they get about their case and less they can be objective. I spend a lot of time as a mediator in addition to handling my own cases, and I can see this happening all the time.
- Attorneys become myopic. You become so immersed in the fight you only see the strengths, not the weaknesses. You become intoxicated with your own facts and turn a blind eye to the negative aspects of your case.
- This problem with objectivity is especially bad when the plaintiff's attorney has lost cases with you before. I tried to settle a case with a plaintiff's attorney and I had handed him his ass about six months before in another case. He did not want to listen to me explaining why he was going to lose this case, too. He's stilted, kept saying the same stuff to me. Some attorneys can't see the forest for their own trees. He had his case in a box and if the facts didn't fit in the box, he didn't care.

When asked what he would like to change about other attorneys, a plaintiffs' attorney with a general civil practice said, "Attorneys don't make clients be realistic. Clients are in la-la land and attorneys need to sober them up."

18.2.5   Premature Assessments and Intransigence

Some attorneys feel pressured to provide clients with an evaluation during their initial meeting or shortly after the attorney accepts the case. Even when couched as a preliminary analysis, these early assessments tend to anchor client expectations and, due to the consistency bias, force attorneys to stick closer to an initial assessment than may be justified by information later acquired through discovery. Information inconsistent with a preliminary opinion may be disregarded, and the attorney and the client may remain committed to a premature assessment:

- Most attorneys shoot from the hip at the beginning. They feel they have to have an answer immediately for their clients, and clients want at least a range of opinions. But their opinion changes over time and that creates a lot of problems.

They've created an unrealistic expectation that will be perceived as them being wrong if they change their opinion. That's why good attorneys do it gradually over time.

- Facts change – most often it's a failure to appreciate the risks. We all believe what we want to believe. It's hard for anyone, including me, to abandon their beliefs.
- One [error] is the lawyer's assessment of the other attorney and the other is thinking you know all the facts when you don't. This is particularly true if you are talking early in the negotiation. So much settlement and negotiation occurs before discovery is completed, and the parties get locked in with those things before they even know what the evidence will be. I've had plenty of cases where the lawyer on the other side thought he could beat my ass, but he was wrong.
- The plaintiff starts visualizing, "I'm getting a new car in October." The idea that this case is worth a new car won't go away no matter how much the facts change. This is the single biggest cause I see. The case looks good at the beginning, and this does not change even when the case changes, even when it's not the same case you thought it was. The lawyer is emotionally, economically invested and cannot dump it.
- Most attorneys get more objective when the case gets closer to trial, but even if they've told the client the beginning number was just to start things, the clients anchor on that first number. As a rule of thumb – and this has been the way for a long time – the plaintiff's demand is usually twice what they want. But clients think the first figure is what they're entitled to, and this potentially creates a false expectation.

A study attorney with a mixed practice deals with changes in case evaluations directly: "You have to educate your client, and when Susie says 'You told me that this case was worth X,' you say 'Yes, I did, and this is what's happened after we first talked.' I want to teach them because I'm responsible for a result."

18.3   Lack of Trial Experience

Many study attorneys are convinced that the greatest barrier to accurate case evaluation and sound settlements is lack of trial experience. Clients unfamiliar with the legal system may be surprised to learn that attorneys advising them of probable case outcomes may have little or no trial experience:

- Inexperience – we are getting a whole bunch of litigators with no trial experience. When you compare the 1960s with today, the number of cases tried to verdict is very small. . . . Today you can't get associates close to a jury trial. You have relatively inexperienced attorneys in this field. You would be shocked by the actual number of cases tried. Because of that, the ability to develop that intuitive sense of what jurors will see gets lost.

- When I first went to work at one of those big Wall Street firms the partner I worked for had never put a foot in the courtroom except for a few motions. Lawyers who handle corporate cases rarely get to trial because it's so incredibly costly. How many cases can you try if they take a year to try?
- A lot of plaintiff lawyers do not have experience trying matters, but they represent themselves as though they do. They're looking to make a deal, not enforce a deal.
- A lot fewer cases are tried these days. You have to be unafraid to lose if you are to be a good trial attorney. In my first year I tried nine cases. Young attorneys today don't want to try cases and cases don't get tried. You can be a *Super Lawyer* without ever going to trial. ... Now all of a sudden no cases get tried.
- There are very few attorneys who actually try cases but lots of attorneys who call themselves litigators. A client needs an attorney who is willing to take a case to trial. You definitely need to let them know you are ready, willing and able to take cases to trial.

Lamenting attorneys' lack of trial experience, a managing partner states, "If you're a surgeon, you should be in an operating room. If you're a trial lawyer, you should be in the courtroom trying cases."

Inexperience contributes to poor case evaluation and negotiation skills, many study attorneys contend:

- I will tell you there is a large difference between how a trial lawyer evaluates a case and how a lawyer who spends his career settling cases evaluates cases. Their motivation is infringed upon by the fact that they have no experience in trial. They do not share that with the clients because they do not want to lose the client. It definitely affects evaluation. Their cases are easier to resolve because they are more interested in resolution more than getting the last dollar that the client is entitled to.
- Attorneys take cases with no intention of trying them and then spend most of their time trying to talk clients into settling them.
- In only a small minority of plaintiff cases the lawyers are willing to try a case, only a small minority. Insurers keep dossiers – they know who is going to try cases and who won't.
- It used to be a good plaintiff's counsel lost more cases than they won. But they would get great settlements because everyone knew he would try the case.
- Plaintiffs need to be aware of what their jurors are like and to know that jurors see things very different from attorneys. Plaintiff attorneys seem to develop an idea of what a hypothetical juror will see in the case instead of a real juror. In high-value cases, this is why we have jury consultants.
- My attitude about settlement is different from some other med mal defense attorneys. They have a young, frightened physician and they settle it. I think that's bullshit. You can't be afraid to lose a case.

A similar concern about the effect of attorney inexperience on case evaluation is voiced by law professor Kevin McMunigal: "The element of evaluation requires predictions about liability and damages involving factual issues and tactical considerations such as a jury's likely reaction to particular witnesses, evidence, or arguments. One would expect a lawyer lacking in trial experience to operate at a disadvantage in assessing the prospects at trial in terms of both liability and damages."[5]

18.4   Inadequate Skills

The study attorneys note that many attorneys do not have an adequate skill set to evaluate and negotiate cases. Apart from inappropriate attitudes and inexperience, some attorneys lack subject matter expertise and are unfamiliar with evidence law. Also missing from some attorneys' skill set are the abilities to properly analyze a case and develop a coherent and persuasive strategy.

18.4.1   Lack of Subject Matter Expertise

In some cases, an attorney simply lacks subject matter expertise. This deficiency takes three forms: failure to conduct adequate legal research, inexperience in a specialized practice area and ignorance of the legal effect of key evidence. These shortcomings seriously impair case evaluation:

- First you have the guy who doesn't have a skill set. He's representing a client in a construction defect claim and wants $500,000 for a $40,000 case. The attorney doesn't know what he's doing. He has no subject matter expertise, no experience in handling these cases. You don't know who he is, you've never heard of him.
- Attorneys sue on a lot of claims where they do not understand the elements of the cause of action.
- You'd be surprised how many defense attorneys do not understand the "going and coming" rule. They sit through the deposition and don't understand what the witness is saying, and then try to argue the opposite of what their witness said at trial.
- A lot of attorneys are afraid to dance with the doctors. I am not afraid to dance with the doctors. You should know your medicine. If you miss out on that, you may undervalue your case, which is just as bad as overvaluing it.
- Most of the time the attorneys did not understand the significance of my questions during depositions and don't realize the case for them was over back then. Too many young attorneys are sent to depositions and don't know how to shut up the witness.

---

[5]McMunigal, Kevin. (1990). The costs of settlement: The impact of scarcity of adjudication on litigating lawyers. *UCLA Law Review*, *37*, 833, 857.

18.4.2 Unfamiliarity with Evidence Law

Lack of subject matter expertise is compounded by ignorance of evidence law. Fundamental to effective trial representation is a basic understanding of the rules that govern admissibility of evidence, but some attorneys have not acquired that knowledge, presumably due to a lack of trial experience:

- A fair amount of misevaluation comes from failure to predict expert testimony that will come in – how will the damages evidence actually be presented? From the plaintiffs' side, the biggest problem is not understanding how evidence will come in. Because of the frequency of trials, the level of knowledge of the rules of evidence has deteriorated significantly. Ten or twenty years ago, a 10-year lawyer was entirely different as far as knowledge of evidence. Misunderstanding the rules of evidence in a critical way is now fairly common. I've seen entire cases lost because an attorney did not know how to get evidence in.
- The value of a case depends on what a jury will see or won't see. So if you don't understand evidence and what's not going to be admitted, you can't evaluate very well.
- Around here we say your job is to get your evidence in. We're not responsible for what the jury does, but it is your fault if you can't get your evidence in.
- A lot of time they don't understand evidence and haven't thought about how they're going to get something in or keep something out. With business records some attorneys haven't studied the rules closely enough. In that case I just tried, he [opposing counsel] did not plan for it [an evidentiary issue] and had not objected within the time required.

Although the Evidence Code is one of the shortest codes, it also is one of the least understood. Because trials are rare, it has become common to watch direct and cross-examinations in which "counsel had not troubled to think through how the rules of evidence would limit the varieties of admissible proof."[6]

18.4.3 Inability to Accurately Analyze and Evaluate

The ability to accurately evaluate a case depends not only on recognizing the salient factors but also knowing how to prioritize and weight them. Study attorneys express concerns that other attorneys overlook critical factors and, once considered, incorrectly analyze them:

- The lawyer who has more life experience can evaluate cases with considerably more skill. Many defense lawyers are tyro lawyers – neophytes with minimal life

---

[6]Tigar, Michael. *Nine principles of litigation and life* (p. 184). Chicago: American Bar Association.

experience. They have a checklist approach to everything. They don't have the tools to make the analysis. You see them at a deposition with a legal pad and a checklist like this [grabs a legal pad, grips it on each side and then lifts the pad to cover the lower two-thirds of his face].

- People have a tendency to ignore how a preexisting asymptomatic condition can be aggravated. Defense lawyers and carriers tend to think it's a rarity when there is a cause between an injury and a preexisting condition, but minor accidents can cause significant injuries. In the case that brings you here today, the other side missed that – just plain and simple missed that. They were blinded by the fact the driver was fine. But the passenger was seriously injured because the lady was older and had a preexisting condition.

- I think it's because sometimes evaluation is strained in attorneys because they are not skilled in evaluating the course of human conduct. As Will [Rogers] – I can't remember his last name right now – said, "Common sense is the least common." Despite good intentions and best efforts, there's a life experience component that cannot be taught. As a result, many attorneys have judgment that's not well suited to case evaluation.

- A single fact can make a difference in a case, if you can get it in. In one case, sure, technically, he [the plaintiff] was right, but he had had 24 beers. The attorney had not taken enough time worrying about how the plaintiff was going to be seen by the jury. You have to pretend you're a juror.

- They say, "I've got a nice client, she's Puerto Rican" or "she's from the Bronx." They're looking at some dynamic that they should not be. They're not looking at the specifics of the case. They're also not realizing that the jury may be able to identify with my client as well as yours. They assume everyone hates [defendant]. They think, "I have a great client and a fantastic injury." I tell them, "I agree that you have a great injury, but you still have to get over me." I will be constantly asking the first question, "Whose fault is it?" I will say, "This is an unfortunate accident and she even has residuals." I'm not going to run away from the facts. But that is not the first question you have to ask. The first question is, "Who's at fault?" I try to tell them, "You have to get past the first question before injuries are even considered."

When attorneys have narrow evaluative skills, they may fail to see all dimensions of the case and overlook connections between superficially unrelated events. Irving Gingold, a trial attorney who had practiced for 58 years, describes "insufficient analysis" in the "burned baby" case:

> One of the largest cases I had involvement with ultimately resulted in a structured settlement of $16.5 million. A prior lawyer was consulted by the client because of a superficial burn on her baby's stomach. Nothing was done. The client stated her baby was born at Hospital A and then transferred to Hospital B. I went to the home to see her baby and learn why they transferred her. I observed the child was unable to neither sit up nor crawl. In our discussion, the client said her daughter is slow and might be retarded.
>
> Instinct led me to obtain Hospital A's records of both baby and mother. The records revealed a failure to properly fetal monitor the baby and perform a timely C-section. This was a cause of the severe brain damage suffered by the child. Did the prior lawyer make a

mistake? In my opinion, yes. He should have properly interviewed the mother and asked the question, "Why was the baby being transferred from Hospital A to Hospital B?" Had an in-depth interview been done it would have shown there was more than one case. I'd call it insufficient analysis.

18.4.4 Lack of Strategy

Apart from lack of subject matter expertise, unfamiliarity with evidence law and an inability to recognize and properly weight salient factors, some attorneys fail to devise and implement a strategy:

- Strategy is almost a lost art. With young attorneys, they do something because they can. They do it because they can do it and they can bill for it.
- Attorneys have knee-jerk reactions and file cross-complaints automatically without considering the consequences. You need to resolve differences between other defendants before going to the jury or at least put them on hold.
- If a lawyer starts to lose, they lose confidence in the case. The reasons they're losing usually are not evaluated well enough. But a case starts to get a losing feel and attorneys don't like to handle cases that are problems.

The failure to develop and implement a strategy, a defense attorney notes, reflects a larger problem: "They don't spend time sitting in that backseat as a juror thinking, 'What will they think?'"

18.5 Bad Habits

Inadequate skills may be exacerbated by poor work habits. The habits most detrimental to effective legal representation, according to the study attorneys, are failure to independently verify the client's story; failure to review records; failure to learn the case and evaluate the witnesses; and failure to prepare for depositions, mediation, settlement conferences, and trials.

18.5.1 Failure to Independently Verify Client Information

Whether through lack of industry, naïveté, or an unswayable loyalty to clients, some attorneys accept information from clients at face value and fail to independently verify its veracity:

- As far as plaintiff cases are concerned, what I see on a fairly regular basis is lack of preparation, lack of full knowledge of the facts. They may know the client's perspective but not witness information or information in the client's own background.

- How other attorneys evaluate clients and their cases kind of depends in my experience. I will say this – and experience is the key to all of my cases – a really good attorney when he sits down with his client he should be able to make a judgment regarding liability. This is first – then he moves to damages. He makes an independent judgment regarding liability and damages, and I don't think a lot of attorneys do this. They take the client's word and start making demands.
- Taking the client's word is the biggest mistake. . . .. This is more likely to occur on the plaintiffs' side. If you don't watch out, they will embellish.
- Jurors are looking for who has the whiter hat, who has the darker hat. This is why it can be a problem believing what the client says and disregarding contrary information.

A plaintiffs' attorney attributes the disinclination to challenge and independently verify client information to law school education and a sense of professional commitment: "As an advocate you want to believe in the client and you want to advance their agenda. That's what we're trained to do in law school, and that's what we do."

18.5.2   Failure to Review Records

Many defense attorneys mentioned the frequency with which they found incriminating evidence in plaintiffs' records, and both plaintiffs' and defense attorneys noted that some plaintiffs' attorneys did not thoroughly examine their own client's records:

- The majority of time the plaintiff's attorney has misvalued the case. I've handled hundreds of settlement conferences as a volunteer mediator, settlement conference judge. Countless times plaintiff's attorney comes in and says the client has to have surgery, but if you look at the records the physician says, "may need surgery." Sometimes I ask them, "Show me the MRI, show me the report," and they don't have it or don't know how to read it.
- I also think that there are a lot of plaintiff attorneys who don't properly screen the cases, don't look at the client's medical records, don't see the things we see. It's very rare to get a phone call from someone who knows the plaintiff, to get a call about something that the plaintiff is doing, something that he shouldn't do. We generally find something in plaintiffs' own records, like a different statement about how the accident occurred at the bottom of a medical record. [Interviewer: Is this because the defense attorney is paid by the hour to review the records and the plaintiffs' attorneys may have different financial incentives?] That accounts for some of it. I also think that with the best plaintiff attorneys this doesn't happen to them. A lawyer is a lawyer.

- Many plaintiffs' attorneys make a superficial analysis of a report or the records. They find a statement or a contradiction in the records but lack the knowledge to know whether it shows the doctor did not meet the standard of care. They don't know the science of it [medical practice], and that is why we want smart people on the jury – to understand the science.
- People value cases differently at the beginning or the end. They have not even valued the case initially and don't know what's in their own files or haven't even gotten the documentation. Ninety percent of plaintiffs' attorneys are surprised by what we discover in their own records. Most of my impeachment comes right out of plaintiffs' own files, which they don't even look at much of the time. I'm doing their due diligence for them. It's the lack of effective valuation by plaintiff's counsel that makes me look good. It's not me; it's plaintiff's counsel that makes me right.

18.5.3 Failure to Learn the Case and Evaluate Witnesses

Even when attorneys have carefully examined the records, they may fail to take the additional steps of thoroughly investigating the facts, interviewing the client and witnesses and listening to the deponents:

- The major shortcoming in the system is that it's all about information. For the system to work we need perfect information, and we don't have it. I'm a "heat" attorney and handle only the hot cases like wrongful death and catastrophic injury, so we've got a willingness to thoroughly evaluate the case. Small players don't spend money to get information like talking with peripheral witnesses. So they rely on their clients and don't independently get the facts. There's no extra return on getting information in small cases, so it's not done. It kind of makes financial sense but means that a lot of the small cases are really bad cases.
- In my experience many plaintiff attorneys have not even met the client. Their paralegal is doing the discovery and they meet the client for the first time a few minutes before the deposition.
- In a case I just had the insurance company took video of the plaintiff lifting, moving, doing all sorts of gardening things – all of the things he said he couldn't do anymore. The plaintiff's attorney was not paying attention to what the client is doing. We got the goods on the client and it caused the case not to go to trial.
- We don't listen very well at depositions. The technological age is not conducive to depositions. The other day an attorney showed up at a deposition and sat down with two BlackBerrys and her laptop. She was using them throughout the deposition – never paid much attention to the witness. One of the main purposes of a deposition is to evaluate and report on how a witness comes across at a deposition, but some attorneys are doing other things. On the defense side, probably the most important factor is what kind of witness does the other side make?

246 Mistakes and Oversights

- When their client comes across to me as someone who won't be believed, it's not a matter of a difference of opinion. The plaintiff's attorney usually agrees with me when I say, "Your client is a bad witness." They just haven't thought about it before or a lot of times haven't met the client before the depo.

The failure to investigate strikes some study attorneys as ironic because modern discovery has made investigation easier by requiring the disclosure of witnesses and authorizing their depositions. As one study attorney mused, "When I started practicing you didn't know crap about your case – it made it a lot more interesting when the trial started. If I had followed that old rule about not asking any questions on cross that you don't already know the answer to, I would not have had any questions to ask."

18.5.4 Failure to Prepare

The fourth bad habit noted by the study attorneys – in addition to the failures to independently verify client information, review records, and learn the case and evaluate witnesses – is lack of preparation. This habit is evident in all phases of litigation, from taking a deposition without adequate preparation to starting a trial without subpoenaing necessary witnesses:

- As a pro tem [temporary judge], I've seen how unprepared attorneys can be. You have to communicate the point [to the judge], draw the picture of the points that are most relevant. The reason attorneys are unprepared is that they're too busy, not taking the time for that case.
- Some attorneys do not put in the time and effort. That is a mistake. But they still bill the clients accordingly. This mistake is equally applicable to both bars.
- Sometimes you get people unprepared and they are forced to settle. They don't get their subpoenas out. They're not ready for trial.
- Many have not properly prepared their client for deposition. I ask them the questions that they have to establish for each cause of action or sometimes to establish a complete defense to the case, and their attorney does not understand that the case has fallen apart right during the deposition. In a whistleblower case, just taking one example, intent is an important issue, and the plaintiff testifies the opposite of what they would have to prove. The attorney often doesn't even see or realize the significance of what the client is saying. They're not helping the client protect them from themselves.
- In mediation, I enjoy walking in when the guy there does not have a clue. It puts the defense attorney on the proverbial hook for running up the tab and not reporting.
- Ninety percent of the court settlement conferences are useless. It's very rare that anything happens at those because lawyers don't know their cases.
- When an attorney is careless or is not detail-oriented in one aspect of the case, it usually shows a habit. It carries over into everything.

- I have sat in settlement conferences where the judge asked, "How old is your client?" The attorney would say, "That's something I don't know." The judge would say, "How can we figure out the cost of care, pain and suffering for how many years if you don't know the client's age?"

18.6   Conflicting Incentives

For some attorneys, money has a strong and insidious effect on case selection, evaluation and negotiation. Study attorneys are concerned and occasionally skeptical about potential conflicts between a client's desire for a reasonable financial resolution and an attorney's desire to operate a financially successful practice. This conflict, they explain, may be aggravated by the incentives inherent in hourly billing arrangements, contingency fee agreements and billable hour requirements.

For plaintiffs, an attorney's financial exigencies may conflict with the client's interests:

- Self-interest and amount of time are where attorneys fail their clients. This depends on the size of the case, too. In the smaller cases, below $25,000, lawyer's financial self-interests often predominate over the client's interests. Part of this is the system, due to overhead, court costs, experts' fees, and the fact you cannot interrupt the production line to spend time in court trying cases. I used to defend those cases, so I know how those cases are settled. In the claims meetings, we used to ask, "Who is the plaintiff's attorney?" The most important issue is who is the plaintiff's attorney because we knew that almost all of them would not take it to trial. We used to say, "Oh, don't worry about that case, he needs to pay the overhead." So we made low offers and they got taken.
- [T]hey drink the Kool-Aid. I drank the Kool-Aid, too, in my first five to ten years in practice – before I got fat and lost my hair. Certainly in contingency fee cases attorneys are co-venturers with their clients and they see stars and brass rings. Plaintiff lawyers tend to overvaluate because they make more money and become habituated to their evaluations – it becomes a habitual thought.
- Cases get settled because of overhead. For the small guy, overhead may mean paying the rent and his secretary. For someone else, overhead can include a vacation home, hookers, cocaine, and two Mercedes. It doesn't matter how big it is, everybody lives to the maximum and for them it's still overhead. It drives small cases as well as larger cases.
- Another element is you tend to have mediation at the end of the case and often either or both parties have run out of money. There's the "I can't pay my attorney anymore" reality. The attorneys know it's over. The attorneys can't keep working without being paid, but the client doesn't want to settle. This pits the attorney against the client. There's lots of this.
- Most attorneys do not realize that winning is resolving a case earlier rather than winning at trial. This oversight comes from naïveté and a desire to earn money.

Some attorneys think they may need to justify their keep. Many of these cases require court approval of the fee – minor's compromises – and attorneys justify the fee by the amount of time spent. If the case settles early on, the court could decide to award a smaller amount.

For defendants, hourly billing arrangements may pose a conflict between the attorney's financial incentives and the client's desire to promptly resolve a case:

- Typically what happens is you will write a demand letter before you file a complaint. So when the attorney gets the case he is not going to discuss settlement because he has not billed anything yet, so they have to justify their existence. One day I'll be talking settlement with them and think we're making some progress and the next day I get a load of discovery from them instead. They say they need to know if there's anything else out there and it doesn't matter if it is a simple case and you're credible – it's their livelihood and they're going to go through the motions no matter what.
- If the attorney is being paid on an hourly basis, then obviously there's a reason to keep the case going. Hopefully, most lawyers don't let that influence them much. But there is obviously an incentive there.
- Defense attorneys do not have the same issue as plaintiffs' attorneys. I called a defense attorney recently to talk about a case with clear liability, a case that would not be tried. It wasn't as clear as taking the wrong leg off, but it wasn't that far from it either. I said, "This looks like a case that should be settled before a complaint is filed." He said, "That's not going to happen. This is how I earn my living." He does not make money settling; he makes money working it up. So it's not a mistake for the attorney, but it's a mistake for the carrier. They have different incentive structures, so it's not a mistake for the attorney. But it may be a mistake in getting your economic incentives mixed up with the client's interests.
- On the defense side this is all about insurance money. They are trying to think of all the reasons a case is worth less. But this masks objectivity for good reasons, but it's not helpful for predicting outcomes. But it is helpful for people's pockets.

The study attorneys' concerns about financial incentives are consistent with interviews of attorneys, claims managers, monitoring counsel, mediators and expert witnesses conducted by law professors Sean Griffith and Tom Baker. In their extensive studies of securities class actions, they found that "[m]any of our partici-pants said that the lawyers involved in the case on both sides also have an incentive to delay settlement: defense lawyers so that they can continue billing the file, and plaintiffs' lawyers so that they can show sufficient effort to justify a large fee under a lodestar approach."[7] On the plaintiffs' side, monitoring counsel told them, "in jurisdictions where there is a lodestar approach to fee awards, there tend not to be

---

[7]Baker, Tom, & Griffith, Sean J. (2009). How the merits matter: D&O insurance and securities settlements. *University of Pennsylvania Law Review, 157*, 819.

early settlements, because [this] rewards the plaintiffs' lawyers working the file – notwithstanding . . . an acknowledgment on all parties that there is decent liability." On the defense side, monitoring counsel reported, "Defense counsel will work a case until they have decided they have earned enough money and then they will tell you it's time to settle."[8]

18.7 Inadequate Communication Within Law Firms

The structure of large law firms may itself be an impediment to sound case evaluation. A key feature of modern large law firms is "leveraging" – assigning work to associates and maintaining a high associate/partner ratio to increase profits per partner. Leveraging is a business model that started on a small scale in the 1970s and has proven to be remarkably successful at increasing law firm profitability. As Paul Lippe, founder and Chief Executive Officer of Legal OnRamp, explains: "Like so much in the modern law firm model, the explosion in associate hours, rates and leverage began with the Cravath IBM antitrust defense in the 1970s and 1980s, when the firm discovered that in the quintessential 'bet the company' case, IBM would willingly pay full freight for associate time on massive and pretty routine document review, and that in turn would drive up Cravath's profits dramatically."[9]

Although leveraging may be a successful business model, it has severe limitations as a decision-making model. The fundamental weakness of leveraging is that it tends to concentrate information in associates and decision-making power in partners. Because associates handle discovery, partners may become dependent on information conveyed by associates who often lack the skills, independence and experience to fully evaluate witnesses and evidence. Leveraging and the related reporting requirements often attend a "chain of command" communication style. That type of hierarchical reporting structure historically produces some significant information gaps and has the potential to provide decision makers with what they want to hear instead of what they need to hear.

The study attorneys were aware of the pitfalls of leveraging. Some of the plaintiffs' attorneys exploited the communication gaps and evaluation deficiencies caused by leveraging, while the defense attorneys took active measures to prevent them from occurring:

---

[8]*Id.* at 819, fn. 236, 237.

[9]Lippe, Paul. (2009, February 11). Law firms' 2011 scenario and the end of leverage. *The American Lawyer.* Among the 50 highest-grossing law firms, leverage has increased from 1.76 in 1985 to 3.54 in 2010. Kessenides, Dimitra. (2010, May 10). The AmLaw 2010: Catching up with the class of 1985. *The AmLaw Daily.* Available at http://amlawdaily.typepad.com/amlawdaily/2010/05/classof1985.html.

- There's a breakdown in how a lot of firms structure communication. In most cases an associate does all the work-up. In this case, the associate was not sophisticated enough to realize the impact of the witnesses.
- [Interviewer: Does the economic structure of firms push work down to less experienced attorneys who may not appreciate the significance of some deposition testimony or evidence?] I deal with the name partner, not the associate, so this is not a problem with me. In reality, it's worse than that. It's an enormous feature of the defense firm, which no one will say is true. To make a profit, they have to give associates as much work as they can take. There's also haphazardness in assigning cases – according to what the next day or next week's schedule requires. That's the economics of the situation.
- How do I make sure I'm getting accurate information from associates and they're not filtering facts? I really try to keep a pretty close eye on the attorney. I know they are less experienced. You get a sense for their judgment level. I don't really follow the Socratic method, but one of the great ways to teach attorneys is to ask questions, to probe – "Why did you say this in the report [to the carrier]?" – because I don't take it at face value. If anything is outcome determinative, I make sure what is being told is sensible.
- In larger firms, they are dependent on the associates. They work together very well. The associates are working the file, and the partner is picking it up and taking cases to trial all over Southern California. You have to depend on them and what is being said is correct. I have the ability and the opportunity to get better insights into what the associates are doing. I'm working side by side them, not on top. I try to train them.
- A mistake a lot of young lawyers make is they meet with clients and experts and take their word for it. This happens because kids want to report good news to the carrier. But it's hard to turn the insurance companies around if your evaluation changes and you've spent months giving positive reports. I tell attorneys to report bad news when you have bad news. Cross-examine the experts and your clients – ask questions, quiz them. Make sure they know the facts and the shit they're saying. Make them show they can back up what they're telling you. I want to push them early on.

In response to the question, "Is evaluation impaired because partners or clients do not receive critical information from associate attorneys?", a plaintiffs' attorney with substantial prior experience as a defense attorney replies, "Potentially what you said is true. Part of that is changing. But in the run-of-the-mill case, it can't be any other way. If you understand this, you run circles around the defense."

An attorney who had supervised litigation for an insurance company before attending law school thought that homogeneity in law firm attorneys also contributed to stilted communication and narrow case evaluations. He describes the advantages – both professional and economic – obtained by firms with a variety of attorneys:

- Just like a jury does, there's a collective wisdom with a jury panel that does not always go your way. The better you are at understanding that dynamic, the better you'll do at trial. If you're in a firm where they only hire all of their attorneys from Yale or Pepperdine or USC – like so many firms do – you're practicing with a narrow band of backgrounds and approaches to life.

- A firm in L.A., one of the firms I worked with, had a bar and had a great range of people – dec [declaratory] relief people, law and motion, trial attorneys. . . . Someone would describe a case and they would discuss it. You never say to anyone, "That's a bad idea." But you should question and challenge the other attorneys you're working with. It's good for young attorneys because if they can't handle it from attorneys in their own firms, how could they handle it in court?

- This is the danger in firms that become too much the same. . . . That's a serious problem and tells me the case may not be analyzed right. I look for firms that have become mechanical. I look for firms that are a little rough around the edges.

- In China, centuries ago, they would break the cycle of control by the warlords by shifting the commanders. It's the same way with law firms; they need to seek a diverse employment base. Differences enrich you. Firms that have attorneys from the same background, they create a stony, uniform product. [A major law firm] recruits from everywhere and that's why I think they're still in business.

- What is it going to do with your ability to expand your practice base? You need diverse attorneys to reach out into new business areas. When you look at the history of firms that developed new practice areas, it wasn't the large, uniform firms; it was the firms with diverse groups of attorneys.

This belief in the value of diversity is supported by extensive research demonstrating that heterogeneous teams are more creative, achieve better negotiation results and display stronger problem-solving capabilities than homogeneous teams.[10] In attempting to apply uniform recruiting standards, law firms may be promoting uniform thinking patterns to the detriment of their clients.

---

[10]See Page, Scott. (2008). *The difference: How the power of diversity creates better groups, firms, schools, and societies.* Princeton, New Jersey: Princeton University Press. Zhong, Chenbo James. (2001, Fall). Group heterogeneity and team negotiation. *Kellogg Journal of Organizational Behavior,* p. 5. Simonton, Dean K. (2004). *Creativity in science: Chance, logic, genius, and zeitgeist.* Cambridge: Cambridge University Press. Nemeth, Charlan J., *et al.* (2004). The liberating role of conflict in group creativity: A study in two countries. *European Journal of Social Psychology, 34,* 365–374. Sawyer, Keith. (2007). *Group genius: The creative power of collaboration.* New York: Basic Books.

Part V
Learning and Advice

Chapter 19
Learning

In Part V of this book, "Learning and Advice," the study attorneys consider whether case evaluation and settlement negotiation skills can be taught and, if so, how attorneys become better evaluators and negotiators. This focus on developing expertise necessarily raises three questions. First, are case evaluation and settlement negotiation skills part of an innate skill set that some attorneys have and others simply never possess or are incapable of developing? Second, are law schools teaching students to be effective evaluators and negotiators? Third, what resources are available to law students and attorneys who are serious about improving their evaluation and negotiation skills? The study attorneys address these questions in this chapter and attempt to provide some practical advice for accelerating the development of expertise.

19.1 Teachability

A threshold question is whether evaluation and negotiation skills are teachable. The tremendous variability in attorney performance suggests that the skills essential to accurate evaluation and adroit negotiations may not be teachable or are very difficult to learn, requiring a broad range of intelligences to master the law and understand the subtleties of human interaction. The study attorneys express disparate views regarding the prospects for teaching evaluation and negotiation skills, many concluding that those skills could be learned but could not be taught. Among the attorneys expressing skepticism, these thoughts are illustrative:

- You can teach a running back all the plays, but they will need instinct – you cannot teach that.
- That's a really difficult question because it seems like you almost have to have a sixth sense. I have to answer that question by saying, "No." There are just some very savvy people around in this world, and they just have a sense of what a case is worth. ... Having this "X" in the equation – that's why I mention savviness.

It's like an unknown but some people know it, even if they can't explain it. I think case evaluation is a carryover skill. You can see it in someone's sense of humor, how they gamble in Las Vegas, and how they evaluate cases – probably has a lot to do with maturity.

- Negotiation? That's kind of a gift. Ted Williams practiced a lot, but without his height and shoulders he never would have made it.
- Someone has to teach you how to play the piano, but not everyone becomes a great pianist. You cannot teach finesse. Even when you look at good musicians, you see they all went to great schools, had great teachers, but some perform at an entirely different level.
- You have to tap into your own experience. They [younger lawyers] may not appreciate what it takes to get that experience. I don't know if you can teach that. You have to be able to judge character and see through the BS.

Noting that some attorneys simply lack ordinary sensibilities, a defense attorney states, "I question whether, if someone is emotionally tone deaf, I'm not sure whether they will ever hear the music."

A middle-ground position, asserting that some skills are teachable while others are innate or grounded in singular personal experiences, is reflected in these remarks:

- Yes and no. Yes, because you can learn what counts. You can learn it and you can make it better. But you can't learn balls.
- Do you have children? They come out a certain way and they have a genetic makeup. We do something with it nobody knows. With the right genetics and proper training you can teach an attorney to be a really good lawyer, mediator, and trial attorney. But [Andrea] Bocelli is Bocelli. You can't make a Bocelli.
- Yes, you can teach it, but a large facet is experience. You can teach what to look for, but you can't change the mindset of the attorney. I was a claims adjuster for [major insurer]. I would discuss how to evaluate a case with new adjusters – jury verdicts, reports, discussions, calls to witnesses. You can lead a horse to water, but you can't make them drink.
- You can teach them the numbers part of it and tell them to look at the *VerdictSearch* reports but I'm not sure you can teach the rest of it.
- It takes a long time to learn how to see the emotional impact of clients or the opposing party. But you can be trained in that.
- Some attorneys think you're born to be a courtroom lawyer. You can argue it either way, but some attorneys have the gift, the ability to relate to jurors early in their career. Young lawyers can be trained and taught to evaluate witness potential.
- It can be sweetened or nurtured. But let me say this – some people just should not be trial attorneys. It has nothing to do with being a technically competent attorney. Lots of technically competent attorneys aren't very good at relating to people. But if you want to be a trial attorney, you can't be a humanoid. You have to be about energy.

A commercial litigation attorney observes, "Evaluating a case is an art, much more so than picking a jury." His firm conducts weekly workshops to teach attorneys case evaluation and negotiation skills. "With good training and experience, you can develop that art," he believes. "There is an experience component and a training component."

Acknowledging the difficulty of developing case evaluation skills, some attorneys indicate that the education process is more inferential than directive, more of an inquiry than an instruction:

- You can take a young lawyer and ask them, "Did you like the witness? Why?" You can't ask every question, but you can encourage their minds to think about the right questions.
- You can learn over time the difference between a really bad case and a not-so-bad case just through comparison of cases they've handled and witnesses they've seen. They can learn a few things like that and should have at least a level of awareness they can identify those factors. If they don't know that, and I tell them to watch for that, it's like my friend's six-year-old son who asks her about sex. She's comfortable with the question and gives him an explanation. But even if you give them a complete answer, they keep asking the same questions because there's no context. It just washes over them. I would hope attorneys have that context to understand these things if they're litigating cases, but you can't be sure. It's something they can learn, but I don't think I can teach it. They learn it as they go along.
- Part of case evaluation you can teach. You can teach awareness. There are things you have to look for. You can watch with them sitting with you. My teaching tool is a book written in the 50's, *The Education of a Poker Player* by Yardley. This book teaches you to read people. You either develop your instinct or not.
- I can take a depo for three days and not understand how to use that at trial. Those lessons you don't learn by watching. We try to pass on the skill to younger attorneys. We give them new cases and then we supervise them, get actively involved in the management of those cases. We ask them, "What do you need to look for? What are the questions you need to ask?"

Because case evaluation skills seem to require a special blend of judgment, curiosity, sensitivity, insight and maturity, an individual's development as a case evaluator may be blocked at an early stage by an overriding sense of conceit, smugness and self-satisfaction. People who are convinced they already are functioning at a superb level may never be motivated to scrutinize, test and improve their evaluation skills. Self-confidence, consequently, can be a major impediment to self-development. A study attorney who taught at a law school expresses her concern about the overconfidence she observes in law students:

> You couldn't teach them. Being a lawyer is about learning how to think different, and for some law students with an attitude of, "I'm fantastic, aren't I special?" you can't teach them. It's that attitude, "I'm special and you're not." They'll have a very difficult time with litigation. Remember, the judge's ego is even bigger than yours.

Other attorneys mentioned a persistent defensiveness on the part of inexperienced attorneys. "New attorneys don't want to hear what's wrong with their cases," a managing partner comments. "There's a lot of defensiveness and attorneys take umbrage when you point out the problems in their cases."

Although confidence may seem to be a desirable if not a requisite attitude in a trial attorney, it frequently masks inexperience and may lead novice attorneys to believe they actually possess the legal acumen they are attempting to project. A study attorney describes the enthusiasm and confidence exhibited by inexperienced attorneys and explains how these attitudes can be counter-productive:

> They will tell you what's going to happen at a trial – what evidence the judge will exclude – when they hardly know anything about trials. I helped one new attorney . . . He called me a few days into the trial and said he was having some problems, especially with evidence coming in. Then he said, "But I'm getting better. Tomorrow I'll be even better." I thought, "It's already over." You can learn a lot at trial, but you can't be an inexperienced attorney and go into a trial thinking you know how everything will happen and then start learning in the middle. I talked with him after the trial and he said, "I was just hitting my stride when it was over." That poor client – it may have cost them their business.

"Maybe I'm getting cranky as I get older, but the newbies are worthless," this study attorney states. "They can't follow the rules or make an argument, and it's a rule-generated field, a profession run by rules."

19.2   Law School Education

If case evaluation and negotiation skills are teachable – or at least can be imparted to some degree – it is reasonable to ask whether law schools are already teaching these skills. But when the question was put to the study attorneys – "Did any course in law school teach you how to be an effective case evaluator or settlement negotiator?" – only three attorneys responded affirmatively.[1] Those attorneys spoke enthusiastically about trial advocacy, legal writing and negotiation courses. Other attorneys looked dumbfounded, as though the question itself was ridiculous. Illustrative responses, often delivered after long pauses, are:

- No. Law schools don't teach too much about that. It's completely theoretical. When students come out of law school all they have is theories. I listen to these attorneys and think, "You obviously have never had a trial. That's just bullshit."
- My personal belief is law school is irrelevant to the practice of law. This is why young attorneys make a lot of mistakes.

---

[1]In the 2010 Law School Survey of Student Engagement, 53% of first-year law students and 57% of third-year law students stated that law school had prepared them well for "understanding the needs of clients." This small increase suggests that law school education had little impact on students' confidence about their ability to enter law practice.

- No one trains you for this. We're teaching them skills [in law school] that are not the skills to try or evaluate a case. So little of the law goes into a case until a trial. It's really not the law but the facts. The kids do not know how to apply law to facts. They're not learning how to practice. They're not going to Catholic school or synagogues either – where you at least learn you can't lie, cheat or steal.
- No course in law school. Law school should be geared toward preparation of hands-on trial advocacy. I didn't know anything about trying a case or evaluation when I passed the bar.
- Law school did not prepare me to practice law. It was preparing me to teach law.
- In my last year of law school I sold Ford automobiles. I did not go to any classes. I guarantee you this was the most valuable course I ever took in law school. Selling cars instead of going to class was the best thing I ever did.

One defense attorney was taken aback by the question: "Law school? No, zero, never was a topic, never was a subject matter. We did not even learn the basics of litigation."

In reflecting on their law school experiences, the attorneys provide some insights into what is missing from the curriculum:

- Students don't learn in law school that judges don't always follow the law and sometimes completely ignore it. I've had judges even challenge me to appeal a ruling which I knew was completely wrong. ... The first thing is there should be a class for people who want to do PI and focuses on *Jury Verdicts Weekly* and finds out about what happens in each county. You really have to get a sense of what happens in cases, and students need to learn what jurors actually do. You need to learn the factors that juries rely on in deciding the award. They need to see what really happens.
- In law school they should have basic courses in negotiations. Students should read the same books the trial lawyers do [turns chair toward shelf behind desk and pulls out David Ball's books *Reptile* and *David Ball on Damages*]. These books show how to create a link to jurors. Law students need to learn that you have to show that a defendant broke a rule that protects all of us, not just the client in this case, how it's a breach of society's rules, not just a jury instruction. Law schools need to teach basic negotiation skills – the art of negotiation, the art of settlement and the art of mediation. Students need to learn the opposite of what they think they're supposed to do – which is to fight all the time. This applies in everything from personal injury to business transactions, regardless.
- Law students should take the same continuing education courses for new lawyers. Maybe they are and maybe they're taking these types of courses now, but they definitely were not available when I went to law school.
- It's absolutely insane to make clinical optional, even if it's just client intake.
- One of my beliefs is you get out of law school without any practical experience. At a minimum, every law student should be required to do one deposition, one discovery motion and a half-day of at least sitting in a trial and watching. This basic education is deemphasized in legal training.

A fundamental problem with law school, a plaintiffs' attorney explains, is that "you don't have a context to understand it." He recalls representing a client in a high-visibility case a couple of years after law school graduation. As a result of the media coverage of that case, his Evidence professor called him and "asked whether I was the same [attorney's name] who was in his class. He said he was reading about me in the newspaper." The attorney replied, "Yes, and I'm finally getting what you were trying to teach."

19.3 Resources

Given the limitations of law school education, how can attorneys acquire and improve their case evaluation and negotiation skills? The study attorneys answer this question by directing attorneys to mentors, attorney organizations, courses, books, volunteer activities and self-instruction. A plaintiffs' attorney offers this advice on resources:

> First, have a good mentor. Hopefully you're a member of a firm that has someone who really knows what they're doing. Second, on the plaintiffs' side, join the California Association of Consumer Attorneys and attend their meetings, their educational seminars. Go to the conventions and courses like the "Masters in Trial" program and listen to people who have the experience. When I started, I read the books by trial lawyers I admired – their styles, their philosophy. Back in those days it was Goldstein [*Lane's Goldstein Trial Technique*]. Now they should be reading *David Ball on Damages* and attend those types of meetings, even at a financial sacrifice. I would also tell them not to be afraid to ask someone in the plaintiffs' bar what they think about the case. On the defense side, join the ADC [Association of Defense Counsel] and attend their programs.

Other study attorneys strongly recommended similar resources, the benefits of which they described below.

19.3.1 Mentors

Mentors are the resource most frequently mentioned by the study attorneys. Looking back on their own careers, many study attorneys recognized the enormous benefit of working with superb attorneys and being able to observe, practice, question and consult with them. Some of the study attorneys had started their careers working with stellar trial attorneys and, during decades of practice, had already mentored a new generation of venerated trial attorneys. Consistent with their own career development and the models they had provided for new attorneys, they strongly recommended that attorneys either take advantage of an established mentor program or initiate such a program:

- If you can be mentored by someone there is nothing better than that. One trial with a good lawyer is better than being locked in an office for five years in one of those large defense firms.

- Hitch your wagon to the star of someone who knows what they're doing. Make a connection on both sides of the table and ask a lot of questions. Talk to a lot of people.
- It is really important for young attorneys to develop a mentoring relationship with an experienced attorney they admire. This may be more difficult for female litigation attorneys.
- [W]e need a mentor system where each new attorney gets set up with an experienced attorney and meets with the mentor once a week to discuss their cases and ask, "What do you think this case is worth?"
- I would say the most valuable thing you could do is see if you could get an experienced attorney to let you sit in on aspects of the case – a mentor to help you learn from your mistakes. You can discuss the correctness of your theories, talk about other cases, whether a 998 [offer of compromise] is made, who the parties' attorneys are. I'm doing it now with an attorney. I took him to a videotaped deposition. This is invaluable.
- It is a lot easier to learn from someone who's been through a lot than to learn it on your own. If you can find an attorney with experience and success and they're receptive to learning through informal education, it's worth its weight in gold. The best thing is to find a mentor.

Mentoring relationships have become increasingly rare as law firms have become increasingly profitable. Noting that many law firms now emphasize short-term metrics like billable hours, law professor and former Kirkland & Ellis partner Steven Harper writes, "Each individual's drive to attain and preserve position in accordance with such metrics leaves little room (or time) for the personalized mentoring that turns good young lawyers into better older ones. There's no metric for measuring the future contribution that mentoring makes to the current year's average profits-per-equity-partner."[2]

If an attorney's law firm does not have a mentor program or an attorney is not working within a firm, it is imperative to seek other attorneys' opinions:

- Read the literature and be willing to talk with other lawyers. There are lots of attorneys who are willing to help you because someone did it for them. You can be sure of the willingness of other lawyers to share their viewpoints on cases.
- Case evaluation is experience. That's the only way you know. Starting off, you don't know anything. So you get it from the people you hang with. My advice is to make yourself available to receive the wisdom of your peers – hang out with other people.
- Talk to other attorneys. To be able to persuade jurors you need to have inputs from a lot of people; you have not experienced what other people have. This is critical.

---

[2]Harper, Steven J. (2010, July 19). Where have all the mentors gone? Available at http://thebellyofthebeast.wordpress.com/2010/07/19/where-have-all-the-mentors-gone/.

- They need to work with a good defense or plaintiff firm initially, even if their intention is to be a solo. Attend seminars. Tag along to mediations whenever you can. Talk to people. I still bounce the value of a case around with other people who have been in the profession.

19.3.2 Courses and Organizations

Many of the study attorneys belong to a local chapter of the American Inns of Court and are members of the American Board of Trial Advocates (ABOTA). They encourage other attorneys to join an Inn, attend ABOTA programs and enroll in other continuing education courses:

- Another organization is the Inns of Court. Mentoring is very much a hallmark of the Inns of Court. It's an opportunity to intermingle with other attorneys and judges.
- A couple of other tools are ABOTA's "Masters in Trial" program. There's a mini-version of it. It has a panel of jurors and you can listen in on the jurors' deliberations. That's another example of tools young lawyers can use to reach out.
- Take some of those Gerry Spence courses. As a plaintiffs' attorney, it was very difficult for me to go drink the Kool-Aid. I'm not as emotive as the Gerry Spence crowd. They teach you to get into your client's shoes. One attorney even goes and lives with his client so when you tell the jury about the client's loss you know what you're talking about. This approach is not appropriate for every case. You have to have a sense of proportion. But it's effective with major injury cases. If you don't understand the client's pain and just go in and recite facts, you will not get the client's case across to the jury.

Law students and new attorneys may not know that the American Inns of Court are open to a broad range of practitioners, as former California Superior Court Judge James Gray writes: "Each of the chapters of the American Inns of Court is comprised of experienced attorneys and judges, middle level practitioners, younger lawyers, and sometimes even law students, and each chapter meets once per month during the school year to 'talk shop.' Afterwards, the chapters put on educational programs dealing with some phase of the practice of law. But the underlying reason for these chapters is to focus on excellence, civility, professionalism, and ethics."[3]

---

[3]Gray, James P. (2010, November 15). The American Inns of Court: Keeping the legal profession on track. *San Francisco Daily Journal*, p. 7.

19.3.3 Publications

The study attorneys urge other attorneys to accelerate their professional development by reading *VerdictSearch*, trial practice books, popular books on sales and negotiations and judicial profiles published by legal newspapers and local bar associations:

- Read the books, articles, depositions of people who have been successful. Those things are out there everywhere. *The Art of Advocacy* – read that. Look at the best examples, the highly recommended. The schools need mandatory reading lists of advocacy, negotiation, mediation books, more real-life sources.
- Read a lot of jury verdicts and when you get a case you don't know the value of, talk with a lot of lawyers. Get empirical information and evaluate your client as a witness.
- It's also OK to read a book. One the first books I read was *The Art of Cross-Examination*. I still use what I learned from that book.
- Watch jury sheets. Have an idea of what different juries are doing in different cases.
- Don't place artificial numbers on what you think the case is worth. Check it out in the reports like *VerdictSearch* reporters. Look for similar injuries. No two cases are the same, but it gives you some idea of what the value is.
- Check out the prior depositions of experts. Look at the cumulative index from *VerdictSearch* for experts. The defense tends to go to the same well, so you should look at how those experts have testified before.
- The trial judge is a very important factor. Judicial profiles are available. Attorneys should look at those. I get calls from other attorneys all the time and we share information about judges and things like how they want voir dire done.
- Read books on sales and negotiations. At the end of the day, a lawyer is a very specialized sales person. At your core, you're a salesperson to the client, opposing counsel, the mediator, the judge, and the jury. You have to look at it from that perspective. There's all kind of literature that tells you about the psychology of persuasion, how people believe things.

19.3.4 Volunteering and Immersion

In addition to seeking the counsel of mentors and obtaining the benefits of organizations, courses and publications, new attorneys need to take initiative and volunteer for assignments and assume responsibilities outside their comfort level:

- I just finished doing associate evaluations, so this is fresh on my mind. Associates are always asking what they should do in negotiations – how they should respond to the other side, where they should start, what they should say. They ask if they can listen to me to see what to do. I tell them they're welcome to, but you just have to jump in and do it yourself. There's no single way to settle a case and you have to start doing it yourself.

- Handle a lot of cases. You have to have a knowledge base, have to have experience, and to get that base you have to take on a lot. We encourage attorneys to take cases to trial.

- In addition to preparation and knowing everything there is to know about the case, the most important thing is experience. I was not in the top of my class so I was not stuck doing depos in a large firm. I was trying cases from my first year. There is no substitute for getting in there. We try to get younger attorneys involved in some aspect of every trial – opening statement, examining a witness, some part of every trial.

- The most valuable thing I did was shortly after graduation. We volunteered to represent the students arrested in demonstrations [in the late 1960s] – three attorneys, ten defendants. I learned more in six weeks of that criminal jury trial than I ever learned in law school. I had no idea what I was doing, made a lot of mistakes, but I learned a lot. The best thing you can do is volunteer – take a PD [public defender] case.

- Young attorneys have to take any opportunities they can get. Contested arbitrations are a good place to start. Being second chair is also a valuable experience. You have to volunteer for opportunities. There is a glut of attorneys so people will work for public entities for nothing. They're [public entities] broke anyway so of course they'll take the help.

"Nothing is better than going to court and just being there, to get into court and watch how people work," advises a defense attorney.

As two of the study attorneys remarked, volunteering to work for a public entity – typically a district attorney's office or a public defender's office – can be of immense value. The Sacramento County District Attorney's office, for example, lost 20% of its attorney positions due to funding reductions and has attempted to mitigate the impact on its misdemeanor unit through the Volunteer Attorney Program. To participate in the program, attorneys must make a minimum two-month commitment and are expected to conduct at least two trials per month. Commenting on her experience in the program, an attorney who handled five jury trials states: "it provided a rare opportunity to prepare cases and participate in jury trials, allowing me to hone my courtroom skills and to become a more confident, effective litigator. Overall I was amazed at the vast experience and knowledge that I gained during my three-month assignment."[4]

---

[4]Scully, Jan. (2010, December 1). Join a DA, see a courtroom. *Daily Journal, Supplement* p. 12.

Chapter 20
Advice

In this chapter, the study attorneys respond to the question, "If you could give some advice to new attorneys to enable them to become better case evaluators and negotiators, what would it be?" Their responses are expansive, embracing many aspects of an attorney's life and practice: health, attitudes, clients, legal research, pre-trial preparation, trials and self-acceptance.

20.1 Health

The most consistently overlooked factor in trial practice courses and books is the sheer physical impact of a lengthy trial. A masterful command of the case facts and the relevant law is of little value if the attorney has not developed the physical discipline and stamina necessary to remain energetic and level-headed during weeks of argument and examination. Trials are the Olympics of law, and they test attorneys' physical endurance as well as their mental acumen:

- This is a very stressful field. I always lose five to ten pounds during a trial. In very few endeavors do you have someone doing their very best to stop you from doing your very best.
- Getting a case, processing the file, while those emotions are strong, being on trial is like no other experience in the litigation cycle. You worry about your client, the jury, what they want to hear, what's going on with the judge, what is the witness going to say, what will the next witness say. It's a battle unlike any other experience I've ever had. The day you don't have that tension is the day you know you should hang it up.
- If I get five hours of sleep it's a miracle. Trials are brutal. I'm [over 70] years old. I don't know how much longer I can do it. [Interviewer: Does it get any easier with experience?] No, that's not the way trials work. In each trial you have to be paranoid, out-work the other side, try to think of every argument they might make and what you're going to say to counter it. You have to have a competitive spirit to play in this game.

- You're in front of an audience. My emotions are running strong any time I'm in a courthouse. I can't tell you the number of times I've had to change my shirt. There have been times my whole body aches at the end of a day. Henry Miller [author of *On Trial: Lessons from a Lifetime in the Courtroom*] wrote about the stresses of being a trial lawyer. You can't take these for granted. You can take on vices and end up being short with people.

Effective litigation attorneys do not have to be athletes, but they do have to be careful custodians of their health. Bad habits, compulsions and addictions that inflict minor damage in a well-controlled, relatively predictable business law practice may ruin an attorney's career in a litigation practice. The public, incessant nature of a jury trial eliminates the private moments life otherwise affords to hide, work around and recover from frailties and indulgences. Vulnerabilities in an ordinary life become fatal at trial because a physically unfit or emotionally impaired attorney cannot perform effectively in front of a judge and jury for the weeks necessary to complete a major trial.

Recognizing that trials are enormously stressful and attorneys have to be vigilant in maintaining their physical health and emotional equilibrium, the study attorneys comment:

- I urge kids to get exercise and eat right and take care of themselves. If we were a manufacturer making widgets, we could just make more widgets. We could do whatever we want with ourselves because the machine is taking care of everything. But in trials, we are the machine. In trials you sleep three to four hours per night. You cannot go to sleep because your mind is still working. You get sick after awhile.
- I can tell by the angst in other attorneys what they're going through. They don't have the energy to walk the walk. You need to realize burnout in yourself.
- Lawyers do not take care of themselves. Alcohol seems to be less of a problem. The old guys drank heavily and still made it to court the next morning. But drugs may have become more of a problem now.
- I tell law students, one, "Never give up on yourself" and, two, "Never give up on your cause" because it's easy to become discouraged in this game because you're up against some really bright people in this business.

An attorney's reference above to Henry Miller seems apropos. In his book, *On Trial: Lessons From a Lifetime in the Courtroom*, Miller advises, "Keep fit, be ethical, take vacations, have many interests, laugh, do not take yourself too seriously, love your work, be creative, face up to hard problems."[1]

---

[1]Miller, Henry G. (2001). *On trial: Lessons from a lifetime in the courtroom* (p. 163). New York: ALM Publishing.

20.2   Attitudes, Beliefs and Outlooks

William James, the eminent psychologist and philosopher, considered attitude to be both revealing and determinative: "I have often thought that the best way to define a man's character would be to seek out the particular mental or moral attitude in which, when it came upon him, he felt himself most deeply and intensely active and alive. At such moments, there is a voice inside which speaks and says: 'This is the real me!'"[2] For committed litigation attorneys, that mental or moral attitude shines when their cumulative experience and advocacy skills are perceptibly advancing a client's cause during a negotiation, deposition, hearing, or trial. To develop that experience and level of skill and realize that moment when attitude, engagement, and performance crystallize, the study attorneys suggest that young lawyers start with these beliefs and outlooks:

- I tell young attorneys to, first of all, trust their own judgment and then be open-minded. We forget jurors do not have much experience, so if you have common sense you can come in as a brand-new attorney and ask, "What do I think about this case?" Sure, there's no substitute for experience, but you should trust your own judgment. Don't abandon your own ideas.
- Think outside the box. Think of someone you really care about and think of all the ways you could solve the problem. Avoid accepting things at face value.
- Try not to think it's a game. In the long run, they'll benefit from not acting like it's a game.
- Don't be afraid but know your limits. Don't be fearful – don't create limits that don't exist, but be mindful of those that exist.
- We had one attorney here who was great with juries. You could just see it in the courtroom. But he was lazy, wasn't willing to put in the time. Unless you're industrious and have the people skills, you won't make it.
- Be conservative. When you have more experience, you can take risks.
- The best advice I would give is PAD [pay attention to detail].
- You should find one area of practice you're comfortable and familiar with and build that one area.
- Don't be cocky for the first 10 years.
- Listen, learn. But don't automatically assume that what you're being taught is necessarily the best thing for you.
- If you are resourceful, you will be successful. I spent a couple of hours [as a temporary judge] trying to settle a case at a MSC [mandatory settlement conference]. After a while it became apparent that the doctor would not consent, so the case would not settle. At the end of the conference, the attorney asked me, "What type of jurors would you select?" I had listened to the parties for two hours so I had a good sense of the case. That's the type of initiative and curiosity that makes an attorney successful.

---

[2]James, William. (1920). The Letters of William James. To his wife, Alice Gibbons James, 1878.

20.3 Loyalty to Clients

"The qualities that are most valuable in any profession are the ones which cannot be bought at any price; and they are plain ordinary guts and loyalty," declared federal district court judge Harold Medina.[3] Of all the qualities essential to professional satisfaction and success, Judge Medina elaborated, "loyalty to one's client through thick and thin stands, in my judgment, at the very head of the list."[4] Reflecting a similar conviction that loyalty to the client is paramount, the study attorneys offer this advice:

- I would tell them first and foremost, never forget your duty is ultimately to your client. Until the legal profession gets back to recognizing that your fidelity is to the client, not worshiping the almighty dollar, you must always remember you first have to perform your duty to the client.
- If you want to have a rewarding career, get to know the client and spend time with them.
- Practice what you learned in law school. Hopefully, that included a course on ethics, fidelity, attorney-client privilege. You can't let anything get in the way of your duty to clients.
- There are all kinds of reasons you can go down the wrong path. If you're honest and true to the client, you'll be honest and true to yourself. That is the key. As the partner said to me when I first started practicing in the 1960s, "There's always room for another attorney, a good, honest attorney." He was right. It just works. Lord knows there are plenty of ways to get misguided in this profession.
- I have lost cases but I always feel I gave it my all. A good lawyer should never go to bed thinking, "I gave up on my client."
- The thing to do is don't get carried away with trying to impress the boss and burnish your reputation by climbing over other people in your office. If you just focus on helping the client, you will be OK. And your client will be OK. You'll have a flow of clients. Your boss will hear good things and they'll know you're honest and hardworking. It's a bit like politics. You do a good job, and the politics and the next election will take care of themselves.

---

[3]Virtue, Maxine Boord, (Ed.). (1954). *Judge Medina speaks* (p. 168). Albany, New York: Matthew Bender & Co.

[4]*Id.* at 292. Quoted in Bradford, Glenn E. (2002, July-August). Losing. *Journal of the Missouri Bar*, *58* (4), 208.

20.4 Independent Judgment

Although an attorney owes a duty of loyalty to the client, ethical rules also impose a duty to "exercise independent professional judgment and render candid advice."[5] The duty of independent judgment may seem like a constraint on the duty of loyalty, but in fact those duties are complementary; the client's interests cannot be furthered ethically when the attorney's role is merely instrumental. As part of the duty of independent judgment, study attorneys recommend that attorneys maintain their autonomy, scrutinize prospective clients and independently verify client information:

- Do not give clients a number initially. Be patient with your evaluation – you need to know everything about your case and the client. The most important thing is do not give clients unrealistic expectations. If the client does not come back, that's fine. Another case will come along soon. Be candid with a client.
- Trust but verify. Never tell your client that you don't trust them, but don't just rely on what the client tells you.
- Before you take any case, interview your client in depth. Don't gloss over the weaknesses. If you think it's a weakness, the other attorney will definitely exploit it. Go through the [Judicial Council] form interrogatory list of questions and question whether the client has committed a felony. Know your client.
- Never take a client who talks about suing their doctor or another lawyer. You can tell they are litigious. Stay away from people who seem to be taking advantage of the system. That's how the jury will see them as well.
- Independently verify everything the client tells you. As Ronald Reagan said in his talks with Gorbachev about disarmament and Gorbachev said, "I have the feeling you don't trust me." Reagan said, "I do trust you. I just believe in trust and verification." This requires a little more work. It's easy to trust. It's harder to verify every fact that will be material at trial.

The importance of independently verifying facts and resisting client pressures to provide an immediate assessment is reiterated by law professors Stefan Krieger and Richard Neumann: "Clients often want the lawyer to predict immediately whether the client will win or lose. In nearly all instances, you cannot make that prediction."[6] They warn that a premature assessment "raises the risk of error" and advise attorneys to "check the law or investigate the facts, or both."[7]

---

[5]A.B.A. Model Rules of Prof'l Conduct R. 2.1.

[6]Krieger, Stefan H., & Neumann, Richard K. (2007). *Essential lawyering skills* (p. 106). New York: Aspen Publishers.

[7]*Id.*

20.5   Client Participation

In his groundbreaking book, *Lawyer and Client: Who's in Charge?*, Douglas Rosenthal examined the effectiveness of "traditional" and "participatory" attorney-client relationships. Clients following the traditional model "trustingly and passively delegate responsibility for the decisions involving their problems" to the attorney.[8] But under the participatory model, clients are "active participants in the professional-client relationship, informed of the choices and their attendant risks, involved in the problem solving, and sharing responsibility for those choices with the professional."[9] After studying 60 personal injury clients, Rosenthal concluded that "clients who actively participate in the conduct of their claim get significantly better results than those passively delegating decision making responsibility. The main explanations offered are that clients can play a constructive role in appraising and assisting the performance of their attorneys and that continuing client appraisal of lawyer performance is warranted by the frequency with which attorneys perform ineffectively in making personal injury claims."[10]

A study attorney who also serves as an arbitrator in attorney fee disputes urges attorneys to adopt a participatory approach to clients or, at the very least, to explicitly confirm the client's preference for a non-participatory role if that is the case:

> Some lawyers do not communicate key events in the case to the client. The client may have something important to say, but the attorney never knows about it until it's too late to do something about it. Attorneys have a tendency to assume that the client either does not know about something or isn't interested in knowing. An attorney might retain an expert witness, for example, and find out later that the client knew someone who might be better or charge less. Or the client might know something about the expert you didn't know.
>
> Some attorneys take the "you're flying first class" approach with clients – lie back, put your earphones on, listen to some music, and I'll wake you when you get there. That is a mistake. Clients want to be involved. It's better to make a decision together. The saying that "it's easier to ask for forgiveness than permission" does not apply to the legal profession. You will miss opportunities.
>
> Law traditionally has been somewhat paternalistic. You want to help people and many attorneys take this attitude of "I'll take on your problem." But this is not a good way to approach. Assume your client wants to be involved. Then you'll have a lot fewer problems at the end of the day. Act like a true fiduciary. Whatever role you assume with the client, make it explicit.

---

[8]Rosenthal, Douglas E. (1974). *Lawyer and client: Who's in charge?* (p. 143). New York: Russell Sage Foundation.

[9]*Id.* at 154.

[10]*Id.* at 144.

20.6   Legal Research

Legal actions are often commenced for strategic or symbolic purposes and, due to time and financial constraints, essential legal research may be delayed until after the complaint is filed, or skipped altogether. The study attorneys express concerns regarding incomplete and careless legal research:

- Research your case. People do not understand what they plead. This is more of a problem in employment and school issues when attorneys get beyond a basic tort case and if you allege something beyond your area of specialty. Attorneys don't research the law and what they're pleading. They don't understand it. Attorneys do not take the time to understand what their case is or how to plead it. In any complicated case you have to understand what you're doing. Spend your time researching.
- Expertise is really important. If you're a generalist, you have a bunch of clients, and the dirty little secret is you can make a living settling those cases. But eventually you come up with someone who works up a case, knows what he's doing and you'll have problems.
- Make sure you research what you're doing.
- Another thing I should mention – maybe it goes without saying – you have to be technically up on the law. Damages is just one example. It's evolved and the courts have refined the collateral source rule – how medical expenses have to be treated. There's lots of other stuff. It takes a commitment and time to keep up with the law.
- It really helps to know the law. You may not know the facts with certainty, but you can at least know the law.

Staying current on the law may seem elementary, but the pressure to meet billable hour requirements often relegates non-billable, general legal education to the lowest priority. Reading the advance sheets, reporters, bar publications and digests of new legislation rarely has a deadline or a billing code, yet it is a discipline that distinguishes professionals from mere timekeepers.

20.7   Pre-Trial Preparation

Preparation, writes Keith Evans in *Common Sense Rules of Advocacy*, "is the best investment of them all. There's no substitute for preparation, and lack of it is always found out."[11] Emphasizing the primacy of preparation, the study attorneys advise:

[11]Evans, Keith. (2004). *Common sense rules of advocacy* (p. 42). Alexandria, Virginia: TheCapitol.Net.

- First of all, there is tremendous opportunity for someone starting off because most people don't work very hard.
- It's easier to get surprised when you've been superficial, not focusing on the case and not giving it the attention it deserves. Preparation is 98% of it. You can't be lazy.
- Have all your facts ready. Know your case well, backward and forward because personally you'll be more comfortable.
- Don't be superficial. In order to really evaluate cases you have to be willing to put in the time to make sure you have all the information.
- As part of verification, get a witness statement. Don't assume people will say the same thing at trial just because that's what they told you when you talked a year or two before trial. Some things turn on future events, and some witnesses change their testimony as their circumstances change in the future.
- Preparation – prepare briefs and exhibits. It's all about preparation, all hard work.
- Knowing your case backward and forward – and caring. You have to give a damn about people.
- It's preparation that wins cases. ... I have stressed the importance of getting a non-lawyers' perspective, knowing the plaintiff's history, turning over every rock, knowing the law, always talking with people and knowing what appellate courts find sustainable.

The study attorneys place particular emphasis on a careful and thorough review of all case documents:

- Be sure you're prepared. You have to read it all. Read every stinking thing. Do it yourself. I'm a great believer in delegation, but you cannot delegate this. They may not see the gem in the records. Sometimes it's just one sentence in a stack of medical records that can turn the case.
- There's no substitute for doing the work yourself with the documents.
- There are two things I emphasize. One is thinking outside the box. The other is following leads, the importance of looking at everything – is there a divorce record, is there a criminal record? You should look at everything, not so much because you'll find something but because you'll have the confidence you know everything. You'll know you didn't overlook anything.
- Get the records – do your homework, put in the time, research your causes of action. With plaintiffs' attorneys there's a tendency to delay preparation. They don't put in the time until close to the end because they aren't billing by the hour. If you don't prepare, you will get burned. On plaintiffs' cases you need to do it unless it [the case] has so little value it wasn't worth it to begin with.

Succinctly describing the critical importance of preparation, a plaintiffs' attorney who frequently serves as a temporary judge states, "Preparedness is probably the one word that separates good lawyers from bad lawyers."

20.8   Trials

Although trial practice is beyond the scope of this book, some study attorneys proffered this advice regarding general techniques and strategies:

- The lawyer's job is to make every case unique. You have to make your case non-frivolous, show why your client is unique. You don't want a defense attorney to say this is just another frivolous case. Personalize your case – make the jury like you, like your client, and make him believable and sympathetic.
- Jurors look at a case with a degree of scrutiny, just like they would if they were buying a car. You have to be able to tell them, "Here it is, take it for a test drive." If the customer finds a problem on their own that you have not disclosed, they wonder, "What else is wrong with this car?" That's why you have to be open with the jury.
- Cross-examination is the skill you have to develop on your own. Better be sure you don't get too far. We've all had a case where you go too far, and the witness gets you. We all get carried away with our cross-examination.
- Stay away from the King's English. No one wants to hear that crap. Even highly educated people want to hear questions in ordinary, conversational terms.
- You have to watch what you're doing. . . . One of the things I don't like to do is reach for too much. I like to take what I can grab with one hand. Otherwise, the jury slaps me.
- You've got to know your audience. The presentation is very different between a bench trial and a jury trial. Another thing is the advice I received in a journalism course on editorial writing: reason logically, argue emotionally. If you reason emotionally, your reason will fail. If you argue without emotion, your argument will fail.

A defense attorney noted that "attorneys tend to be redundant. We lack confidence and think we have to say something over and over for someone to understand." This insight is consistent with jurors' frequent complaint, "That lawyer thought we were stupid because he kept telling us the same thing all the time."[12] Reporting on his consulting firm's interviews with jurors, David Ball states: "One of the biggest complaints we hear when interviewing jurors is that the lawyer was condescending. This is not always a matter of tone. It is also due to over-repetition."[13]

---

[12]Ball, David. (2005). *David Ball on damages* (p. 363). Louisville, Colorado: National Institute for Trial Advocacy.

[13]*Id.*

20.9 Self-Acceptance

The distinctions between learning and imitation, between improvement and emulation and between adherence and adaptation become clearer as an attorney progresses from acolyte to professional. New attorneys initially observe and listen to attorneys more experienced in case evaluation and trial advocacy, and they eventually recognize that they cannot be just like those attorneys in their use of language, their mannerisms, their display of confidence and their insights into judges, juries and case strategies. Even the best attorneys serve only as models, not moulds. Emphasizing the importance of individuality and self-acceptance, the study attorneys urge attorneys to follow their own style and realize that personal authenticity still has greater force than a near-perfect imitation of another attorney, however distinguished and admired:

- Your summation, your passion, to convince the jury – it comes from within. [I] can't try the same case that Harvey Weitz [eminent New York trial attorney] can. I can't do it and I don't try to do it because it's not me. It's a double-edged sword because I can't be as persuasive and powerful as the best-known trial attorneys, but no one can be as strong as me being myself.
- Good trial lawyers have to be comfortable with themselves.
- I had the good fortune to be second chair with three separate attorneys. Each had his own style and I learned a lot about how important it is to follow your own style and not try to be someone else.

Underpinning this advice to follow your own style is a more subtle message that, for many attorneys, the first and hardest task is to find that style and then to give it a presence.

20.10 Précis

A managing partner whose firm represents both plaintiffs and defendants gives this broad, practical advice:

Always run things by other people – attorneys and non-attorneys.

Don't think you know everything.

Don't be afraid to create a situation where there is a good cop/bad cop situation so you're not afraid to get into a negotiation with someone more experienced than you. Create a layer for you to learn and collaborate with other attorneys at your firm – "I have to run this by Mr. X."

Don't get emotional; don't get emotionally vested. You have to stay objective for the client at all times.

Don't be bullied or intimidated by how respected or reputable the other attorney is. Don't let it sway you.

Use the process to ask a lot of questions and learn. Don't be afraid to use the "Columbo" approach. Say, "I'm new at this – tell me why." Information is where it all is, that's the power. You get more information when you're open about your inexperience.

Don't be afraid to say you don't know the answer.

Don't confuse passion and emotion. I think it's a requirement of the job for an attorney to be passionate. But getting emotional is when the attorney takes on the client's emotions and they get upset and start yelling and screaming because they are feeling the same way as the clients.

Good trial lawyers maintain credibility. It's not OK to puff things up and in closing argument be asking them [jurors] for something you haven't proven. . . .

You have to adapt. Being willing and able to adapt is paramount especially because you might find out [during the trial] why the other side is offering so little or demanding so much for the first time. Case valuation evolves at all times. What if the judge says, "You can't do that." What if you can't get some evidence in? You have to be prepared for everything.

The same case will be tried differently with a judge or a jury. Your demeanor has to change with the witnesses, too. If they're credible, why in the world would you attack them? The only time you can get into an aggressive cross-exam is if they have earned it.

If the client wants a case resolved early, they have to understand they have got to accept less or pay more. There's a time continuum for settlement.

We're not perfect – we can't always predict what a jury will do.

Don't underestimate the other side's ability to put on a case that supports their settlement position.

Chapter 21
Conclusion

"The kind of work we do, the cases we take, the way in which we accept or defy injustice: the entire body of our work speaks to the world about our values," writes Michael Tigar. "It tells the world whether and how much we believe we can get justice in the present state of things."[1] This book, hopefully, shows not only the kind of work the study attorneys do and the cases they take but also the values that underpin their motivations, attitudes, styles, strategies, techniques and concerns about the legal profession. The study attorneys believe we have an imperfect but roughly fair system of justice, and they believe they are responsible for obtaining the benefits of that system for their clients. When their case results fall short of their goals, they look inward for explanations and avoid the easy answers available from blaming "runaway" juries and deceptive adversaries. Although they acknowledge the civil justice system has flaws, their thoughts and efforts are focused on developing persuasive narratives and themes, anticipating evidentiary problems in proving their cases, overcoming biases against their client and realistically assessing how jurors will perceive witnesses and decide cases.

The study attorneys have a track record of accomplishment, but rather than relying on old routines and schemas, they remain critical of their own performance and continually evaluate and attempt to improve their analysis, presentation and judgment. Their candor about their own mistakes demonstrates that they are conscious of shortcomings and use those experiences to enhance their professional skills. They also are acutely aware of the limitations and biases of their own views and regularly solicit insights from a broad range of people. This constant process of forming ideas and opinions, questioning them, and testing them among lawyers and non-lawyers prevents them from becoming overconfident or underprepared.

The study attorneys' case evaluation skills are analytical and holistic, deliberative and intuitive, intellectual and visceral. Their advocacy is passionate, factual, knowledgeable and adaptable. In dealing with jurors and judges, they rely on a large

---

[1]Tigar, Michael. (2009). *Nine principles of litigation and life* (p. 281). Chicago: American Bar Association.

R. Kiser, *How Leading Lawyers Think*,
DOI 10.1007/978-3-642-20484-5_21, © Springer-Verlag Berlin Heidelberg 2011

collection of experiences and a wide range of senses to find universal themes, arguments and concepts that meet legal standards and moral expectations. Despite a high level of confidence in their opinions and skills, they are receptive to jettisoning strategies when they clash with new evidence or fail to resonate with jurors.

If the study attorneys' characteristics had to be described in four words, they would be responsibility, respect, resourcefulness and resiliency. The study attorneys seek and assume responsibility for results. Although they understand that numerous factors are beyond their control in every case, their energy is fixated on the elements they can shape and direct to deliver an outstanding result. A sense of respect pervades their practice, extending to clients, jurors, mediators, judges, and adversaries as well as the civil justice system itself. When respect is unwarranted, it is withdrawn reluctantly, proportionately and without vindictiveness. Their sense of respect also envelops a trait essential to health, perspective, judgment and balance: self-respect. Responsibility and respect, in turn, are complemented by resourcefulness – a force integrating creativity, intelligence, practicality, tenacity and industry to accomplish the client's objectives. And when strategies prove ineffectual, clients disappoint or jurors push back, the attorneys are resilient, recovering quickly and learning from the setback. All of these traits are merged into this simple yet comprehensive advice from one study attorney: "When things get difficult, you have to suck it up. Deal with the problem because that is what you are – a problem solver."

Index